TWO BUGS
ON
BIKES

Our middle-aged gap year cycling across
Europe and Africa

JACQUI WEBSTER

HEMBURY
—BOOKS—

Two Bugs on Bikes

First published by Hembury Books in 2025
www.hemburybooks.com.au

Copyright © Jacqui Webster

Two Bugs on Bikes

The moral right of the author has been asserted. All rights reserved. No portion of this book may be reproduced in any form without permission from the author and publisher, except as permitted by Australian copyright law.

The author and publisher have made every effort to contact copyright holders for material used in this book. Any person or organisation that may have been overlooked should contact the publisher.

 A catalogue record for this book is available from the National Library of Australia

JACQUI WEBSTER

I'm dedicating this book to the two most important men in my life.

To my partner Joe McNamara, who was the inspiration behind this journey and who is the most courageous, compassionate life and travel companion anyone could wish for. I would follow him to the end of the world and back. He always tells me I'm a lucky girl!

To my Dad, John Webster, who lost his battle with cancer in 2015. I still miss him everyday. He was with me for every step of this journey. Dad always told me that you make your own luck!

Two Bugs on Bikes

ACKNOWLEDGEMENT OF COUNTRY

I would like to acknowledge the traditional custodians of the land on which this book was written and where I live and work — the Gadigal people of the Eora Nation and the Darkinjung people of the Central Coast. I pay my respects to their Elders, past and present. I also extend my respects to all Aboriginal and Torres Strait Islander people, the original story tellers of Australia, whose enduring connection to the land, culture, and community continues to inspire and guide us.

JACQUI WEBSTER

TABLE OF CONTENTS

ABOUT THE AUTHOR..*vii*
PREFACE..*viii*

PART I MOROCCO AND EUROPE 1
   IN AWE OF THE ATLAS 3
   BREAKING THE FAST 12
   THE RACE IS ON 20
   RAIN ON THE RIVIERA 33
   WHY DON'T THEY LIKE US? 45
   BRINGING A KNIFE TO A GUNFIGHT 54
   BEARS IN THE BALKANS 59
   INCONVENIENT CATS 67
   DANCING WITH THE GREEKS 76

PART II AFRICA 93
   TWO LEFT SHOES 95
   LAND OF A THOUSAND HILLS 105
   OLIVIER 118
   CHANCE ENCOUNTERS 126
   WE ARE THE STARS 140
   RUNNING WITH KENYANS 157
   SCALING THE SUMMITS 170

THE MEDICINE MAN 176
THE SPICE ISLANDS 185
TWO BUGS 197
NOT YOUR REGULAR CRUISE 204
THE LONG ROAD TO LUSAKA 215
HIPPO DODGING ON THE ZAMBEZI 225
PRECIOUS AND THE CHICKEN 232
A ZAMBIAN CHRISTMAS IN ZIMBA 239
TOO CLOSE TO THE EDGE 242
THE ELEPHANT HIGHWAY 246
SURVIVAL IN THE DESERT 255
UNUSUAL ESCORTS 269
ACKNOWLEDGEMENTS 289
EPILOGUE 294
REFERENCES 298

JACQUI WEBSTER

ABOUT THE AUTHOR

Growing up on a farm in Yorkshire, England, Jacqui Webster always wanted to be a writer. Still, it wasn't until she traded her beach house and job as a public health professor in Sydney for an adventure across two continents by bicycle that she finally decided to write a book.

With over thirty years of experience working to improve food policy, Jacqui began her career in the UK, before moving to Australia in 2007 and completing her PhD in Public Health at the University of Sydney. Jacqui is currently a Professor in Public Health at the University of Technology Sydney, passionate about improving food systems.

While training for triathlons in 2010, Jacqui met her partner Joe, the driving force behind their cycling trip. They spend their time between Sydney and the Central Coast – when they're not travelling. A strong believer in embracing life fully while inspiring change and making a difference, *Two Bugs on Bikes* is Jacqui's first book.

PREFACE

I didn't start out on the trip with the idea of writing a book; I just kept a journal to record our experiences. Even when I approached Jess Mudditt, who later became my book coach, I was still only thinking of some kind of photo-story coffee table book that I could print out and give to family and friends. I just needed someone to help me complete it.

However, as our discussions evolved, Jess helped me realise I had the material to write a travel memoir. I'd always wanted to write a book, and so thought I'd make a start and see where it took me.

Likewise, while we didn't start our trip with the idea to ride through Africa, I've dreamed of travelling through Africa my whole life. I just never expected that it would be on a bike!

My partner, Joe, and I planned the journey together, but this was really his adventure. Joe, who was forty-six when we set off, became a father when he was just twenty, so had missed out on travelling while he was young. I'd never married or had children and had travelled a lot throughout my life. At fifty-one and having been with Joe for thirteen years, I felt fairly settled. My work was rewarding and I loved my home life – particularly swimming every morning at MacMasters Beach on the Central Coast. It was hard to put it all aside. At the same time, I didn't want to be left behind while Joe went on an epic adventure. So, I had to follow him.

Both of us had been in our jobs for a long time, me for seventeen years and Joe for twenty three. We had a bank of long service leave to use so it was a good time to do this. Still, I was worried. I'm committed to my work. For the last thirty years I've worked for NGOs, government and research institutes to improve food environments. Much of my previous travel has been linked to my work, and I was anxious that I'd find it hard travelling for a year just for the sake of it. When I told colleagues I was taking a year out, they immediately assumed I was doing what many academics do, taking a sabbatical at a different academic institution or with an international organisation. When I explained I was going to ride a bike for a year, they were shocked. "Won't you feel guilty?", "What about your students?" and "Aren't you worried about your career?" were common responses. I admit I did have some doubts. I felt I should be doing something more meaningful with my year. But while we toyed with the idea of trying to link the trip to a cause or raise money for charity, we felt that might detract from the spirit of adventure, and didn't want any ties.

So we agreed we would just set off and see what happened.

I guess deep down I knew that whatever happened with my work, it was important to do this for my personal life. Taking a year off to cycle across the world was Joe's dream, and he didn't want to do it without me. Having originally planned to set off in 2021, our plans were set back by the global COVID-19 pandemic, which gave us an extended time to prepare. We didn't worry about training as we were already relatively fit from triathlon training. But Joe was fanatical about getting the right kit and spent hours researching the different routes.

We already had bikes which we'd ridden on previous multi-week cycle tours in Australia and New Zealand. Mine was an entry-level Polygon gravel bike with alloy frame and carbon forks with a rear rack. Joe had a sturdier Soma steel frame gravel bike with front and rear racks. We were trying to keep things as simple as possible in case of any mechanical issues, so both bikes just had a single chain ring, with 38-millimetre tyres and a front dynamo to charge the lights. We set off with Ortlieb bags on the racks (mine just on the back and Joe's front and back) for our clothes and camping and cooking gear, with handlebar boxes for sunscreen and snacks. We also had our phones mounted on the handlebars for navigation.

We made sure we had good quality lightweight camping gear and upgraded to a lightweight three-person tent with two vestibules, so we had plenty of space while camping. We had a Trangia stove for cooking and a power bank for charging our phones when we were in remote areas with no electricity. We felt pretty well organised.

But no amount of planning could have prepared us. We set off for Morocco in March with mixed emotions, not knowing where our journey would take us or what would lie in store for us when we returned.

JACQUI WEBSTER

PART I

MOROCCO AND EUROPE

Two Bugs on Bikes

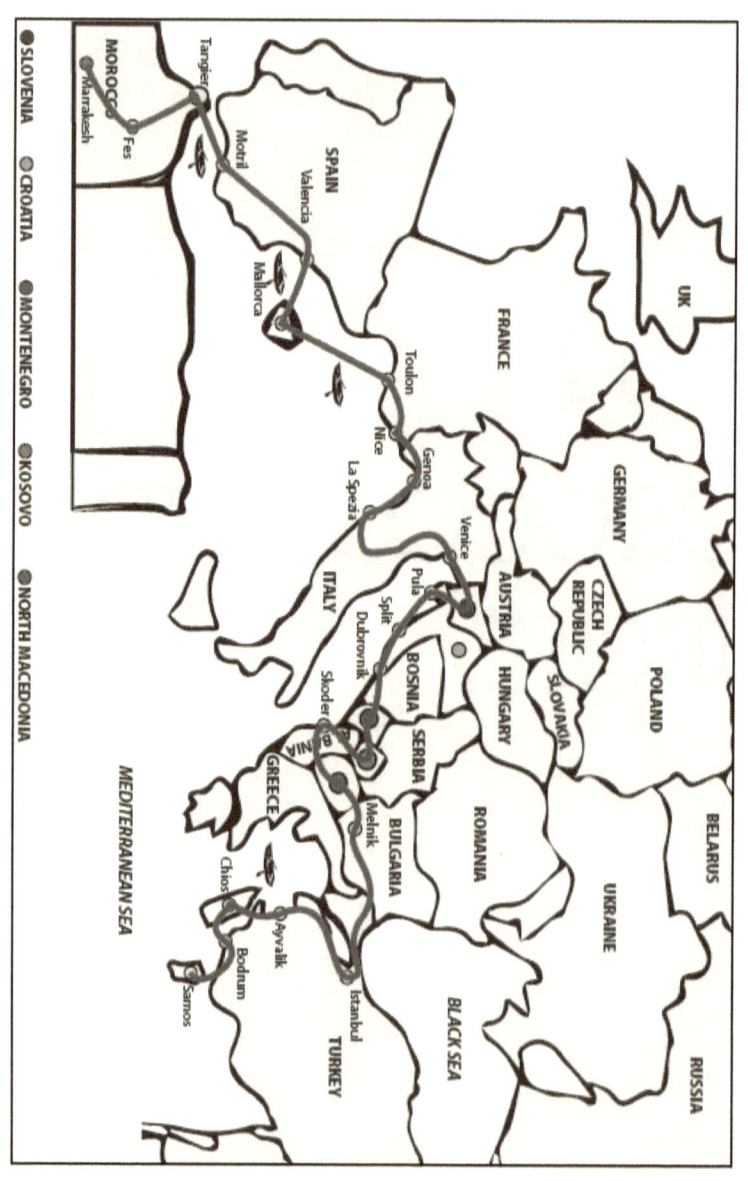

-1-

IN AWE OF THE ATLAS

"I can't believe we're actually doing this!" I shouted, wheeling my heavily laden bicycle between motorbikes, horse-drawn carts piled high with dates and oranges, and stalls selling spices, ceramics, carpets and French pastries, as we weaved our way out of the bustling alleyways of Marrakesh.

In no time at all we were cycling on smooth tarmac with a well-marked cycle lane on the two-lane highway heading south towards the Atlas Mountains. Ahead of us, snow-capped peaks rose from the horizon like a mirage. My shoulders started to relax, and a wide grin slowly spread across my face as we fell into a rhythm.

Four hours later the picture was vastly different. We'd cycled up hill after hill. My heart was pounding and sweat was pouring down my neck. I strained, standing up, trying to force one last pedal stroke before jumping awkwardly off my bike to avoid falling. I rammed the brakes on to stop the bike sliding back down the hill. My whole body was shaking.

"This is way too hard!" I yelled out to Joe, who was dismounting ahead of me.

A line of cars and trucks were parked on the corner and a crowd of men in traditional Berber clothing watched us, their faces a mix of curiosity and concern.

"I told you it was a dumb idea to cycle up into the Atlas Mountains on the first day," I grumbled as Joe sat down at the side of the road and started to unwrap a nougat bar we'd bought in the bazaar the previous day. He smiled weakly, looking apologetic and defeated.

"I may have underestimated how hard it was going to be with the bags weighing so much," he confessed.

"No way, José!" I replied, trying to find a sense of humour.

With all the bags, which included cooking and camping gear, Joe's bike weighed about fifty kilograms, and my bike was thirty-five kilograms – the difference in weight intended to balance out our difference in strength, particularly when climbing hills. We had climbed about a thousand metres but still had a fair way to ride, including another 400 metres of climbing before we reached our destination for the day.

I left Joe munching on his snack and made my way up the bank, seeking some solitude in the landscape. It was exactly what my sagging spirits needed. The rugged Moroccan mountains loomed in the distance, their stark presence forming a dramatic backdrop against the clear blue sky, grounding me in the moment. The earthy tones of the valleys stretched out below and a group of white goats was huddled together under a dying argan tree, creating an iconic scene in the dusty landscape. I inhaled deeply, allowing the stillness to wash over me. Tears pricked my eyes as the emotional toll of the past few weeks hit me, the mad rush of wrapping up at work, the emotional goodbyes with friends and family in Australia, the whirlwind of catching up with loved ones in the UK, and the exhaustion of long-haul flights. I took another big breath, fighting back the tears and trying to take in the view. Then, just as suddenly, a wave of exhilaration swept through me and I felt a smile spread over my face in anticipation of the adventure ahead of us. Pulling out my phone, I snapped a picture, one of the thousands I would capture over the year ahead. But somehow this one felt different. More than just a snapshot, it marked a moment of a transition, a reminder that sometimes the most meaningful journeys start with a deep breath and a decision to take the next step.

The original plan had been to cycle from Selby in the UK (near where I was born and grew up on a farm, and where my mum and sisters still live) to Singapore (which was about as close to Sydney we could get without flying). However, since it would still be cold in Europe when we kicked off, we decided to start in Morocco instead. We'd do a loop of the country before getting a boat to Spain and continuing east through Europe towards Malaysia. We were nervous about Morocco due to the challenging physical terrain but were intrigued to learn more about the culture. Now, as I gazed at the mountain range, my exhaustion dissipated and excitement for the adventure ahead fizzed in my veins.

Wandering back to the road, I found Joe scouring Google Maps to find somewhere to stop and eat. He pointed out a restaurant called Dar Adali (meaning Adali's home), which was just one kilometre away and looked lovely. We pushed on to find the place had spectacular views, but all the tables were reserved. After some negotiation, the friendly owners agreed to bring us bread and olives with honey and olive oil. It was simple but delicious and we consumed every last crumb before lying down to relax for around an hour.

We thought we had about twenty kilometres left to ride that day, with a few big climbs followed by a long downhill to Ouirgane. But shortly after lunch we missed a turn, so had to backtrack and found ourselves on a gravel road between houses, heading out into farmland. We persisted, but the track deteriorated into big ruts before disappearing altogether. We turned back. The only other route was an extra fifteen kilometres via Moulay Brahim and Asni, meaning we now had more than thirty kilometres left to ride, much of it uphill.

We were already completely spent, but had no choice. I reluctantly climbed back on to my bike, struggling to find the strength to follow Joe.

"I'm not sure I can do this for a whole year!" I yelled in exasperation at his back.

Moulay Brahim is a small rural hillside town with a population of just over 8,000. It's named after a Moroccan Sufi saint who practised a form of Islam valuing peace, love and tolerance, emphasising inward meditation to reach a connection with God. The town is a popular spot for tourists and nature enthusiasts coming from Marrakesh to enjoy the mountain air and stunning views. Six months after we rode through it, it was decimated by an earthquake. Dozens of people were killed in the rubble of the clay brick and cinder-block houses following the quake, which had a magnitude of 6.8 and was reported to be the biggest that had hit a North African country in 120 years.

The descent through Moulay Brahim was cobbled and steep and the climb back up through the town even steeper. A local showed us a shortcut, which seemed great until we came face to face with about 200 steep steps that we had to carry our bikes up, taking it in turns to help each other lift the heavy loads.

Descending out of the town was much more fun. We flew past people watching and waving from the hotels and street cafes. The kids were pouring out of school, smiling and shouting *bonjour* and *hello*. It was magical – I would have pinched myself if I weren't clinging so hard to my handlebars.

We finally arrived in Ouirgane, a Berber village in the heart of the Toubkal National Park, at around five o'clock. At just under ninety kilometres and more than 1,600 metres of climbing, our first day's ride had been too far and too hard. Auberge le Mouflon, a lovely homestead near a stunning lake run by Rachida and her family, was exactly the kind of sanctuary we needed.

"Can you eat too many olives?" asked Joe. We were sitting in the beautiful garden waiting for dinner, tucking into another large bowl of olives with oil and lemon.

Soon our host emerged with a feast. "I source all the produce from local farmers," Rachida told us as she served up chicken tagine, salad and freshly made khubz (a kind of cob loaf), followed by peppermint tea. She pointed out the orange, lemon and olive trees in the garden surrounding us and explained that she made her own olive oil.

We devoured the meal. Joe raised his glass in a toast. "We did it, babe!" he said. "Well done."

"It was tough," I replied. "It was so hard going up that hill past all the cars at the side of the road. I could barely stay upright!"

"I know," Joe said. "Let's try and make the rides a bit shorter and easier until we get a bit fitter."

Joe had already mapped out the first few days' rides and together we'd identified places to stop along the way. We agreed to cut the next planned ride day in half and found somewhere that looked like a good spot to stay in between.

We slept like logs that night.

In those first few days in Morocco, we were blown away by the kindness of strangers.

The next morning, we went in search of a shop to buy supplies for lunch. We bought bread, cheese and olives, and some nuts and roasted chickpeas for snacks. This exchange took forever as the woman in the shop – Latifa – only spoke a few words of French but she was incredibly patient, helping us to find what was needed. She also insisted we meet her six children, take photographs and exchange phone numbers (so we could send them all the photos) before we left. Latifa is still sending me messages to this day!

The next day we stayed with a Berber family. The son, Said, lived in Marrakesh but had supported his parents to host foreign guests and advertise online. He couldn't join us, but we talked to him on the phone to find out how to reach the beautiful homestead, up high in the mountain village of Ijoukak. The whole family welcomed us and gave us fresh mint tea.

The Berbers, also known as Amazigh (which means free people), are one of the oldest ethnic groups indigenous to North Africa, and make up around 30% of the population. Their arrival in Morocco predates the Arabs and they are known for their close connection to the land, distinct languages, music and dancing, as well as traditional crafts like weaving and pottery.

Sitting outside the house admiring the view, we were joined by two young girls. They were about ten years old, with long hair tied back in braids and wearing tracksuit pants and jumpers. Like the owners of the homestead, they spoke only the local Berber language, Tamazight, so it was difficult to communicate, but we tried to learn a few words. Joe took out our playing cards and we taught the girls to play Snap. They laughed self-consciously and stayed with us until they were called back to their families for dinner. Joe smiled as they left. We felt we had shared a special bond.

Later that afternoon, more children – girls wearing traditional Berber outfits of lightweight cotton dresses with a belt and headscarves – joined us as we wandered around the village. Traditional Berber-style houses made of mudbrick and stone, with flat roofs, were set against a backdrop of rugged mountains towering over deep rocky valleys and contrasting patches of green agricultural land. The girls beckoned for us to follow them and led us down to the river, where we crossed on the stepping stones and enjoyed the soothing sound of the water. On the way back, the girls picked us berries from a tree and showed us into a small mudbrick dwelling with a round clay oven, which was where the local bread was made.

It was a touchingly enriching way to explore the small town, which was still relatively untouched by tourism. The girls wanted nothing, but we gave them a few coins for their time. They ran away holding hands and giggling.

Inspired by the authenticity of these cultural exchanges, we relaxed into an easy routine: we woke early, ate a huge breakfast, usually eggs with bread and fruit washed down with hot coffee, packed our things and then set off on our bikes. Each day we had a clear route in mind, having planned it the night before. But we never knew what the road was going to offer us.

White-blossomed trees lined the edges of terraced fields that stretched out over lush green valleys with traditional Berber villages dotting the landscape, as we climbed up into the High Atlas. The Tizi n'Test pass road was narrow and steep as we snaked our way up the hundreds of challenging hairpin bends overshadowed by rocky cliff faces. Hotel Belle Vue was balanced on the edge of a hairpin bend about 2,100 metres above sea level at the top of the pass. Sitting writing in my journal that evening, after a cool shower as the sun was setting over the mountains, I reflected on the journey so far. We'd only been cycling for three days but had already met so many people.

Most people were amazingly friendly. They shouted out of cars and waved as we flew down hills, making us feel like champions. Conscious of the need to respect the Muslim culture in Morocco, we'd tried to dress conservatively, opting for loose T-shirts and long shorts rather than tight lycra. This seemed to be working. I'd only felt admiration from other women so far – and no animosity from men.

But not all places were the same. Leaving the Atlas Mountains behind, we rode through Sidi Ouaaziz, a small town in the Sous Massa region on the road to Taliouine. On entering a cafe, I suddenly became very self-conscious. There were only men in the cafe, and all were wearing traditional dress. They just stopped and stared, unsmiling. Even the young boys didn't greet us. It was the first time I'd felt unwelcome anywhere in Morocco and we made a conscious note to pay more attention to the clientele before entering places from then on.

We pulled into Taliouine scorched, stressed and hungry after a seriously painful long, hot ride battling headwinds, across unwelcoming terrain. A small village surrounded by hills, Taliouine is slowly nearing extinction, its proximity to the Merzouga Desert meaning the conditions are too harsh to bear. We checked into Hotel Saffron, named after the most expensive spice in the world,

Two Bugs on Bikes

which Taliouine is famous for. But the souks were silent, no one was trading in saffron, and the once majestic Glaoui Kasbah was crumbling.

"This scene is like something out of the apocalypse," I remarked as we battled our way east along the famous Route of a Thousand Kasbahs towards Ouarzazate, the Hollywood of Africa.

We were surrounded by arid land with huge boulders towering on the edge of hillsides. A large solar farm sprawled behind the city, adding to the eerie feel. It was easy to see why it had been a location for many movies, including *Game of Thrones* and *Mad Max*.

The small guest house we'd booked for two nights so we could rest turned out to be on the edge of the city overlooking an airstrip. Not exactly what we'd envisaged. The noise from the nearby road meant relaxing by the small pool was going to be impossible. We were hungry, so decided to head out for lunch.

"Cheers!" we said, as we had our first beer of the trip in a lovely little French Moroccan restaurant nearby the guest house. Ouarzazate is not really known for its food, but this place had good reviews and we thought it was time to spoil ourselves. We were the only people there and the waiter hovered around us as we decided between the pigeon pie or the goat tagine. The food was delicious, and it was good to escape the heat.

Strolling around the souks after lunch, I was keen to linger and learn about the different foods, but it was too hot, and we bickered. Joe wanted to go back to the hotel.

"I'm tired; I don't want to be walking around in the heat on my afternoon off," Joe complained. I felt exhausted too but I didn't want to waste my afternoons sleeping.

"What's the point in cycling through all these places if we don't take the time to explore?" I retorted, following him reluctantly.

Back at the hotel I felt unsettled. This wasn't how I'd envisaged this trip. I'd expected to be camping or staying with locals, not battling the heat all day then collapsing in a hotel room, looking at four walls while Joe was sleeping. This wasn't where I wanted to be. I needed to be out in nature. I was also worried about my mum, who was about to turn seventy-eight. My sister had called that morning to let me know she was in hospital again, having had recurring nosebleeds. They were waiting on the results of the tests. I wanted to call but it was already too late back in the UK. I was feeling anxious and guilty. The few days that we'd spent on the farm before flying out from Manchester to Marrakesh hadn't been enough. A year seemed a long time to be away on a crazy adventure, particularly when Mum wasn't well.

"Ouch!" Joe shouted out, watching me with a look somewhere between bemusement and fear as a large, near-naked woman grabbed the waistband of his boxers and roughly poured a bucket of cold water over his private parts. She then slapped him on the shoulders and indicated that he should turn around.

I was lying on a concrete slab in a pair of paper knickers. I shut my eyes as a gallon of hot water was sluiced over me and another large, sweating woman leaned over me, rubbing my skin with a rough glove. I had just come out of a sauna and been doused in freezing cold water, and now my skin was peeling off in shreds as the woman scrubbed me down, grunting incomprehensible instructions in Arabic and nudging me to turn over or stand up.

Two hours later we emerged from the hammam, humbled and glowing. The traditional bath and massage was the perfect remedy for the heat and stress, slapping us out of our worries and giving us strength to continue our journey. It wasn't just the exhaustion that had been shed, but the physical and emotional tension we'd been carrying too. We walked out revived and well rested, ready to embrace the road again.

~ 2 ~

BREAKING THE FAST

"*T*his seems an unlikely place for a guesthouse!" I called out to Joe as he navigated through the winding tracks, past piles of rubble and dead trees.

Kalaat M'Gouna means 'fortress of the river Gouna', in the Valley of the Roses. In late spring the small city is literally covered with roses. They bloom during the month of May and tourists come from all over to walk the paths of the river and inhale the perfume of the roses mixed with the scent of almond trees and wheat fields.

It was late March, and there were no roses when we turned off the tarmac road after cycling eighty kilometres from Ouarzazate. We followed the dusty track left and right through crumbling ruins of old Berber houses. Eventually arriving at a big wooden door with a metal bolt and a simple sign declaring MAROC DES MERVEILLES (the wonders of Morocco) above it, we were greeted by a young boy who led us through the corridor to a charming room with low ceilings and two single beds with Moroccan blankets.

"I love this place," I exclaimed to Joe, smiling and collapsing on the bed.

The young boy served us peppermint tea and homemade biscuits as we waited for the guesthouse owner, Abdul, who was eager to meet us and take us for a tour of the area before dinner.

Abdul made up for his limited English with his enthusiasm as he led us on an agricultural hike around the area.

"All sowed by hand," he said, gesturing over the wheat fields where the herons were nesting. He pointed out apricot, almond, peach, fig and olive trees, as well as the rose bushes that the area is famous for.

"Traditional Berber bridge," he explained as I tiptoed behind him, balancing on the rickety construction of logs laid across the river, leading us towards the ruins of the old Kasbah that the town is named after. Joe stood close to me as we listened attentively as Abdul told us about the festival of the roses, where the women wear headscarves adorned with flowers and the children wear garlands as they parade around the town celebrating the rose harvest.

"It sounds exquisite," I said. "How come there are so few people living in the town now?"

"Not enough work," explained Abdul. "Rose harvest is seasonal, and people come from the surrounding areas. Most young people move to the city. My children go too."

Back on the roof terrace, overlooking the vast, rust-red landscape as the sun was setting over the horizon, we were treated to another exquisite homemade dinner.

"All food grown in nearby fields or sourced from market," explained Abdul, as he served us Moroccan salad, olives and a chilli dip for starters, followed by turkey tagine for main, and oranges and bananas with cinnamon for dessert.

We collapsed into bed content, laughing about how much we'd learnt about Moroccan food and culture in just one day.

The days passed by quickly after that. We got into a routine of planning and riding, settling into different roles with Joe working out the routes and me finding places to stay. We got better at accepting that some days would be amazing, while some would just be ordinary. The quest for food and supplies to fuel us on our rides was never-ending. While in some places, strangers at the side of the road would flag us over and feed us olives and bread with olive oil and honey, in other places we could ride for hours without finding anything to eat. In the small village of Tilmi, we asked around for food and soon had half the town trying to help us, showing us to the shop (which was just a hole in the wall) and then running off to different houses to gather other things, including couscous, bread, coffee, carrots, onions and tinned fish.

We needed these supplies when we were left to our own devices at the Ighounba Inn, just after Ait Moussa Ouichou, at the base of Tizi n'Ouano, one of the most remote passes in the Atlas Mountains. We were miles from anywhere and it was the most basic place we'd stayed at. There were a couple of rooms with bunk beds and one bathroom with drop toilets. It felt like we were the only guests to have stayed there for several decades. We'd arrived without booking and there was no food, so we cooked our own dinner on the camping stove overlooking the misty mountain that we were planning to cycle up the next day.

"Goodnight, my friends. I'll come back early to cook breakfast." The innkeeper smiled and locked the door behind him. It was 8 pm and he was going home to his family.

It was dark and eerie and strange staying alone in the old inn but we slept well, and the innkeeper was back as promised early the next morning.

Just how alone we were on this trip was made clear the next day as we started the climb up Tizi n'Ouano.

"Ouch!" I gasped. My wheels had slipped in the gravel, and I'd fallen sideways off my bike, hitting my head on the rocks. Luckily, I was wearing my helmet and there was only a scratch on my shoulder, but I felt rattled.

We had turned off the main road and were climbing up to the pass on the rugged gravel track. There was really no reason to go here other than bragging rights, but Joe was insistent that it would be an adventure. I'd followed reluctantly. I was tired, and after falling I couldn't help thinking about how bad it might have been if I hadn't been wearing my helmet.

Joe looked back and, having checked I was okay, was now laughing

"It's not funny," I said, rubbing my head. "How would we have been able to get emergency services out here?"

"You're okay," he replied. "Come on, let's get going now."

I felt frustrated. The climb was tough. We couldn't see much because of the clouds that were rolling over the hillsides. After reaching the summit and rolling in the small patch of snow that was left at the top, we quickly donned our rain jackets to protect us from the wind and the rain as we set off down the other side. I wasn't sure it had been worth it.

After several hours descending in the freezing cold, our hands numb with pain, we came across La Grotte Auberge, a humble traditional Berber inn about ten kilometres outside Agoudal. We rolled up to the door hoping for food and warmth and were not disappointed. Wrapping ourselves in warm blankets, we drank hot, sweet Moroccan tea while the owner, Abdul, stoked the stove to make us a hearty vegetable tagine. The walls of the inn were adorned with Moroccan carpets, pictures of the nearby caves and newspaper cuttings of other people's adventures. The warmth of the inn after expending all our energy outside in the cold reminded me of sitting by the fire in a pub in England after a winter's walk and I smiled at the comforting memory. So often you have to do the hard stuff to get the rewards. If we hadn't taken the route over the pass, then we wouldn't have had the experiences of staying in the deserted inn at the base of the climb or meeting Abdul at La Grotte Auberge. As we hugged Abdul goodbye to get back on our bikes again, it felt like we were leaving an old friend.

We dropped down to Imilchil, a small village of about 2,000 people in the valley of Asif Mellulen (the white river). Imilchil is known for the traditional Berber betrothal festival, where people from the neighbouring villages come together to find a husband or a wife. The annual festival grew out of the legend of the two lakes where two young people from different tribes fell in love, but their families forbade them to see each other. They cried themselves to death, creating the neighbouring lakes of Isli (his) and Tislit (hers).

Arriving hot and tired at the local guesthouse, we weren't in the market for a husband or wife. But we were easily persuaded by our charismatic hotel worker, Baboo, to visit the weekly animal market the next morning. Rows of cars and trucks were parked on the roadside leading to an enclosure teeming with cows, sheep, goats and donkeys. Men in traditional dress stood around eyeing them.

A baby goat was thrust into my arms and immediately I was smitten as it nudged my face gently.

"You buy?" said one of the men, smiling mischievously.

"I wish I could take him," I replied, "but I don't think he would fit on my bike!"

In the nearby food market, huge plates of grains and pulses were displayed in colourful, oversized plates alongside piles of citrus fruits and bundles of greens. There seemed to be no shortage of fresh foods here, despite the cold climate and distance from the commercial centres.

But accessing enough food and clean drinking water are increasingly a challenge for many indigenous people in Morocco, who are deeply connected to the land. At our next rest base, Hotel Gîte Mourik, the owner, Hammid, explained how it had been hard to sustain the fruit crop over the last few years because of the harsh climate and the drought.

"We used to get a good yield from the apricot trees," he said, "but now they are all dying."

Hammid and his wife, Rashid, are some of the lucky ones, making a reasonable income from their beautiful guesthouse.

"Many people in the High Atlas only have work as labourers or agriculturalists, which barely brings in enough income for food and heating," Hammid told us. "The future of these people hinges on water. They are constantly anxious about when the rains will come. Now climate change is impacting the weather making them even more vulnerable," he said.

Meanwhile, Ramadan was starting. Joe and I were feeling anxious about our own ability to find food to eat while most people would be fasting.

JACQUI WEBSTER

"Where are you guys from?"

We had just pitched our tent by the shores of Lake Ouiouane for our first night wild camping in Morocco. The sun was starting to go down, casting a shimmering amber light over the water. Joe had gone to wash in the lake. My stomach lurched when two Moroccan men wearing jeans and leather jackets drove up on a motorbike. They had friendly faces and seemed to be lovers, but I wasn't sure we were allowed to camp here.

"We're Australian and travelling by bicycle," I said, gesturing to the bikes under the tree.

The taller man asked a few more questions about where we had come from and what direction we were heading in. Then he put his hand in his pocket and pulled out a card.

"I'm a policeman," he said. I took a deep breath. We'd heard so many negative stories about policemen following cyclists in Morocco, telling them it's for their safety but ruining their experiences.

"This is my number," he added. "I work in the next town. Pop by and have a coffee when you're passing."

A warm smile spread across his face, illuminating his kind eyes. He patted the other man on the shoulder, and they climbed back on the bike. They were obviously a couple.

"Enjoy yourselves and call me if you need anything!" he shouted as they drove off up the hill.

I relaxed and released a shuddery breath. Joe returned from his wash in the lake, and I recounted the story.

"A gay policeman in Morocco?" he said. It felt unlikely in a country where homosexuality is criminalised. "That's probably lucky!"

We set off late and didn't have time to pop by the next day, which was a shame. Despite all the stories we had heard from other cyclists, that was the only encounter we had with police in Morocco.

Lake Ouiouane wasn't the most idyllic spot for camping. There was litter everywhere. Two stray dogs rummaged through plastic bags of waste food and rubbish that had been left by daytrippers. We'd had a tough ride that day and needed a wash, but the lake shores were muddy and strewn with debris. Despite this, it was good to finally get the tent out of the bags. We set up camp, unrolling our lightweight mattresses and sleeping bags in the tent and setting out our table and chairs overlooking the lake. We cooked vegetables and couscous on the camping stove and crawled into the tent just as it was getting dark.

A few days later, I was breathing hard, barely moving, pushing my bike up a gravel road with the city of Fez fading away behind me. We had flown downhill into the city, weaving past cars, trucks, horses and carts and motorbikes. With a population over 1.2 million, Fez is the second-largest city in Morocco, its old town situated on the banks of the Oued Fès (the Fez River). Arriving through the backstreets, we witnessed people living in shacks, burning rubbish and begging for food. Later that night we soaked up the atmosphere in the souks as people ran around frantically, buying fresh dates and chebakia and other honey-drenched treats to take home to their families in preparation for breaking the fast.

In a remote town called Nefzi, halfway between Fez and Tangier, we met Foued, our guesthouse host. He was also fasting. When he asked us what time we'd like dinner we said that we'd wait until it was time for him to break his fast and eat together. He served up a sumptuous feast of tagine, couscous, breads, olives and fresh fruit and insisted that we keep eating even when we were about to burst. Later he took us up to the terrace where the local men were all hanging out drinking (mainly tea) and smoking (mainly hashish) and playing a card game. Joe confused the game with the Italian card game briscola and tried to join in, humiliating himself – much to the amusement of the locals who couldn't speak any English.

We continued north, battling headwinds along the coast, carrying our bikes up the stairs in the beautiful Blue City of

Chefchaouen, and exploring the souks in the university town of Tétouan.

At the port in Tangier, we again found ourselves waiting to break the fast. We'd ridden more than eighty kilometres that day and were hungry. The roadside cafe was almost full, with truck drivers sitting at tables, plates of fish and eggs and rice in front of them. We asked for a menu and were told there was only one option. This was the meal they served at Ramadan.

The sun was setting as we sat down to eat. The waiter brought our food. Joe immediately picked up his fork and was about to eat. I put my hand on his wrist and suggested he wait. All faces were turned to us.

As the sun dipped below the horizon, the muezzin made the call to prayer and the men smiled and gestured for us to eat. A chorus of Bismillah! (in the name of Allah) erupted as we ate our last meal in Morocco, marvelling at how far we had travelled and how much we had learnt. We would take with us a lasting impression of the generous Moroccan hospitality and openness to strangers, of the contrasting complex Arab and Berber cultures and of the deep Moroccan spirituality blending Islam, Sufism and indigenous beliefs, infusing daily life.

~3~

THE RACE IS ON

"**C**ome on!" I urged Joe. "Let's get away and make a start up the hill before all the cars."

The ferry was pulling into the port at Motril, on the southern coast of Spain. After having only one beer during all our time in Morocco, we'd had a late night, drinking with some young German travellers we'd met in the queue. Retiring to our cabin, we were rocked to sleep by the drumming sound of the engine as we sped 265 kilometres across the Western Mediterranean.

Now, listening to the hum of car engines starting and the ferry's chains clanking, I was buzzing, ready to start the next phase of our adventure. Joe was less excited, knowing that we had to cycle just over seventy kilometres, mainly uphill, with a total 1,500 metre climb up to Granada. The ramp lowered, and a whole new world opened out before us.

We cycled straight out of the bustling port, along the modern waterfront, into the charming old coastal town of Motril. As we bumped along the cobbled streets, we admired the blended architecture, the white Andalusian houses with terracotta rooftops reminiscent of the region's Moorish past. Graceful horseshoe arches opened out to charming courtyards, providing a glimpse of Motril's deep-rooted cultural heritage.

Several hours later, after cycling up hills looking over the Rio Guadalfeo, with the snow-dusted Sierra Nevada mountains in the background, we kicked back in a bustling cafe in the small town of Talará, eating fried calamari with a house salad and crusty bread, washed down with sparkling mineral water.

"This couldn't be more different to Morocco!" I said, gulping a glass of cold fresh water.

It was Wednesday lunchtime, and most people seemed to be immaculately turned out in work attire or smart casual. At every other table people were drinking wine, which seemed slightly surreal after Morocco. Also different was that no one seemed to notice us or have any interest in what we were doing. We'd grown accustomed to the constant attention and people queuing up to ask us questions about our journey in Morocco. The indifference of the people here was strangely unnerving. On the other hand, the familiar comforts, including the fact that we could drink water straight from the tap and go to the bathroom knowing it would be clean and there would be soap and running water, felt like a bit of a relief.

It was a long haul to get to Granada that day, but we were impressed by how good the roads were and how much distance the passing cars gave us. After a brief stop in a bike shop to fix the bottom bracket on Joe's bike, which was spoiling the serenity by making a clunking sound every time we went uphill, we tackled the last few steep kilometres of cobbles up to the Albaicín, the old Moorish quarter, in Granada. From the cute rooftop terrace outside our room in a family guesthouse we gazed at the majestic views over the Alhambra.

It was a relief to have a rest from the bikes for a while. We spent two days unwinding and wandering in the city, ambling along the beautiful cobbled streets lined with orange trees, soaking up the melodies of the street music, and savouring the sumptuous summer salads. We walked around the gardens of the Alhambra, admiring the ancient Islamic architecture and enjoying the breathtaking views of the Sierra Nevada mountains. We had a lovely evening strolling through the bustling Plaza Nueva, before enjoying a meal at a flamenco show. We also caught up with some old friends of mine.

Steve and I had met in San Francisco when I was travelling between university years. He was also from Yorkshire. When I'd rocked up to the hostel to find it full, they'd told me there was a room in a long-term let that two English guys were staying in. Steve and Wolfgang (from Austria) were working as builders, earning a bit of extra cash to supplement what they earned as musicians busking their way around America on a gap year. Steve was twenty-nine and had abandoned his successful job in marketing and sold his house in London to fund his travels before going back to England to retrain as an osteopath. Once fully qualified, he moved and set up a business in Spain. We immediately hit it off and spent the next few days exploring San Francisco together and going to concerts. We stayed in touch over the years. Steve always encouraged me to follow my dreams and travel, including going to live in Spain myself for a year after I finished university.

Now, more than thirty years later, I was keen for Joe to meet Steve and his family. We climbed up the banks, past vegetable gardens and goats at the back of the Albaicín towards the famous heritage-listed Sacromonte, to find his apartment at the top of the hill. Steve and his wife, Christine, greeted us and introduced us to their twin sons Sid and Sam, and Steve's father, David, who was visiting from Yorkshire. David was an excellent jazz pianist and Sid and Sam had also grown up to become talented musicians.

"This was where we played during the COVID lockdowns," said Steve, pointing to one side of the balcony. "Erica, the singer, was over there," he said, pointing up to a row of townhouses in front, "and Abe, the other guitarist, was up there." He gestured to another balcony. Steve and the boys played keyboard, bass and drums. After struggling to hear their neighbours on the other balconies, they managed to wire the apartments together and link up to the speakers so they could regularly treat the whole neighbourhood to uplifting music.

"It was an amazing feeling to play together even though we couldn't see each other, knowing that the people stuck in their apartments were enjoying the music. Sometimes the clapping and cheering would go on forever," he said. Sam and Sid, who were now eighteen, nodded in agreement and showed us the article that had appeared in the local paper.

Christine explained how she had dedicated her time during COVID to improving her cooking skills at home. "It was one of the strictest, longest lockdowns in the world," she said. "The streets were deserted but there was a strong sense of community. The neighbours organised bulk orders of fresh asparagus, beans, meat and cheese to be delivered to each other's houses."

Tucking into the delicious fresh food, sipping crisp white wine and enjoying the relaxed conversations about life was revitalising. Joe and I had become closer over the last few weeks' travelling. We'd learnt to anticipate each other's needs and be more patient. We talked for hours, planning routes and recounting different experiences. We were happy alone together. But the time with Steve and Christine, the twins and Steve's father was a reminder of the simple joy of family life and the richness of time with friends that we'd left behind.

Back on the road a few days later, we were stunned by the spectacular beauty of the national parks of the Sierra de Segura as we headed east towards Valencia. We stayed in a cave house and cooked on an open fire in Benalúa. We rode for twenty kilometres seeing nothing but olive trees on the way to Cazorla. Ancient churches balanced on the edge of hairpin bends above the cascading aqua blue rivers of the El Tranco de Beas dam.

"It's harder to get food in Spain than it was in Morocco during Ramadan!" Joe said as we arrived at another town during siesta to find everything closed. We had ridden too far again and were starving. Worse, I was starting to feel like I was coming down with something.

"My throat feels sore," I moaned.

"We need to keep going if we're going to catch the ferry to Mallorca," he replied. It was the holiday season, so we'd decided to book ahead for the ferry. We now realised we hadn't allowed enough time.

Two Bugs on Bikes

We pushed on for another long, hot day, much of it on an old railway trail with little shade. Arriving at the town Chinchilla de Monte-Aragon, we discovered that the camping site where we'd planned to stay was a concrete jungle full of large campervans. So we'd kept riding and were now perched on the side of a rock, hidden by trees, at the top of a hill where we planned to wild camp for the night.

I was gazing over the valley as Joe stood naked behind a rock, washing himself with a bottle of water.

"Wow. Check out the view!" I exclaimed.

"Thanks!"

"I mean the city and the castle," I replied, laughing. "Look at how the light is changing."

We pitched our tent as the last rays of light left the sky, and sat on the rock eating seafood paella made with canned seafood, sharing a bottle of red wine.

The sun was setting behind the medieval castle, casting warm hues of golden light across the rugged landscape. A cascade of colours – pink, orange and purple – cloaked the whitewashed houses. The sound of festive music wafted gently towards us as the Easter procession made its way through the main square in the city below us.

"Don't you wish you were down there soaking up the atmosphere instead of hiding away up here?" I asked. I felt anxious, despite the fact that it was now dark and no one was around.

"No. I just want to be here with you, enjoying this view," Joe said, pulling on his puffer jacket and beanie and lighting the stove. He put his arm around me and pulled me close so I could rest my head on his shoulder.

I slept fitfully that night, drifting off to the sound of distant laughter as the last of the revellers left the town and waking every time I thought I heard a car driving up the hill, my heart racing, convinced we were going to be discovered and arrested. Every shadow felt like a potential assassin.

"I'm not sure wild camping is for me," I declared the next morning, pulling my cycling clothes over my rumpled hair and rubbing my bleary eyes. My body felt stiff from the cold ground and the tension.

"We'll get better at it," Joe said.

We had read so much about other bikepackers' tales of wild camping – awakening to awe-inspiring mountain vistas or falling asleep under the starry skies, far away from the hustle and bustle of the modern world. I wanted to make sure we didn't miss out on these more meaningful experiences by always staying in paid accomodation, but as I stood there rubbing my sore shoulders, the reality felt a world apart from the idyllic images I'd imagined. I was beginning to wonder if it was worth the stress.

Alcalá del Júcar is a beautiful old town nestled in a dramatic canyon formed by the Júcar River. We locked up our bikes near the bustling artisan market and draped our cycling clothes over them to dry so we could explore the town.

After smashing out sixty to seventy kilometres of hilly rides each day for the last few days, it was good to get off our bikes and explore a new town.

"Look down here!" I nudged Joe and we peered through the jail-like bars on the huge windows of the Cuevas del Diablo (Devil's Caves), a bar halfway up the hill. The turquoise-blue river formed a stark contrast to the rolling green hills in the distance. We had crossed the Roman bridge and climbed the narrow cobblestoned streets between well-preserved white houses and past the beautiful sixteenth-century church of San Andrés to reach this quirky bar, which was owned by a former matador called Diablo. Books and artefacts lined the narrow corridors connecting the different rooms of the cave.

I browsed the markets and found some beautiful handmade emerald-green enamel earrings (I couldn't carry much on the bike, but I'd decided I was going to treat myself to a new pair of earrings from every country). Meanwhile, Joe snoozed on the sandy banks of the river, somehow managing to shut out the noise of the crowds and the music from the nearby market. We were both exhausted. I envied his ability to sleep wherever he was but also wondered what the point of cycling so far was if he was just going to sleep when we arrived.

"We should head off and find a place to camp," I told him, waking him from his siesta.

"Yes, I suppose," he sighed. "Are you sure there's nowhere to stay here?"

"Not for less than three hundred euros a night."

We had a pretty good budget for cycle tourists but couldn't afford to blow it all in the first month.

That night we camped about twenty kilometres out of town in a little grassy field by the river. A Spanish couple had already set up camp at the back of their campervan. We went through the now-familiar routine of putting up the tent, rolling out the mats and sleeping bags inside and then setting up the stove and food on the camping table outside the tent. We then washed ourselves and our clothes in the river before settling down to read and write for the evening.

"I can't find my glasses!" I said in exasperation the next morning, emptying bag after bag onto the grass, desperately trying to find them. I had been wearing them before I went to bed the night before, but now they were nowhere to be seen. We unpacked the tent again and checked all the pockets inside the tent, but to no avail. I still had my sunglasses, but needed my normal glasses for the evenings if we were out anywhere after it got dark.

Joe looked on in bemusement.

"What are you smirking at!" I snapped.

"It's just hard to imagine how you can still lose things," Joe said, chuckling. "We're carrying so little and there's a place for everything, but you still keep managing to lose things."

"You're not helping!" I snapped back. I couldn't decide whether I wanted to laugh or cry.

After retracing my steps again for the tenth time I finally gave up, putting on my sunglasses and saying goodbye to my other glasses for the rest of our trip in Europe.

That day we cycled 100 kilometres and climbed 2,000 metres. While the views were incredible, the long days were taking their toll. I had woken up that morning sneezing. My head was throbbing and my chest felt tight. I wanted to stop earlier on in the day's ride to camp at a beautiful spot by the river, but Joe pointed out that camping in the national park was strictly forbidden, so we pushed on to a government campsite: Cuevas de las Palomas.

The site was packed full of screaming Spanish kids – the absolute last thing my aching head needed. We tried to find a quiet spot and pitched our tent and set up our camping chairs to rest and relax.

"Why do they have to keep their car engine running?" I grumbled. I was standing up, bristling with anger and ready to march over to the neighbouring young couple and give them a serve.

"Sit down," said Joe. "It's probably just so they can have light while they're eating their dinner."

Another hour later the couple were playing cards with the engine still running. The noise of it grinding away was driving me crazy.

"I can't handle this anymore! The point of camping is so we can be out in nature! I'm taking them this camping lamp." I grabbed the lamp and stalked towards the young couple.

"Hola!" I called. I tried to sound friendly as I asked them if they wanted to borrow the lamp so they could turn the engine off, pointing out that it was a bit noisy, and we wanted to go to sleep.

"No, thanks," said one of the young girls. "We don't need a light. We were just charging our mobile phones. We'll turn it off now."

"Gracias," I said. "Have a good evening." I walked away, shaking my head in disbelief. "All that noise just to charge their phones?" I said, crawling into the tent and collapsing on to the mat beside Joe, who was reading. I shut my eyes and tried to sleep but felt irritated. I didn't want to be in this busy place surrounded by other people. Joe seemed relaxed and content. "Try to sleep," he said. "You're not well and need rest. Nothing will seem as bad when you've had some rest."

Several days and an overnight ferry later, I was feeling better and was keen to make the most of our few rest days in Palma de Mallorca, before we set off cycling across the island. Joe was inside sleeping, having finally succumbed to whatever bug had been plaguing us both for the last few days. I explored the old town and sat for a while in the shade of the stunning Gothic cathedral, which towers majestically over the bay. Swinging my legs over the side of the wall, looking out over the sea and scribbling a few notes in my journal, I felt relaxed and free. I was getting used to this way of life.

Mallorca is a cyclists' heaven and several days later we were whooping with joy as we twisted and turned our way down the twenty-six hairpin bends of the famous Sa Calobra descent, on one of the most iconic cycling routes in Europe. Every turn revealed another dramatic view of rugged mountains towering over deep valleys as we rolled down towards the sparkling Mediterranean Sea. The climb back up was something else, with gruelling steep switchbacks that seemed to never end. We'd left our bags with the old man selling orange juice and hot chocolate in a little cafe at the top of the climb, so we were much lighter than usual.

Back at the cafe, our touring bikes again laden up with bags were quite a spectacle for the many lean, lycra-clad cycling enthusiasts who were stopping at the cafe for a quick drink and an energy gel. We looked completely out of place and certainly not very competitive in our loose merino T-shirts and baggy shorts.

"I reckon you can catch them," Joe challenged me as we ground our way up another tough hill towards the end of the day. Ahead were two professional-looking middle-aged male cyclists that we seemed to have been trailing for a while, neither catching them nor falling behind.

I stepped on the pedals and prepared to suffer for a while as I tried to gain on them, Joe tucked in tightly behind me. Cycling most days for the last two months was starting to pay off and I felt strong and in control as my heart rate picked up and my muscles reacted to the increased oxygen pumping through my blood, slowly but surely pushing me faster up the hill. The look on the lead guy's face as he clocked me gaining on him was classic. The race was on!

"Nice work, babe!" Joe said as we stopped at the top of the hill, waiting for the group we'd passed to get to the top. The guys shook their heads in disbelief then shook our hands and asked where we were from. We were all exhilarated from the exertion and breathing heavily. We shared some stories about cycling through Morocco, climbing through the Atlas Mountains, and then through the mountains in Spain. The men were from Bristol in England, and like most of the other groups that were riding here, were on a training camp. They explained how far they had cycled that day, making excuses for being beaten on the climb by a girl on a touring bike. They were curious about our travels.

"Spain is spectacular but feels a bit familiar," I told them. "We felt more alive and physically and culturally challenged in Morocco."

"We miss feeling like rockstars and having people waving and shouting hello everywhere we go," Joe added.

"I've heard that the kids can be aggressive and throw stones at cyclists in Morocco," one of the men remarked.

"That only happened to us once," Joe said. "It wasn't fun, but it can happen anywhere. Ninety-eight percent of the people we met were friendly and wanted to talk with us, and even invited us into their homes."

"I'd love to do something like that," said one of the guys, "but my wife wouldn't want to come with me, and I wouldn't be able to be away for so long on my own."

"See how lucky you are?" I said to Joe that night as we snuggled into our sleeping bags in the campsite at the old monastery that night. We had been reflecting on the fact that our shared passion for cycling meant we were able to share these incredible experiences together.

After struggling through mainland Spain fighting sickness while racing to catch the ferry, in Mallorca we started to relax into a more forgiving routine, riding for a few days then resting, soaking up the sights and meeting people along the way. We stayed an extra night at Monastery Lluc and took a day trip to the quaint town of Pollensa before riding onto Port Alcudia. We planned our routes using the Komoot app, scouring travel blogs to get ideas and using Google Maps to find interesting places to stay. We had time to spare. The next place we absolutely had to be was Split in Croatia, where we were meeting my sister for her fiftieth birthday celebrations in June, but other than that we were free to just plan day by day and stop where we felt like it along the way.

The deal I'd made with Joe before setting off was that we could camp for a couple of weeks but then we had to have a few nights in a spa hotel. For our last night in Mallorca, we'd booked a flashy hotel in the port town from where we'd catch a ferry back to the mainland. The room had been heavily discounted, and we arrived to find it was a large, glitzy place with a vast open reception area looking out to an expansive pool. Glass lifts ferried guests to the different floors.

"You can't keep your bikes here," the receptionist barked as we walked up to the desk. "You need to take them down the road where there's a garage and you can pay for them to store them there."

"No way," I said. "That's crazy. We've been travelling for forty days all through Morocco and Spain and this is the biggest place we've stayed. Surely there must be somewhere for the bikes. What about all these rooms?" I waved my hand at a row of empty offices near the reception in the hotel.

So far on our trip, people had gone out of their way to find us a nook under the stairs or space in a storeroom for the bikes. On several occasions the bikes had even had their own room at no extra charge. It seemed so unreasonable that such a large, expensive hotel wouldn't let us keep them there and we were going to have to pay to store them.

We were planning to wake up before daylight to cycle one of Mallorca's iconic routes – the Cap de Formentor to the lighthouse – so it would be a pain to have to store the bikes somewhere else. The receptionist seemed completely indifferent to my protest.

"Please wait over there until your rooms are ready," she said sternly, pointing to a seating area.

We sat down timidly on the white fabric sofas, feeling grubby in our sweaty cycling clothes after several days camping.

"I'm not sure I'm a fan of big hotels," I whispered to Joe. "I miss the charm and personal touch of the little guesthouses."

"Yeah," Joe said. "I'm not feeling the love either."

A few hours later our outlook had completely changed.

"I'm not moving from here!" I was stretched out in the spa bath on the terrace of our executive spa suite, leaning my head back in the bubbles and holding my glass out for Joe to top up with wine.

"Pretty good, huh," Joe replied, laughing. "The sunset is going to be fabulous."

After waiting a while in the hotel reception we'd been approached by the manager, who told us that there had been a mistake with the bookings. We'd booked a discount double online but somebody had just taken the last double in the hotel at the same time, so there were now no more doubles available. We looked at each other in frustration.

"We've upgraded you to the rooftop spa suite," the manager continued, smiling. "There will be room for the bikes on the balcony. You can take the bikes in the lift. Here is your key card. Enjoy your stay."

We ran around the room like children, opening the fridge and stroking the white fluffy robes before checking out the balcony.

"I'm not going to want to leave to go out to a restaurant tonight," Joe said.

"Let's cook on the camping stove!" I suggested.

"Great idea! Let's get some supplies in town when we go to the bike shop."

I couldn't stop grinning watching Joe cook chorizo paella on the camping stove in his white robe while I lounged in the luxurious bubbles.

"What an awesome way to spend our last night in Spain," I said. "What are our stats?"

Joe checked Komoot on his phone. "Just over 900 kilometres with more than 13,000 metres climbing," he said.

"Over fourteen days," I added, "with five nights camping and one night on a boat. Not bad."

We quickly calculated how long it would take us to get to Split in Croatia at the same pace and agreed we were on track.

"Let's try not to book anything else in advance so we don't have to race again," I said. "It hasn't been much fun being under so much pressure. I want to make sure we enjoy the ride and have time to explore places along the way."

"I agree," Joe replied. "We'll take it easier from now on."

The next evening, after an early ride down to Cap de Formentor to beat the crowds of cyclists (and there really were crowds!) and a day chilling by the beach, we boarded the ferry for the twenty-three-hour trip to Toulon in France.

JACQUI WEBSTER

~4~

RAIN ON THE RIVIERA

I wheeled my bike up a rocky path off the road towards the beach and leaned it against the wall, taking a deep breath as I looked out over the sparkling turquoise waters of the Côte d'Azur. Waves gently lapped the pebbly beach that stretched out towards the Esterel Massif in the distance. I took off my shoes and socks and pulled my T-shirt over my head, tiptoeing over the rocks towards the sea.

"It's absolutely freezing!" I told Joe between gasps. My skin tingled and I could feel my senses coming alive.

"About sixteen degrees, I think," he replied, diving in and taking a few strong strokes out towards a cluster of rocks where we swam for a while looking for fish.

This was the first time we'd swum in the sea since we'd set off on our trip nearly six weeks ago.

Back home in Australia, we'd moved from Sydney to the Central Coast during COVID and now spent most of our time near the beach. We swam most mornings, sometimes about a kilometre, but other times just in and out. We found the challenge of getting into the water whatever the weather restorative for our mental health, but even in the winter months it rarely got below sixteen degrees.

After sharing a baguette and a lovely raspberry tart from a beautiful French bakery in the small town of Salinas, we continued along the V65 cycleway, part of an extensive network of greenways in France for hikers, cyclists and other non-motorised vehicles.

"So much for camping on the beach with a view!" Joe laughed. We were at Port Grimaud, a small coastal village in a bay near Saint-Tropez. We'd put up our tent in the allocated spot on the campsite that had cost us thirty euros. In front of us was the shiny wall of a gigantic new campervan, completely obscuring any view we might have had.

"That thing's the size of a small hotel," I exclaimed.

"Imagine travelling with all of that stuff!" Joe said.

The beauty (and one of the challenges) of travelling by bike was that you could only bring the bare essentials. We were each carrying two cycling outfits, plus a couple of outfits for day or cool evening weather. I had one pair of long pants, one pair of shorts, one skirt, one singlet vest, one T-shirt, one long-sleeved top and one lightweight, non-crease dress. And of course, a rain jacket and woolly hat for when it was cold. Everything could be mixed and matched so I felt like I had a few outfit options. We used packing cubes so that things were easy to find. The simplicity was liberating. It was such a stark contrast to travelling in a campervan with everything you needed – they even seemed to have two TVs inside!

It was a different sort of camping and people like us with tents were being squeezed out by the prices that people were willing to pay for a patch of grass. We ate at the campsite restaurant on the beach that night and worked out that the evening's camping cost much more than an Airbnb. Wild camping was difficult and frowned upon in this part of France.

"We might need to take out a special Riviera budget for here," Joe said.

Cycling along the waterfront between the iconic towns of Cannes and Nice with the lush green mountains in the background was something else. The cycle route was well maintained and we passed many other day trippers and even a few other cycle tourists coming the other way. Beautiful people posed in the flash resorts lining the waterfront and elegant yachts bobbed in the harbours, providing a glimpse of the luxury lifestyle.

After another prohibitively expensive night out in Nice, where we mingled with the young folk sipping Aperol Spritzes overlooking the vibrant Promenade des Anglais from a trendy balcony bar, we took a diversion from the coastal road to climb one of the Tour de France routes: Col-d'Èze.

"It'll be easy!" Joe joked when I asked him why we needed to climb to the top. It was early and the air was still crisp and cool as we cycled back along the Promenade des Anglais and out of the city. The terrain slowly transformed from coastal chic to rugged hinterland as we navigated the increasingly steep switchbacks, glancing out to the sweeping sea views with the dramatic mountain ranges in the distance. The 500-metre climb took us about an hour and we posed at the top of the summit for a photo by a statue of an oversized Tour de France cyclist.

Reaching the charming medieval city of Èze, we enjoyed croissants and coffee overlooking the Mediterranean Sea, before continuing our ride.

Several hours later, after some exhilarating descents, we had dodged through a gap in the barriers and were cycling as fast as we could along the famous Monaco Grand Prix racetrack, gaping at the expensive boutiques and restaurants advertising champagne and oysters. Workers were setting up for the famous race the next week. Rows of empty seats and huge TV screens lined the streets along the iconic circuit.

"I'm not sure we fit in here?" I said to Joe as we sat with our feet hanging over the edge of the harbour wall in the shadow of the seemingly endless line of superyachts in Port Hercule. We had leaned our bikes up against a lamppost so we could rest and enjoy our simple picnic lunch of a baguette with brie and cherry tomatoes. "We must look like vagabonds!" A group of smartly dressed people walked by, looking down at us and glancing back to our bikes, tutting as if it were not the done thing to picnic in Monte Carlo. I smiled up at them, not caring what we looked like, knowing that I wouldn't trade the experiences we were having for any amount of riches.

Later that day, after crossing the border into Italy and exploring the beautiful old town of Dolceacqua, we were enjoying an ice cream in the evening when Joe said, "Do you realise we had breakfast in France, lunch in Monaco and dinner in Italy?"

"I know! What a day!"

"It feels good to be in Italy," said Joe, who is half Italian. "I'm looking forward to visiting my cousin and we would have run out of money quite quickly if we'd stayed any longer in France."

That evening we ate fresh pasta with delicious freshly made pesto which the region is famous for. Having climbed up to the nineteenth-century castle where we stopped to look out over the lush Ligurian landscape bathed in the evening sunshine, we meandered back along the cobbled street and over the donkey's back bridge, ducking under ancient arches, past shops and cellar doors, until we reached our guesthouse.

"Remember the last time we were in Italy?" asked Joe softly.

I nodded, tears pricking my eyes. It was a year after my dad had died. Joe had organised everything as I was still struggling to get excited about anything, even a holiday. I flew from Sydney to Rome to meet Joe, who had been cycling with friends. We hired a car and drove down to the Amalfi coast and spent a few days in Positano.

"I know I didn't say so at the time, but I was so grateful you took charge", I said. "When we stopped for homemade lemon granitas hiking in the Valley of the Gods up above Positano, it was the first time I'd felt truly happy in ages."

Joe smiled and hugged me close. "I remember feeling so relieved to see you smile again. And I'm glad we got to see Nonno and Nonna's birth homes in Calabria before we went to Sicily. Do you remember arriving in Strongoli in our hired Alfa Romeo?"

"Yes," I said laughing. "It was like we were the first tourists to go there in two hundred years!" The few elderly villagers still living in the largely abandoned hilltop town had all come out into the main square. They watched and waved in excitement as we navigated our way up the steep narrow streets to the only guesthouse in town. We felt like A-grade celebrities!

Several days later, having left our bikes at the campsite just outside the bustling town of Sestri Levante, halfway between Genoa and La Spezia, we mingled with the mobs waiting for the tourist train to take us to Riomaggiore, one of the five villages that form Cinque Terre (five lands).

I'd been looking forward to visiting Cinque Terre for years, seduced by American travel writer Rick Steves' description:[i] "Tucked between Genoa and Pisa, along a mountainous and seductive six-mile stretch of the Italian Riviera, lie the Cinque Terre – five *(cinque)* traffic-free villages carving a good life out of difficult terrain. Each village fills a ravine with a lazy hive of human activity. Calloused locals and sunburned travellers enjoy the area's unique mix of Italian culture and nature. There isn't a Fiat or museum in sight – just sun, sea, sand (well, pebbles), wine, and pure, unadulterated Italy."

We didn't share his enthusiasm. The pastel-coloured villages nestled into the steep rocks overlooking the sparkling Ligurian sea were stunning, but we felt lost wandering around with the crowds navigating gelato shops and trinket stores. The experience felt contrived and unreal. We were happier back on our bikes the next day, climbing the hills in the rain and catching glimpses of the coloured houses through the fog.

Leaving the Ligurian coastline behind, we noticed the rugged mountainous terrain transform and soften into rolling hills as we crossed the border into Tuscany. Tired from a long day in the saddle after two nights camping, we approached our spa hotel in Fosdinovo in anticipation. We were excited to treat ourselves to some downtime and had booked in advance for two nights, upgrading to a balcony room.

"Here's your rooftop balcony," said the hotel receptionist with a sweeping gesture intended to demonstrate the expansiveness of the view. My heart sank as I looked out at the gigantic grey rooftop that completely obscured any view of the landscape. Old television aerial wires lay abandoned on the ground. An uninviting broken outdoor furniture setting seemed a weak attempt at creating a sense of comfort. The room itself appeared dark and damp, matching the weather outside.

Two Bugs on Bikes

The disappointment had kicked in the minute we cycled up to the hotel door. The place resembled some sort of Italian *Fawlty Towers* scenario but without the humour. The male receptionist at the front desk had been quite rude about our reluctance to leave our bikes in the unlocked car park. This hotel was supposed to be a treat and we'd expected something much nicer for our first night in Tuscany.

"How about *this* view?" Joe asked the next night as we stood looking out over the majestic mountains, which were speckled with white stone. We were camping on the edge of a steep drop outside the Citta di Massa refuge in the Apuan Alps. The area is renowned for the pure white marble mined in the Carrara quarries, used to create the Pantheon in Rome and Michelangelo's *David*.

"Much better!" I replied. We had abandoned the hotel after one night, despite the manager refusing to give us a refund, and were instead camping for free outside a mountain camping refuge for hikers.

Inside, over a homely dinner of beef ragout with freshly made pasta and house wine, we learnt that the refuge was established in 1947 by the Italian Alpine Club to provide a safe resting place and logistical support for hikers and climbers exploring the Apuan Alps. This was part of a broader effort to develop a network of mountain huts across Italy, enhancing accessibility to the country's mountainous regions.

"Maybe we should ditch the idea of spa hotels," I said to Joe later that night, snuggling contentedly into my sleeping bag on the edge of the cliff.

The rides through Tuscany were breathtakingly beautiful, particularly the Strade Bianche, made famous to cyclists as part of the UCI (International Cycling Union) World Tour. The white gravel roads meandered through the rolling hills, fields of yellow and red spring flowers stretching out before us. We settled into a more relaxed rhythm, finding quirky farmstays in the rolling countryside or local guesthouses in the gorgeous towns of Luca and Siena, where we wandered through the ancient cities savouring the sights and stocking up on supplies for the next days' rides.

"This is where he parked the bulldozer!" I pointed out to Joe. Inspired by the novel *My Italian Bulldozer* by Alexander McCall Smith,[ii] we had cycled up to the hilltop town of Montalcino and were exploring the streets, trying to find places where the different scenes were set. In the book, the protagonist, Paul, who has just been ditched by his girlfriend, escapes his stressful city life to come to Tuscany and finish a cookbook that is already overdue. However, he arrives at the airport in Italy to find there has been an administrative stuff-up with his hire car booking, and the only means of transport available is a bulldozer. It's an implausible love story, and we enjoyed reliving the jokes while wandering around the ancient cobbled streets.

"Let's go and taste the Brunello," said Joe. Montalcino has been made incredibly rich and famous by its Brunello, one of the best and most appreciated Italian wines. Sitting in a little terraced restaurant draped in bougainvillea, overlooking the vineyards, we laughed with the sommelier as we tasted different drops.

"This rich red should give you notes of wild berry, liquorice, star anise and leather," he said.

"Leather?" I exclaimed.

"Yes," he went on. "This is because of the ageing process in oak barrels. This Brunello has been aged for five years. Many old red wines have hints of leather."

A few nights later we were sitting sipping house wine at a farmstay in the quiet hilltop town of Torricella, after camping for a few nights and cooking on our gas stove. It was quite a contrast to Montalcino. Arriving in the afternoon, we found the family busy serving a big group of people coffees after a long lunch. Kids were playing in a playground overlooking fields of horses. We took a walk around the farm buildings and stables, where they were schooling a young foal. It reminded me of my family's farm back home in Yorkshire and I felt a pang of homesickness. I had always travelled and had moved to Australia away from my UK family seventeen years earlier, but still felt a strong pull towards my family back home on the farm. I missed hanging out with my niece, preparing the holiday let and looking after the horses. I always wondered what my life would have been like if I hadn't moved so far away. I was looking forward to spending some time with my sister and niece in Split later that month.

For the next few days, our focus was racing the rain. We rolled down from the hilltop hamlet of Torricella in beautiful sunshine and started the 700-metre climb to San Marino, anticipating amazing views from the European microstate perched precariously at the top of Mount Titan. But with every switchback turn the fog closed in around us, and by the time we reached the top we couldn't see much beyond our front wheels.

"Are those your bikes?" asked a security guard who had wandered over to the cafe where we were sipping hot chocolate. He pointed back towards the edge of the square where we'd left the bikes and wet clothes to dry while we put on warm clothes and went in search of food.

"Yes," I said. "Is there a problem?"

"No problem," he replied. "It's just that they are parked in the president's parking spot in front of the palace. The president is on his way."

"That's a problem!" I said, mortified. We ran over to the bikes and quickly moved them to a safer spot.

Initially an independent monastic community dating back to 301 AD, San Marino lays claim to being the oldest existing country as well as the oldest constitutional republic. We were sitting in the main square, the Piazza Della Libertà (Freedom Square) and had unwittingly parked our bikes in front of the public Palace, the city hall and the seat of government, which had been obscured by fog. Looking up now we were impressed by the distinctive Gothic-style building with its striking clock tower. The building is a symbol of the republic's long-standing independence and democratic traditions.

We somehow took a wrong turn descending from San Marino and ended up pushing our bikes up steep roads through the fog before descending back down towards Rimini on the Adriatic at the southern end of the Valley of Po. It was good to see the sea again, but there was something serene and quite surreal about the Adriatic coast at the beginning of May. The beaches were prepped for summer, with rows and rows of posts with ropes strung between them marking out where the beach umbrellas and sun loungers would go for the private lidos. In other places there were lines and lines of unoccupied beds awaiting guests. There were hardly any people around, but we missed the raw beauty of the natural beaches that we were used to in Australia.

The rain was really setting in. Bemoaning our lack of adequate wet-weather gear (we had rain jackets to keep our top halves dry but nothing for our legs or shoes), we tried wrapping our shoes in plastic bags to keep them dry. Many of the hotels and restaurants were still closed and it felt like we were in the wrong place at the wrong time. We managed to find a small serviced apartment in Ravena to spend a few days to dry our clothes and prepare for the next stage of our journey towards Venice, but the constant rain was starting to get to us. We were losing our appetite for exploring more Italian towns and eating mediocre food in overpriced restaurants.

Wandering along the beach towards the promenade later that night, we heard loud music thumping from a little beach bar and went over to explore. A small group of people were drinking and invited us in. A DJ was playing, and it turned out it was his birthday. He'd invited a small group of friends to celebrate and we'd inadvertently crashed his party, but no one seemed to care. We drank too many negronis and danced the night away, stumbling back along the beach in the early hours of the morning and crashing into a heavy sleep.

After chugging along in the rain for another day we finally reached Chioggia, a charming town at the southern end of the Venetian lagoon.

"Benvenuti, venire!" ("Welcome, come in!") said Giovanna, the owner of the small Airbnb we had booked.

"We're soaking wet!" I exclaimed, pointing to the muddy bikes.

"No problema," Giovanna said, grabbing my bike and steering us inside, where she insisted we give her our clothes so she could take them home to wash, and made us coffee while we showered.

"What an amazing welcome," I said to Joe later, as we were wandering through the picturesque winding streets along the canals and over bridges.

"Just lovely," replied Joe. "It makes such a difference when you meet someone and they are welcoming and interested in your story."

Giovanna had asked us heaps of questions about our trip and our lives at home and shared with us her story of moving from Milan to set up her charming little Airbnb in Chioggia. We'd been missing those connections while cycling in the touristy areas along the coast. It probably explained why we'd been feeling a bit lost and were missing friends and family.

Chioggia is known as Little Venice because of its similar canals and architecture, but it's less crowded, making it peaceful and relaxing to explore. The colourful buildings reflect a blend of Venetian and traditional styles and it's famous for its bustling fish market, which adds to the town's lively atmosphere. We enjoyed a glass of wine and a pizza at a bar while we mapped out how to get to Venice mainland the next day. No bikes are allowed in the city, so instead we would need to catch a ferry and cycle eleven kilometres along the cute Pellestrina island, enjoying its quaint, pastel-coloured houses and relaxed lifestyle, then jump on another ferry to Venice Lido, where we could leave our bikes in a hotel before catching a ferry to Venice for lunch and to spend the afternoon.

Arriving in Venice by boat was a completely different experience to when I had travelled there by train with my sister when we were Interrailing around Europe more than thirty years earlier. The spectacular ornamental buildings and churches tower majestically over the sparkling water, with boats, punts and barges all jostling for position coming in and out of the canals. I told Joe how my sister and I had arrived only to find out that Pink Floyd had played a free concert on the water the night before and everyone had watched from the cafes or punts on the river.

"Everyone we met was asking if we'd seen the epic show and we were so disappointed to have missed it," I recalled, smiling and thinking of how long ago it seemed now.

Following a good tip from another cyclist we'd met on the way, we stayed on the ferry as it weaved through the different ports so we could get a good view of the city from the canals without having to pay extra for a tour, before disembarking at St Mark's Square. We visited the cathedral and meandered through the little alleyways, tasting different foods before finding a restaurant for an evening of jazz. But it was strange to be without our bikes, which had become part of our identity, and we felt far removed from the masses of tourists as we roamed through the famous streets and squares.

From Venice we headed away from the coast and climbed up towards Udine and the border with Slovenia. Our last two nights in Italy were spent at a mountain farmstay called AleGra, run by Alex and Graciela, where we slept in tiny huts with glass roofs so you could fall asleep looking up at the stars. After a long ride and having to push our bikes much of the last 700 metres uphill on dirt tracks, it was a relief to arrive at the farmhouse and be greeted by Graciela, a warm welcoming Argentinian woman. She showed us where we could wash at the back of the farm house and went off to collect wood to light the stove to warm the water for showers whilst we washed our bikes with a bucket of water.

Alex, her husband and the cook, returned from where he had been collecting honey. "I'm Italian" he said as he brought us peppermint tea to drink by the fire. "I met Graciela in Mexico when we were working as volunteers to help protect communities from human rights abuses."

We were sitting by the fire relaxing and sheltering from the rain. "We've owned property for twelve years now but had to work hard to get the farm and restaurant going." Alex explained. "The restaurant has been popular for a few years now. The tiny huts for guests are a more recent addition: we built them in 2020 during COVID."

The huts were little more than a raised bed with a small amount of space to keep your things, but they had a sloping roof made of glass so that lying on the bed you had a fabulous view of the countryside and the sky above. Alex, who loved sleeping outside looking up at the stars, had initially just built one of the tiny huts for himself, but then friends had visited and said he should build more and start a guesthouse to go with the restaurant.

"We didn't realise they were going to be so popular," he said.

There were just five huts spread out on the side of a sloping meadow dotted with sheep. There was no one else there when we stayed.

Climbing into bed later that evening, full after a delicious meal of homemade pasta and wine, we lay looking up at the stars and watching the clouds move over the night sky as the last light lingered on the side of the rain drenched mountains. We reflected on the challenges of living out here in the mountains.

"Do you think you could live somewhere like this?" I asked Joe, romanticising about the idea of being on a farm with chickens and having to grow our own food somewhere remote. But he was already sleeping.

JACQUI WEBSTER

~5~

WHY DON'T THEY LIKE US?

"**T**wenty-three!" I called out to Joe through clenched teeth as I stood up on my pedals, using every last bit of strength to power me around the twenty-third hairpin bend. We were climbing the iconic Vršič Pass. At 1,611 metres it's the highest pass in Slovenia, with twenty-five switchbacks, each offering a more spectacular view of the rugged alpine landscape than the last. At that time of the year it was covered in red gorse, which contrasted sharply with the bright, snow-capped mountains in the distance.

By the time we reached the top we were exhausted; we leaned our bikes against a wall and tried to catch our breaths.

"That was sensational!" I gasped, collapsing on a bench and breathing in the crisp, cold air.

After two and a half months riding most days, we were beginning to feel really fit, but this climb was still a bit of a stretch with our heavy bags. We'd crossed the border into Slovenia the day before. Bovec was a bustling adventure hub that reminded us of Queenstown in New Zealand. We tasted the burek (savoury pastry filled with meat or cheese and spinach) in a local bakery and drank a few beers in a local craft brewery while planning the climb across the Julian Alps the next day.

"It's an advanced climb only for really fit people," the woman in the tourist information centre had said, looking me up and down. We'd been trying to find out if the pass was open at the top, as for weeks there had been too much snow.

"Just follow the yellow line," another guy had replied when we'd asked him which direction to go.

We left the centre laughing, feeling none the wiser.

The start of the ride had been relatively easy, meandering alongside the bubbling aqua blue Soča River flanked by fresh green pine forests. But once the climb started, we were in for some punishment.

The descent was highly technical, with steep cobblestone switchbacks that were slippery in the damp air. The road was built by the Russian prisoners of war during World War I and various monuments are dotted along the route, adding a historical dimension to the natural beauty.

Slovenia was the first country on this trip that I hadn't previously visited and it was the first time I'd been in the Balkans. I was enjoying relearning some of the history, particularly about the ten-day war when it became independent from Yugoslavia, which it was part of for most of the 20th century. Despite being a socialist state allied with the Eastern Bloc, Slovenia never subscribed to the Warsaw Pact, which provided for a unified military command between the communist states dominated by the Soviet Union. Slovenia continues to operate as a parliamentary democracy with a centre-left government.

We stopped for lunch in the elegant Kranjksa Gora on the Sava Dolinka River. After rolling through endless green meadows flanked by mountains and stocking up on supplies in Bled, we continued along the valley to the smaller sister Lake Bohinj, where we pitched our tent right next to the water. Both Lake Bled and Lake Bohinj were made by glaciers and have thermal springs. Sitting on our camping chairs waiting for our stove to heat, we marvelled at the towering mountains reflected in the glasslike surface of the lake.

"This place is dreamy." I said. "I'd love to hang out here for another day."

Joe's eyebrows knitted together. "But we need to continue and get to Croatia."

"You always want to push on," I bit back. I knew I sounded like a petulant child, but Joe's need to keep moving was exhausting. "I feel like we're missing out on things, just rushing from A to B without having time to relax and reflect, or even explore. Shouldn't we be doing what all the other tourists here do and taking the boat across Lake Bled to climb up the ninety-nine steps to the Church of our Dear Lady to ring the bell and bring ourselves good luck?"

"Why do I need any more good luck?" Joe countered. "I'm here with you, cooking my dinner on a camping stove, looking out at this inspiring view with nothing else to do but ride my bike for the rest of the year. Why should I want to do what the other tourists do?"

He had a point, and I conceded.

But some days I longed to be more like other tourists. Covering much of the same route as the better-known EuroVelo 8, The Parenzana Trail runs along a 129-kilometre stretch of trail on an old railway track that operated from 1902 to 1935, along the Istrian peninsula. Crossing the border into Croatia, we climbed the hill on the grassy track, glancing back at the stunning views as the Adriatic Sea disappeared behind us. The old tunnels, bridges and railway stations of the trail punctuated the route and provided some historical context for it. It had been a lifeline for trade until it was abandoned in the early 20th century.

But as the smooth grass tracks turned into rough gravel, the charming railway tunnels lost their appeal.

"This is impossible to ride," I said, getting off my bike in the damp, dark tunnel to push. "I can't see anything and my bones are literally hurting from the constant bumps."

"It did say it was best suited to mountain bikes," admitted Joe, "but I've read lots of reviews from people on touring bikes who said it was okay."

"Maybe with thicker tyres?" I suggested. "The rocks are the size of footballs. This is definitely not a track for touring bikes!"

In the quiet little town of Krančići, we drank a beer with an old man who introduced himself as Edward.

"There is nobody here. Everyone left after the war," he told us, gesturing to the empty square. "People are starting to come back with tourism, but most of my friends left a long time ago or have died now."

It was less than thirty years since the end of the Croatian war of independence from the former socialist state of Yugoslavia. Almost one-quarter of the Croatian economic infrastructure was ruined, costing billions of dollars. More than 20,000 people were killed and many more refugees were displaced, placing a huge social and economic burden on the country.[iii]

"It's amazing how quickly people forget," I said to Joe as we were cooking our food in the lovely camp kitchen later that evening. "When people think of Croatia now, they think of lovely islands, the beautiful historical cities of Split and Dubrovnik, and *Game of Thrones*. People rarely think of the war, despite the fact that it was the subject of a high-profile international criminal trial that resulted in some parts of the war being declared a genocide less than twenty years ago."

"People don't want to think about these things," Joe replied.

But the old man in the square was clearly still impacted and had wanted to share his memories.

"There's something different about the people here," said Joe, coming out of the supermarket at the end of a long ride a few days later. "I feel like they don't like me. I try to be friendly, but they just stare back at me coldly."

We had been in Croatia for a few days now and, while the scenery was beautiful, we were finding it hard to relate to people. Usually, any people we met were falling over themselves to be nice to us, either because they were genuinely interested in our story or because they wanted to sell us something, but here people seemed indifferent, even standoffish.

"Maybe it's a throwback from the communist era?" I suggested, noting that Russian people were also reputed to be quite stern.

We later learnt (mostly from reading the Cody McClain Brown book *Chasing a Croatian Girl*,[iv] which is written by an

American who marries a Croatian) that Croation people are rarely friendly unless they know you. They actually think it is very strange if you smile or start informal chit chat with them if you don't know them. On the other hand, when you do get to know Croatians, they are very hospitable and will go out of their way to make sure you are looked after. Understanding these cultural differences changed our expectations and this, alongside learning a few greetings in Croatian, transformed our interactions.

"How do you fancy island hopping for a while?" asked Joe, pouring over the map. "We have plenty of time before we need to get to Split to meet with your sister. We could get a ferry from Pula to Lošinj island, and then cycle across the bridge to Cres, then get the ferry to Krk, and then get the ferry to Rab and cycle to the other side, then get the ferry to Pag."

"That sounds like just my kind of adventure!" I agreed, thinking Joe might finally have realised we needed to slow things down.

It turned out my expectation of gentle rides around beautiful islands was misguided. Like the mainland, the Croatian islands are all different in terms of terrain, but a key characteristic is that they are rugged with craggy mountains in the centre. Most of the towns and villages are located at sea level by the water's edge, meaning steep climbs from one to another. The main road through Cres runs along the backbone of the island, which is flattened out, meaning there is little to see. Off the main roads some of the tracks are extremely rocky and hard to ride. It wasn't always the idyllic, picturesque environment you would imagine it to be, but there were some stunning rewards for our efforts.

"I've been subject to misinformation!" said the elderly German cycle tourist, holding out a piece of paper showing us the ferry times from the island of Rab to Pag that day. "They said there was a boat at 4.30 pm and now they are saying there is no boat until tomorrow."

"I know," I empathised. "We also arrived today not realising it was a public holiday and the boats wouldn't be running. We might see you on the boat tomorrow!"

"Only seven bikes are allowed on the boat each day," Joe pointed out as we were eating dinner later that evening. We'd been island hopping for a while now, mostly on car ferries. The boat operating between Rab and Pag was a small passenger speed boat with limited capacity for bikes. "We've already met three other cyclists planning to leave tomorrow. We should make sure we arrive early so we can be at the front of the queue."

By eight the next morning we were perched on the front of the boat, surrounded by twelve bikes tied precariously to the railings. There were more inside. With no life jackets and no safety briefing, we were jetting across the sea between Rab and Pag islands. We shouted excitedly, exchanging stories with two other cyclists who'd joined us on the front of the boat as we bumped across the Adriatic Sea, watching the small speck of land in the distance come into focus.

Pag is famous for Paški cheese, made from sheep's milk. The island is sixty kilometres long and has around 8,000 inhabitants and 30,000 sheep. Arriving by boat, we were faced with a tough climb out of the port. We were going in the same direction as the two other cyclists – Patrick (from the Netherlands) and Jules (from France) – so we decided to stick with them.

We stopped at the bakery just before the town of Novalis for burek and coffee, then continued off road for a while, admiring the strange lunar landscape with steep, smooth rock faces looming over glistening white salt pans across the water. Relaxing into a rhythm, we started to enjoy chatting with Patrick and Jules. We camped together that evening, splitting the cost of a site by the water and enjoying a shared dinner in a nearby bar. It was great to have company and we laughed listening to each other's stories and learning about why we'd all decided to take time out of our lives to explore the world by bike for a while.

The next day Patrick announced that he wanted to take the sheep's trail which was part of the route he was following. I didn't think this sounded like a good idea.

"Sounds good," said Joe immediately without even looking in my direction.

"That is not how I would have chosen to spend my day!" I was starting to lose my mind as my bike bumped over lumps of rock in uneven ruts on the grass trail. The track was interspersed with gates to keep the sheep in different sections. We had to stop and open the gates and drag our bikes through. There were apparently twelve on the route and we had only counted four so far.

"Me neither!" said Joe, looking annoyed. To my surprise he agreed we should quit and head back and after some negotiation, we managed to escape the trail and get back onto the tarmac road towards the main town of Zadar. Patrick and Jules both followed. After a night in a cosy shared apartment drinking walnut liquor with our host, Iva, we went our separate ways, promising to stay in touch and drop in on each other should we happen to be passing through our different homelands.

Joe and I continued island hopping. Dugi Otok is the most remote of the Croatian islands. We headed to Sakarun Beach, a patchwork of azure-blue and black water, very few tourists and just a handful of boats, where we ate the best Greek salad I've ever tasted. The next day, after sleeping at Kamp Kargita, we rode to Sali on the other side of the island.

"Are you seriously going to jump from there?" Joe was clinging to the side of a rock and was about to plunge about thirty metres into the Mediterranean Sea.

Spending the day with a Belgian couple we'd met at the campsite the night before, we'd diverted from the main road near the town of Vela Luka, and attempted to cycle but ended up pushing out bikes up most of the off-road climb to the top of the cliffs so we could swim through the Dragon's Eye and Golubinka sea caves. Leaving my clothes on a ledge, I clambered across the face of the rock so I could jump into the sea further down and we swam together, taking it in turns to dive down through the semi-submerged entrance of the cave and lie on our backs as the mesmerising light reflections from the crystal-clear water bounced off the cave walls.

"Thank you! We would never have been brave enough to do that if you hadn't dragged us along," shouted the Belgian couple as we cycled our separate ways that afternoon.

The climb up to the house we'd booked to stay with my sister and niece outside Split was almost impossible, made worse by the fact that it was raining. We arrived exhausted and rang the bell to find there was no one there. Our host Anton arrived minutes later and opened the gates. They swung open, revealing a stunning newly built two-storey house with a large garden area.

"Don't worry, the workers will stop soon for the weekend," Anton reassured us, gesturing to a large crane and the rattle of the construction coming from next door.

As I took in the view, I couldn't help feeling a bit disheartened. I'd splashed out a fair bit of money so we could have a lovely place to spend time with the family, but it had views over a building site. I couldn't help thinking I'd be happier camping on the side of a hill.

Fortunately, my sister Sam, niece Ella and their partners were thrilled by the house, especially the rooftop spa and gorgeous ensuite rooms. It wasn't long before they had chosen their rooms and were popping champagne and chatting about what to do over the next few days. I joined them, laughing and drinking in the hot tub on the roof. It was great to reconnect, share stories and relax together, though we stayed up too late, which left me with a hangover the next morning. Joe was preoccupied with planning the next few legs of our trip, including working out where he could get his bike fixed as it was still making a terrible clunking sound whenever we cycled up hills.

The next few days passed too quickly. After ninety days cycling through Morocco and Europe, immersing ourselves in different cultures and adjusting to a simpler way of living, our time with family in Split was a bit of a culture contrast. It was clear that our priorities had shifted along the way. They wanted to sit in the sun, but we wanted to relax in the shade. They wanted to go and explore the busy tourist spots and we wanted to stay local and escape the crowds. Their holiday was about indulging and unwinding from their busy lives on the farm, and we had got used to embracing simple pleasures. Joe and I adapted to their agendas, and we had fun on a boat tour to one of the islands and darting around the town on hired scooters.

Our last night together was Joe's birthday, and he wanted to walk up the hill to a nearby restaurant with rave reviews about the local food and excellent views over the bay, while the others wanted to head back into town. In the end, we went our separate ways. I tried to put on a brave face and pretend it didn't matter, but I was crying inside. The family time I had been looking forward to for months was over all too soon, I felt like we hadn't had enough quality time together, and it would be too long before I would see them all again.

~6~

BRINGING A KNIFE TO A GUNFIGHT

We were queuing at the Bosnian border at Ivanica. Joe was leaning forward, resting on his handlebars, looking fairly incongruous in his orange T-shirt and baggy shorts chatting to a group of leather-clad motorcyclists. They were dressed in black from top to toe, with full-face helmets obscuring their eyes. They looked intimidating.

"Where have you come from?" the one nearest to Joe asked in clipped English, gesturing at the bikes.

"Spain," he replied. We learnt a while back that it was easier not to have to explain that we first did a loop in Morocco and took the ferry across.

The men told us they were from Serbia and were heading to Bosnia for the weekend. They wanted to know how far we cycled every day, how we navigated, where we slept.

"Why don't you get motorbikes?" they asked.

"Good question!" I responded.

"We like to stay fit, plus you see more from a bicycle," Joe explained.

They looked unconvinced as they sped off, shaking their heads and laughing with each other.

"This place is really desolate," I said to Joe. We had turned off the main road after the border crossing and were travelling parallel to the Croatia–Bosnia border. The road was just a single lane peppered with potholes and the sky was dark. There seemed to be no one else on the road. The fields at the side were overgrown and every few kilometres there were piles of rubble around the ruins of abandoned houses.

"I'm guessing this place was destroyed during the Croat–Bosniak War and was never rebuilt," I said.

Just at that moment I saw a warning sign for landmines.

"Jeez! Are you sure it was a good idea to cycle this way?" I asked Joe. My stomach began to churn.

As if in response, thunder rumbled in the distance.

"It's a well-marked cycle route," he replied, "but the forecast is for heavy rain. We need to push on quickly."

Seconds later I heard him cursing ahead of me.

"Bloody hell! Not again! Not now!" He swung his leg over the bike and hurried to the back wheel, which had popped and deflated.

"Stay on the road!" I reminded him, suddenly even more conscious of the potential landmines.

I checked the map to see how long we were going to be on this road while he changed the tyre, which he could do quickly now.

"It's about another fifteen kilometres before we're back on the main road to Trebinje," I said.

Back on our bikes we faced an increasingly strong headwind as we bumped over the potholes, slowing our progress even further.

"Is that a bull?" I said suddenly. A herd of cows was standing on the road, staring curiously at us while chewing. Just ahead of them stood a bigger, bulkier creature with a wider head and menacing horns.

"Yup!" said Joe.

"You have got to be kidding!"

"What now?" asked Joe. "You're the farmers' daughter."

I took a deep breath. "We have to just keep going," I said. "Stay to the right so he doesn't feel threatened."

I was breathing heavily. My heart was beating so hard I thought it was going to burst out of my chest as I cycled past the bull, trying to look friendly. Joe followed behind me in silence as the bull watched on.

It never moved.

By the time we hit the main road the rain was pouring down and we dashed towards a petrol station where lots of motorcyclists were sheltering and pulling on waterproof layers. They made space for us outside the shop while we stacked our bikes against the wall and rustled through the bags to find waterproofs.

"Where are you going?" asked one of the motorcyclists. He had taken off his helmet revealing a big, friendly bearded face.

"Trebinje," I answered.

"You planning to stay there tonight? Have you booked somewhere?" he asked. "Do you realise the biggest motorbike festival in the Balkans is being held in Trebinje this weekend?"

We shook our heads in disbelief. We didn't know. We hadn't booked anywhere.

"It's like bringing a knife to a gunfight!" Joe exclaimed as we rolled into the town, motorbikes passing in both directions and groups of bikies sitting around drinking beers on every corner.

After being turned away from the first few places, we managed to find the last room on the outskirts of the pretty town, just across the Trebišnjica River. We showered and lay on the bed for a while, laughing about our day. We had woken up in Split and said goodbye to Sam and niece Ella and their partners, before cycling to catch the ferry to Dubrovnik. The others were also going to Dubrovnik and spending a few days there before heading back home. They wanted to drive, so we'd agreed to say goodbye in Split. Joe and I relaxed on the four-hour journey, watching through the windows as the mainland flashed by in the sea spray. Then, just as we were pulling into port, Sam had called and said they were arriving.

"Why don't you come and meet us for lunch?" she'd suggested.

"Great idea!" I replied.

It wasn't a great idea.

We had to deviate from our planned route to meet them near their Airbnb. While it wasn't that far, Dubrovnik is on a steep cliff, which made it almost impossible to get out of town.

"You were so angry with me," I said, laughing at Joe, who buried his face in his hands.

"I know!" he groaned. "I'd spent ages planning the route so that we could get through the city easily and you immediately just threw the plans out of the window without even asking me."

"I'm sorry," I replied. "But I wanted to have a last meal with them. And you have to admit, the views climbing up out of the city from that road were spectacular!"

"Yeah, except we had to haul our bikes up over the railings just to reach the main road."

The route had clearly been closed to cars, but we'd managed to get through on the bikes. From there it was a steep uphill climb to the border crossing where we'd first encountered the bikies.

"Come on. Let's go party with the bikies. What else could go wrong?" Joe said, pulling me up from the bed.

We wandered over the Ottoman bridge, admiring the watermills and views along the riverbank, and meandered through the cobbled streets to the main square, where we sat down and ordered a beer.

"What currency do they have here?" asked Joe.

"Gosh, I don't even know," I replied, looking it up. "The Bosnian convertible marka, BAM for short, is the only legal currency, according to this."

"Do you take euros?" asked Joe as the waiter arrived with our beers.

"Sure, no problem," he replied.

"That was the most expensive beer of our trip so far!" I said as we left the square.

"I know!" Joe exclaimed. "I didn't realise Bosnia would be so expensive!"

We later laughed when we realised the menu had been in markas and we'd paid the equivalent amount in euros.

"The waiter must have been pretty happy with that tip!" I said as we tucked into a typical Bosnian meal that evening. Joe chose ćevapi (skinless grilled mixed-meat sausage) with somun bread (soft round flatbreads dusted with sesame) and ajvar (spicy red capsicum and eggplant sauce) and I had grilled trout with spinach and potatoes. Everything was fresh and delicious.

Later that evening we wandered over to the festival enclave. There were several bars and a big stage being set up for a concert. Rows and rows of motorbikes were lined up outside a tent with black-leather trouser-clad bikies wandering up and down, checking out the revs. The noise of the engines was incredible. I lined up at the bar to get a drink. Looking around I felt I almost blended in with my black hoodie and hiking pants, but Joe stood out like a skinny cyclist in his mustard merino overtop.

"I don't know how we'll sleep tonight," Joe said as the music cranked up and the bikies started swaying to the electrifying energy of AC/DC and other rock anthems.

Less than an hour later we were tucked up in bed, sound asleep, oblivious to the noise outside. We awoke the next morning refreshed, and ready to take on another country.

JACQUI WEBSTER

~7~

BEARS IN THE BALKANS

Bosnia was our entry to the Balkans. For the next few weeks, we tried to soak up information about these fascinating countries that were characterised by complicated cultures and conflicts linked to their former socialist identities and clashes with communism.

Twenty-four hours after our encounter with the Balkan bikies, we were crossing another border into Montenegro, one of the newest internationally recognised countries in the world. Montenegro (which translates as the black mountain) was part of the former Yugoslavia and then Serbia and Montenegro, before separating from Serbia in 2006.

The Bay of Kotor is a long stretch of the Adriatic Sea with several broad bays joined by narrower channels, surrounded by the Dinaric Alps; tall, rugged mountains that tower majestically over the sparkling water. We descended into the bay as the sun emerged from the clouds, and skirted around the water's edge admiring the pretty medieval stone villages. The water was crisp and cool as we jumped in to refresh ourselves before locating our little Airbnb, where we stayed for a few days to explore the ancient walled city. I walked up the 1,350 steps to St John's fortress to check out the views over the bay at sunset. Joe joined me later and we snacked on fried whitebait in paper cones, wandering around the maze of small alleys, bookshops, quaint hotels and bars of the old city.

We left before sunrise the next day. *"If you can dream ..."* I read out the graffiti on the stone wall of the first hairpin up the Serpentine climbing up out of the Bay of Kotor. The motivational quotes spurred us on to master the steep hills between the switchbacks as we climbed higher and higher.

"If you can fight ... I wonder what the next one says?" I pondered.

"Look at the views from this cafe," said Joe as we stopped, leaning our bikes up against the wall.

"It looks closed," I said.

Joe skirted around the back. "We can get in through here," he called. "Grab the bags with our lunch."

We sat perched on the edge of the cliff on the newly built tables and chairs in the still-closed cafe, eating the bureks that we'd bought from the bakery at the base of the epic climb and staring in reverential silence at the shimmering Bay of Kotor, a slice of blue wedged between imposing mountain walls. The huge cruise ship that had blocked half of the view of the bay when we were at sea level looked like a tiny speck from where we were now, more than a thousand metres above.

Half an hour later, as we flew down the Lovćen mountains after climbing all morning, my heart sank a little.

"Why can't we ever stay at the top?" I said to Joe, only half joking. "We always seem to spend so long climbing just to roll back down again!"

"Happy now?" Joe said later, gesturing out over the expansive views from the hilltop cafe adjacent to our campsite nestled under an old olive tree on the side of a hill, not far from some famous waterfalls. I smiled and nodded begrudgingly. The climb was always worth it.

The next day we took a short diversion to see the oldest olive tree in Europe, the Stara Maslina, located just outside the old city of Stari Bar. Said to be 2,247 years old, the ancient tree's thick, twisted trunk was charred black on one side, supposedly the result of some old men throwing away a cigarette butt while playing a card game. We paid the one euro entry fee and posed for photos, looking somewhat emaciated in comparison to the enormous trunk of the tree.

"Where are you heading?" asked a middle-aged man wearing a long white tunic and a round skullcap. He was standing next to a campervan, admiring the view.

We explained that we were heading up into Serbia and then across to Bulgaria.

"No, no, no!" he said, his face falling. "You must travel through Albania. The coastline is stunning and the people there are so kind and inviting. Serbians are not kind."

Crossing over the border into Albania a few days later, we found the condition of the roads was starting to deteriorate and huge electricity pylons were stretched over the landscape, spoiling what would be lovely views over the lake.

Albania is a developing country that was first independent in 1912, having separated from the Ottoman Empire. It transitioned from being a monarchy to a communist regime, before becoming a constitutional republic after democratic elections in 1992. A period of instability and economic hardship followed. Over the last two decades the country has transformed from one of the poorest countries in Europe to an upper middle-income economy, with agriculture and tourism the major contributors. But the tourism infrastructure still seemed to be evolving.

We'd read somewhere that at Ladis's restaurant you could camp for free, as long as you ate in the restaurant. Rain was forecast, so we set up our tent in a shed on the edge of the lake before escaping into the comfortable shack to read and write by the fire while our dinner of goat stew and oven-cooked potatoes was being prepared by the owner. At the other side of the restaurant, her family played a game of cards.

"Listen to this," said Joe, looking up from the book he was reading: *The Accursed Mountains: Journeys in Albania* by Robert Carver.[v] He told me about kanun, the ancient Albanian code of honour and justice, which was passed down orally over the centuries, serving as a guiding principle for society. It governed many aspects of life, including family, blood feuds and property.

"According to kanun, if someone is killed or dishonoured then the family of the person killed or dishonoured has the right to take revenge. So sometimes these fights span generations and people have to live in confinement all their lives for fear of being killed," he said.

"Does this still happen today?" I asked, somewhat nervously.

"Blood feuds still happen occasionally, but the government is trying to stop them," he said, reading on. "The good news is that one of the worst things that can happen in Albania is that someone can disrespect a visitor, so I guess we can expect to be treated well as travellers."

The next day we woke early for the thirty-kilometre ride to catch the 9 am Komani Lake ferry from Fierzë to Valbonë. The roads were some of the worst we'd encountered, with huge potholes filled with water from the rain. Passing through a tunnel under the dam wall, we emerged at the bustling ferry port where hordes of people were waiting. We were immediately pounced upon by a young man telling us we needed to pay a tax to get on the boat.

"We already have our tickets, which include the taxes," said Joe confidently, having been tipped off by Ladis the day before that this might happen.

We wheeled our bikes to the back of the boat and locked them up. Joe queued to buy a local snack of meat and potatoes in flatbread. Upstairs the ferry was filling up fast. There were no seats inside and people were pushing past to try to find space on the outside deck. As the ferry set off, I couldn't help wondering how safe it was. It was clearly well over capacity.

I was happy to be outside watching the impressive landscape float by. Towering green hills cast a shadow over the azure waters of Lake Komani. The fog melted away as the sun came up over the hills and every turn of the ferry led to more breathtaking views of the mountains and little villages that dotted the hillsides.

"What's that?" I nudged Joe and pointed at a shadow moving towards us on the water.

For the next ten minutes we were slicing through a sea of plastic bottles that had been tossed into the water. It was a sobering reminder of how vulnerable the world is. Both of us talked about how sad it made us feel that the beauty of the lake was veiled in so much plastic debris. Albania is one of the dirtiest countries in Europe and clearing up trash is an ongoing challenge, but much of the country is still pristine.

Rolling off the ferry three hours later, we climbed up into the Accursed Mountains in the Valbonë Valley, the road running alongside a beautiful clear river. Here, blue water bounced effortlessly over boulders, no trash in sight. We stayed in a little family guesthouse and ate in a nearby restaurant.

The next day we hiked back up to the border with Montenegro, drinking in beautiful views of fields of flowers and rugged, snow-capped mountain peaks. For the last few kilometres we slid over the snow to reach the Maja e Thatë pass at 2,050 metres. We'd set off for a stroll that morning and had taken hardly any supplies, so we were starving when we reached the top.

Relief flooded through me when I spotted a sign for food on our way down. We were close to the bottom of the climb but still several kilometres from the village.

"Don't get too excited," said Joe. "There doesn't seem to be anyone here."

"Let's knock on the door," I suggested.

I rapped gently and an old lady wearing traditional dress, a headscarf and a warm smile opened the door. Half an hour later we were sitting at a table topped with a colourful tablecloth and a basket of hot bread, overlooking the picturesque valley dotted with mountain huts. We were brought plates of cheese and pickles, followed by thick jani me fasule, a traditional white bean soup, then homemade cake and coffee.

We ate hungrily, savouring every last bit of food as we rested our legs feeling our energy slowly return.

"So much for a rest day," I said with a wry laugh.

Despite months of cycling every day our legs were smashed from the hike. For the next three days we struggled to walk.

Two Bugs on Bikes

Rolling back down from the valley, we crossed the border into Kosovo.

Chatting to the border control officer about our ride I said, "Albania has been great – we've met lots of lovely people. But we're looking forward to continuing our journey and learning about the people of Kosovo."

"It's the same," he responded. "We are all Albanian."

I laughed at the absurdity of it with Joe later. "Imagine that a border control guy would say that the new country we are entering is the same as the last country."

But chatting to the guesthouse owner in the vibrant town of Prizren, the second-most populous town in Kosovo, we learnt that more than 90 percent of people in Kosovo are ethnic Albanians. There are some differences, our host, Alex, conceded.

"We tend to be better educated," he said. "We speak a different dialect [Gheg] in Kosovo. Most people in Albania still live in the country and follow their ancient traditions. Albanians have a stronger national identity, whereas Kosovans embrace multi-culturalism."

Certainly, in Prizren multiculturalism was evident. We sat on the terrace of our guesthouse looking out over an immaculately maintained Catholic cathedral in a predominantly Muslim country. In the main square, young people wore Western dress while smoking shisha pipes and listening to modern Western music.

Kosovo declared independence from the Socialist Republic of Serbia in 2008, after a prolonged period of conflict where Serbian authorities inflicted many severe human rights violations and atrocities on the Albanian population, leading to a NATO bombing campaign followed by UN administration. It was hard to believe that all this had happened less than thirty years ago.

Later that afternoon, I was staring at my weathered face in the mirror, watching as a young lady with limited English hacked off chunks of my hair. I had shown her a picture of a younger me with shorter hair that I was keen to look like again. She looked doubtful, but committed to giving it a try.

An old man wearing a round skullcap and walking with a stick was resting on the chair opposite. He spoke English and told me about protests that were happening near the border with Serbia. The protests had been sparked by local elections in municipalities with significant Serbian populations. Serbia does not recognise Kosovo as an independent state and tension still simmers.

"Many Serbs boycotted the elections," he told me. This led to the election of ethnic Albanians, which led to riots."

I left feeling somewhat relieved, both that my haircut wasn't a disaster and that we'd make a lastminute call not to go to Serbia.

Somewhat by chance, we stayed at a Serbian guesthouse in one of the Serbian municipalities the next day. We'd been nervous due to the tensions but, while the town felt a little eerie, the guesthouse, Etno Kuća Petrović, was homely. The owner, Lady Snezana, was stereotypically staunch and unsmiling, but made us feel comfortable with a lovely meal of ćevapi and zimnica (pickled vegetables) with potatoes. We slept well that night.

Several days later, after riding across North Macedonia, we were wild camping in the Rhodope Mountains in Bulgaria, having been riding along the ridge admiring the amazing views over the Thracian Plain for the last few days. We'd had a spectacularly peaceful evening setting up camp and cooking in the mountains, far away from everything. It was blissfully quiet. Perfect. But when night fell and we tried to sleep, I couldn't relax.

"Hey babe, wake up. There's something outside the tent," I hissed. I'd read that there were bears in the Rhodope Mountains.

"Go to sleep," said Joe. "I can't hear anything."

Two Bugs on Bikes

"I can hear breathing and munching," I said. "I've been awake for ages. I just need you to look outside."

He grumbled but sat up and zipped open the tent.

"Oh my God!" Joe gasped. "You're right!"

"Oh no!" My heart was racing and I was starting to panic. "What is it?"

"It's a rabbit," he said. "Can I go back to sleep now?"

~8~

INCONVENIENT CATS

Joe had spent hours researching the best route to take to get into Istanbul. We were already tired of Türkiye, worn down by the oppressive heat and the relentless traffic. We had expected to be uplifted by the rich ancient culture, sumptuous food and friendly people. Instead, we cycled past ancient ruins without stopping, the melting tar sticking to the tyres as we trundled painfully slowly along the hot black roads towards Istanbul, on a tight timeline to meet family.

A chance encounter with Clive, another Aussie cyclist, travelling in the opposite direction, reminded us that we were not as tough as many other cycle tourists. We received a WhatsApp message from Clive, a work colleague of one of our friends back home, just as we'd reached the top of a big climb to get to our eco-lodge after another hundred-plus-kilometre day in the saddle in over forty-degree heat.

"You must be in Türkiye by now?" his message said. "I think I'm travelling the other way. Where are you?"

Incredibly, we were about two kilometres away. Clive was sitting on the floor in a petrol station just outside Vize at the bottom of the hill.

"There's no way I'm going back down that hill," Joe said.

I sent Clive the address and directions to our eco-lodge and invited him to come and join us. Clive had also left Australia in March but in the opposite direction, flying to Tbilisi in Georgia and setting off from there. He told us that he liked to travel for as long as possible on a minimum budget. He nevertheless seemed to enjoy the shower and dinner in our lodge while he entertained us with his stories of camping on roundabouts or under highways surrounded by stray dogs or staying with locals in remote villages. Our stories seemed tame by comparison.

Setting off the next day, we were determined to be more intrepid.

"Maybe over there?" I gestured to a shady patch at the back of the park. After another long, hot day, we had cycled to this spot in the hope it might be suitable for camping.

Rusted old oil cans were overflowing with garbage. Underneath a dilapidated picnic table, two stray dogs lurked, waiting for food. Clive had mentioned that if we took food for the stray dogs they would leave us alone. They seemed friendly enough, but I didn't want to get too close.

"There's no water," groaned Joe as we tried to turn on a rusty tap at the side of a derelict building that might have once served as a washroom.

We were tired and hungry. My enthusiasm for wild camping was diminishing by the second, gloom descending over me at the thought of hanging out in this unwelcoming park all evening. We were up high but the trees blocked any kind of view.

"Let's eat something and then decide what to do," I said.

The dogs followed us for about three kilometres as we escaped the park, eventually giving up when we reached the main road.

Istanbul was easily the busiest place we had been on our travels so far, and all our research indicated that it would be a cycling nightmare. "Istanbul, as it turns out, is almost entirely bike-proof," wrote Rebecca Lowe in her memoir *The Slow Road to Tehran*.[vi] "Between the outskirts and the centre lies a labyrinthine mass of urban barbarity designed to vanquish even the hardiest of wayfarers: an Escher-like confusion of ten-lane roadways, vertical hills, jet black tunnels and inconvenient cats."

Luckily for us, Joe's research paid off and, having cycled through every demographic group's habitat, including luxury villas and informal settlements, as we traversed the many layers of the outskirts from the north, we dropped relatively effortlessly into the sprawling city of over 17 million people.

We celebrated with a victory photograph at the Bosphorus.

"We've crossed a whole continent," I said to Joe, feeling emotional with the realisation of what we'd achieved.

The next day, we queued up at the Chinese embassy. We'd been told we couldn't get a visa for China without going back to Australia, but we thought we'd give it one last shot.

Joe handed over our application forms, together with passport photos and flight and hotel bookings. The stone-faced official shook his head and handed the papers back.

"Australians can't get visas here," he confirmed. "You have to go back to Australia."

We left the building feeling dejected. There was no easy way forward from here. We had reluctantly made the decision not to cycle through Iran due to the recent tensions, so we'd been planning to cycle through Georgia to Azerbaijan and then get a ferry across the Caspian Sea. But the land border with Azerbaijan was still closed, plus it was going to take us too long to cycle back across Türkiye from Bodrum in the south-east of the country, where we'd arranged to meet some friends to go sailing for a week. So, we'd been planning to fly from Bodrum to Kyrgyzstan, cycle the Pamir Highway and then cross over into Xinjiang in China and take the train to Beijing. Without a visa for China, we were going to have to fly twice.

"One of the main reasons we're travelling by bike is because it's more sustainable," I said to Joe. "I'm not that excited about having to fly into Kyrgyzstan and then fly out again."

Joe nodded. "I really want to cycle the Pamir Highway, but we're also running out of time."

If I was honest with myself, I'd been feeling anxious about cycling the Pamir Highway, the old spice route, for some time now. Spending several weeks cycling at 4,000 metres above sea level was going to be tough, and also very cold. I knew it was one of Joe's dream destinations, so I'd been bracing myself to get through it for him. But it was starting to seem like I had a way out. Where would we go instead though?

We had seven more months before we were due back at work. Suddenly it all seemed too hard, and I was struck with an overwhelming desire to be back at home, going to work and hanging out with family and friends.

Back at our guesthouse in the north of the city, we scoured maps and the Australian Smartraveller advice.

"Maybe we could just loop back through Europe and visit some of the places we've missed on the way here?" I suggested.

Joe shook his head. "I'm not interested in going backwards," he said. "Maybe we can cross over through Israel. We can't get through Syria of course, but maybe we can take a ferry across to Cyprus and then to Lebanon?"

"I'd really love to ride from Alaska to Patagonia," I said, "but that's too far for six months ... maybe we could just do South America?"

"Venezuela is a red zone, so 'do not travel', according to Smartraveller," said Joe. "You wanted to have a hard rule of not going through any red zones."

This was true. I wasn't comfortable with cycling through areas against official government advice, even though I knew the government's decisions were often political.

I can't really remember how we decided on Africa. We were discussing our experiences to date, how in Morocco every day was different, and we felt really alive. Europe had been fun, but it was more like a holiday on bikes. We were looking for a more meaningful adventure. Joe had been excited about Lebanon and Israel, but it turned out that the ferry that used to run from Cyprus to Lebanon or Israel no longer ran, so that option was out (lucky in hindsight, given that war broke out three months later!). But if we flew to Rwanda, avoiding Egypt, Sudan and Ethiopia, which were part of the classic Cairo to Cape Town route but were currently unstable for various reasons, then we'd have a clear route of mainly green and amber countries (safe to travel according to Smartraveller), all the way from Kigali to Cape Town.

"I've always wanted to travel in Africa," I said excitedly as we were booking our flights later that day. "I just never imagined it would be on a bike!"

Having made our decision, our excitement and nerves started growing in equal measure. Sitting on our camping chairs to fit in with the locals on the banks of the Bosphorus in Sariyer, we discussed our fears.

The sun was setting, throwing flashes of pink light across the rippling river water. Groups of teenagers and families, some wearing Western outfits and some in more traditional Turkish attire, sat around on deck chairs, enjoying cups of tea and snacks by the water. Sariyer used to be a fishing port and many old locals live there, but recently it has attracted more affluent Turkish families and expats, lured by the proximity of the lush forests and charming waterfront areas within easy reach of the bustling city. It felt at once foreign and familiar, and very safe.

"I know Mum is going to freak out when we tell her we're going to Africa," I said. "She'll be convinced that we'll get eaten by a lion or kidnapped by armed rebels." Secretly, I was also worried about these things.

"I'm more worried about the roads," Joe said. "I'm not sure we have the best bikes for the roads in Africa. It'd be good to have thicker tyres, but our bikes won't support them. And I'm worried about getting sick and not being able to get treatment."

Joe had been sick quite a lot since we'd set off travelling and often didn't seem to have optimal strength. I was convinced he had long COVID.

Several days later he was completely bedridden, this time with a serious bout of food poisoning. His son Jesse, who'd met us in Istanbul with his girlfriend, Isabella, was also sick.

The night before we'd been on a fabulous food tour, trying the local delights on the Asian side of the Bosphorus. Joe and Jesse were now blaming the mussels.

Two Bugs on Bikes

Enjoying some quiet time to myself while Isabella rested on the hotel roof, I sat on an ornate mosaic bench by the water fountains outside the entrance of the Hagia Sofia, watching the queues of people snake their way through the entrance.

The thing about travelling by bike is that when you're not with your bike it's easy to feel lost and directionless. When you are with your bike your identity is clear: you're one of those crazy people who cycle thousands of kilometres in search of adventure. People cross the streets to come and say hello to you and find out what you're doing. It's a great way to meet people and spark conversations.

Now, alone, watching all the tourists flock by, I felt like I didn't belong.

I pulled out my journal (now an app on my phone, having spilled a bottle of water over my original notebook) and made some notes about the last few days. When we'd crossed the border into Türkiye, we had been given a few packets of biscuits by some random strangers in the car behind us. Joe thought it was funny that I opened them to check for drugs! Then we were invited to shelter in a garage with a group of farmers in a small village when it started raining. The youngest guy spoke some English and helped translate as we sat chatting, learning about each other's lives. These were the kind of friendly moments we experienced in the rural areas away from the main roads.

In stark contrast, in the city, most of our exchanges were with people who were trying to find ways to extract money from us. Türkiye is known for its hustling tourist touts, but the people seemed more desperate than I remembered from my previous visit, and the friendly jaunts were becoming increasingly irate. The Turkish lira was rapidly losing value against the dollar, and the Turkish people were losing faith at the same pace, angry at the government for the lack of regulation on immigration, which everyone seemed to think was the source of every problem.

It was hard saying goodbye to Jesse and Isabella after five days in Istanbul together. We'd had a sensational time exploring the sprawling souks and majestic Hagia Sofia and tasting fish sandwiches straight off the boats by the Bosphorus, despite the food poisoning. Jesse, then twenty-four, is the younger of Joe's two boys; his eldest, Jacob, was twenty-five. They'd been just eleven and twelve when I met Joe. I'd watched them grow up and, while never feeling the need to take on a mothering role as they already had such a strong network of supporting female role models in their lives, I'd become very attached to them both and loved having them in my life. Isabella had been Jesse's girlfriend since school and we adored her.

Waving them off on a bus to Cappadocia, where they were going to take a hot air balloon flight, we jumped back on our bikes and cycled a few kilometres to catch the ferry across the Sea of Marmara to Bandirma, to continue our journey south-west towards Bodrum, where we were planning to meet up with friends for a week on a boat.

"Do you know what has surprised me most about you on this trip?" Joe said the next morning as we were cycling up a long hill out of Edremet.

"No," I said, intrigued. "Please tell me!"

"That you have been able to completely leave your work behind. I didn't think you would be able to do it. I'm glad."

It was true. I hardly thought about my work, and I never talked about it. The person who'd taken over my job had set a goal to not have to contact me and, apart from one email early on, she'd stuck to it.

"I know, I was nervous I'd need more of a purpose," I said. "I thought I would need to be achieving something to feel fulfilled, but it's been enough just getting from A to B."

"What have you learnt about me?" asked Joe.

"That you always pick every single seed out of watermelon," I laughed.

"I can't believe you don't," he said. "What else?"

"That you are a meticulous planner and have to plan everything! And maybe also that you are probably less inclined towards camping and spending time in nature than me. I thought I was going to be the one wanting spa hotels, but it's you!"

"That's not true!" Joe protested. "I just like to know I can have a shower and a cold drink."

A few days later we were cycling through a forest just kilometres from our campsite when we were stopped by four men carrying machine guns.

We were trying to reach Arden camp, a stunning riverside campsite nestled between the foothills of Mount Ida and the Aegean coast.

My heart thumped wildly. The soldiers were shaking their heads and seemed to be indicating that we couldn't go past and had to go back. But we couldn't understand what they were saying.

"What do you think the problem is?" I asked Joe.

He shook his head. "I don't want to go back, whatever it is. I'm spent."

A few minutes later a group of young Turkish people turned up on a quad bike and translated for us. It turned out there had been a lot of forest fires and the area was closed unless you had a booking.

"Do you have a booking?" asked one of the young people.

"No," I replied. "We only have a small tent and so we always just book when we arrive."

"You'll need a booking," he replied. "Or, they said there is a place a couple of kilometres back where you can camp under a bridge by a river. It's not a campsite, but people camp there and it's outside the national park, so it's allowed."

Joe looked distressed and shook his head. "It's so hot. I really need some shade and a cold drink," he said.

There was no reception so we couldn't book online. Our options were looking limited.

Another exchange with the army guys took place. Then the young guy turned to Joe and said he needed to go with him on the quad bike to the campsite and get a booking and then they would let us in.

I stood by the two bikes, watching Joe disappear on the quad bike with the three strangers, leaving me alone in the middle of the forest with four soldiers. They were glancing over at me and saying something. This suddenly seemed like a very bad idea.

"We think you like to sit," said one of them, wandering over with a chair.

I smiled, realising my fears had been misplaced. They were just being considerate.

That evening, after pitching our tent on the banks of the river and then diving into the crystal-clear water to freshen up, we sipped mint tea and ate gözleme with the hip young Turks.

"I saw your bikes. Where did you ride from?" asked one of the young girls, leaving her group to come and chat to us. She was pretty, with a sort of shabby chic look to her. She introduced herself as Merveet. I immediately warmed to her. She translated between us and the group, fielding their questions about how far we rode every day, where we slept, how we navigated. We asked about their lives, finding out about life for young people in Türkiye, learning about their hopes and dreams. "He said Türkiye is not a good place to be at the moment," Merveet translated. "The government has let too many immigrants in. They are not educated. They don't work. It is costing the country too much money."

We were surprised to hear this sentiment echoed in the younger, presumably less-conservative people.

Merveet was excited when we said we were going to Africa and insisted on getting our details and following us on Instagram.

"I'd love to do what you are doing. You are so inspiring. Stay safe," she shouted as we cycled off the next morning.

~9~

DANCING WITH THE GREEKS

"It's so hot!" I said to Joe, turning over in the tent. "I can't sleep. Let's get up and jump in the sea." It was dark but there was a full moon casting a bright beam over the pebbled beach and glistening water. We were camping on the west side of the Greek island of Chios, having ridden over the mountain range. Our tent was in a little grassy nook under the trees a few metres back from the shore. We grabbed our towels and tiptoed over the pebbles, walking cautiously into the cool water and submerging ourselves.

The water rippled with an other-worldly light as we plunged in. "Look at the bioluminescence," Joe breathed, moving his hand slowly through the water, lighting up a trail of stars.

"It's like being wrapped in a blanket of sparkling lights," I said sinking into the water.

Climbing back into bed we fell asleep immediately, our body temperatures finally cooled to the core and our senses soothed by the magical experience.

We woke to the sound of the water lapping at the pebbles. The sun was just coming up over the hill, casting a beam of orange light along the water. As I looked up, I saw a large ram perched on the edge of the cliff, silhouetted in the morning light.

"We've got company!" I said to Joe, pointing up at the ram.

He laughed and rubbed his eyes. "I slept like a log after our swim."

"Me too," I replied. "Great idea to come to the Greek Islands."

Tired of the heat and traffic in Türkiye, Joe had done some research and worked out that we could get most of the way to Bodrum island hopping through Greece. We'd taken a ferry from Cunda Island (which is connected to mainland Türkiye by a bridge) to Lesbos, where we'd hung out for the morning before taking another ferry to Chios. After a night in an Airbnb in the main town, we rode over the top of the island, climbing up through the dry vegetation, hoping we could find somewhere to camp on the more remote side. We were only about thirty kilometres from Türkiye across the water, but it felt worlds away.

A few days later a catcall rang out as I slipped into the cold water on the island of Samos, just as the sun was rising. "Happy birthday, sexy!" said Joe.

I smiled. I was fifty-two years old that day and felt utterly content.

We'd splashed out for my birthday, booking into a small boutique hotel with a pool surrounded by olive trees.

Back at the hotel, over an elegant breakfast of Greek yoghurt and fresh fruit, flaky pastries and homemade jam, Joe outlined his plan for a ride – a fifty-two-kilometre exploration of the island's beaches.

"It'll be great to ride without all the luggage," he said.

I took a deep breath, torn between the lure of more adventure and the tempting thought of relaxing by the pool all day.

"As long as we're back early in the afternoon so I can have at least an hour to lie by the pool and ponder the state of my life before we go out for dinner," I negotiated.

We headed off shortly later, stopping to buy new tyres in the quaint little town of Pythagorion, named after Pythagoras, the Greek philosopher and mathematician best known for his theorem on right-angled triangles. At the bottom of the cobbled shopping street the road branched left and right (creating two right angles!) and Joe indulged me by looking after the bikes for a few minutes so I could wander up and see the famous Blue Street, where the locals have painted everything white and blue, including plant pots and bicycles, in true Greek style.

After a long, steep climb into a headwind, we had a lovely lunch in Mytilini and then stopped for a swim at the beautiful beach of Posidonio.

"Ouch!" I yelped several hours later as my front wheel hit a big lump of gravel, tossing me sideways into a patch of briars. "This is a nightmare!" I ranted. "How much further do we have to go? What made you think fifty-two kilometres, mainly off road, was going to be a good idea?"

"You're fifty-two today!" Joe replied.

We arrived back at the hotel tired, hungry and bruised, with little time to spare. We jumped in the pool to quickly freshen up before pulling on the best clothes we could find and heading out for dinner. So much for my relaxing time by the pool!

The restaurant Triantaphyllos (Little Square) in the sixteenth-century village of Paleokastro was alive with locals laughing and drinking wine. We were ushered into the only free table at the edge of the square, which was lined with bars and restaurants all draped in purple flowers. Absolutely ravenous after the day's gruelling ride, we ordered whipped feta and roasted red capsicum dip with crusty bread and salad, grilled swordfish with olives and lemon, and a demi-carafe of white wine.

"Let's get more wine!" I said to Joe, feeling energised by the food and the atmosphere.

"Are you sure?" Joe said. "I'm really tired."

"But it's my birthday," I responded, crestfallen. "I thought we might go out dancing!"

"I'm sorry, babe," said Joe. He looked sheepish. "Maybe we should have taken it a bit easier today."

I pushed my plate away with a sigh but smiling. "Let's go home. It would've been fun to go out dancing, but we've got the rest of the year!"

The next morning we caught the ferry to Agathonisi, a small speck of land that divides the archipelago of which Samos is part, from the Dodecanese islands. With only around one hundred and eighty inhabitants, there are just a couple of tavernas and a shop by the port. Joe had been nervous about coming here as it was almost impossible to cycle up and over the island's steep roads, and there wasn't another ferry for two days. We were stuck and there was literally nothing to do.

I was ecstatic. This was my idea of heaven.

"Are you here for the festival?" asked the young woman serving coffee at the tiny taverna where at least a quarter of the local residents seemed to be having breakfast.

"What festival?"

"The festival of Agios Panteleimonas, the famous saint of this area," she replied. "It is tomorrow evening. Boats will start arriving full of people from all the other islands by midday tomorrow. Isn't that why you came?"

"That sounds amazing!" I smiled as I realised my plans for doing nothing were out the window. "Where do we get tickets?"

"You don't need tickets. You can just rock up and pay on the day," she said.

"Where are you planning to stay?" asked an elderly local. He looked quintessentially Greek with his striped T-shirt and beard.

"We don't know yet," I responded a bit nervously. We were planning to check out the beach and wild camp, but locals weren't always happy about this.

"There are some guesthouses up the road," he said, "but they are crazy expensive. If I were you, I would just camp on the beach. No one will bother you."

He pointed out the road running back along the side of the island and said there was a beautiful beach at the end of it, about a kilometre away.

"This place is incredible," I sighed, lying on the pebbly beach in the shade that evening. "This is exactly what I needed."

The next morning, we took a stroll to the other side of the island to see the old fishing port and were greeted by a colony of cats guarding the boats, which were bobbing peacefully in the water. I photographed a small blue-and-white church on the hill on the way back, thinking it looked like the very essence of Greece. Later, over lunch by the water, we watched as boats full of people old and young, the men in shorts and smart shirts and the women in summer dresses, arrived, ready to join the celebrations.

The religious procession snaked its way up the hill to the little Church of Saint Panteleimonas.

"This is so much fun!" I beamed at Joe later that evening, my face glistening with sweat and my shoulders burning as I was swept around the dancefloor to an energetic rendition of "Zorba's Dance".

People, mainly locals from the other islands and a handful of other tourists like us, sat on long benches, feasting on barbecued souvlaki, marinated pork chops and zucchini with watermelon and feta salad. We drank local wine while a folk band played traditional music and old and young alike were dragged into the dancing circle.

We didn't expect to sleep much that night – there wasn't anywhere near enough accommodation on the island for all the extra visitors and we'd heard that the young people simply stayed up all night or slept on the beach. Fortunately, only a handful seemed to find our beach and they didn't keep us awake for long.

"That was our last night camping before we go to Africa," I noted as we were packing up the tent.

"Hey mate!" shouted Simon as we walked into the yacht club. "Look at you guys, all skinny and fit. How are you? How's it been?"

We sat down at a table overlooking the pool and ordered beers. Trevor arrived a few minutes later and we stood up to hug him. It felt good to be with friends again.

We knew Simon and Trevor from our triathlon club, but the idea for the sailing trip was based on reuniting a crew that had kayaked across the Bass Strait two years ago. The Bass Strait crew included Joe, Trevor, Simon and Ollie, but Ollie hadn't been able to join for the sailing trip. I had been part of the Bass Strait crew when Trevor first initiated the plan to kayak the stretch of water from the south of Australia to Tasmania. It was during COVID when travel restrictions meant Joe and I had to postpone our planned departure for our cycling trip. We couldn't leave the country, but we were allowed to leave home to exercise, and kayaking was exercise. None of us were really kayakers before then, and with just six months to train, it was an intense time.

There was only ever a small chance that I was going to see it through, but I didn't want to be left out. During a summer holiday spent kayaking on the big seas between Sydney and Batemans Bay I lost my nerve and decided to quit. The boys kept going and made a successful 350-kilometre crossing over twelve days in March 2021, stopping at remote islands and spearfishing for food along the way.[vii]

The plan to meet in Bodrum was made based on our itinerary. But rather than stay in Türkiye, we decided to sail back across to Greece and explore the Dodecanese islands. In hindsight, this was a mistake. It turns out going through customs on a sailboat is a bit of a headache: the Greeks aren't exactly known for their bureaucratic speed and efficiency.

After an initial hairy crossing from Bodrum to the island of Kalymnos, we spent the rest of the day docked, waiting for our papers.

There were worse places to be stuck for the afternoon. Kalymnos is a stunning island renowned for rock climbing due to its steep cliffs. My eagerness to explore the port town of Pothia was rewarded by the labyrinth of charming cobbled roads snaking through quintessential Greek houses built from local stone and painted an array of gelato shades, with blue shutters and balconies. Cafes and shops lined the waterfront, many selling the sea sponges that Kalymnos is famous for.

Our seven days on the yacht were a welcome break from the bikes, despite the bureaucracy of crossing borders on a boat. The days passed quickly as we navigated our way from one island to the next, enjoying the serenity of the ocean, stopping to swim in caves and spending the nights sipping ouzo after long, lazy meals with locals.

"Look at these guys," I said, pointing to the pod of dolphins dancing around the bow of the boat as we crossed the virtual border back into Türkiye. "It's like they're giving us an escort."

"What a fitting end to a fabulous week," said Trevor, finally looking relaxed now we were on the home stretch.

"I can't believe you're going to cycle through Africa for six months," Simon said hugging us goodbye at the port in Bodrum. "Do you think we'll ever see you again?"

"For sure," said Joe with a laugh. Little did we know that at some points during our time in Africa we'd be thinking the same.

Joe playing cards with the local Berber kids in Ijoukak, Morocco

Taking a break *on the way up the Dades Gorge, Morocco.*

Breaking the fast with Foued, Nefzi Guest House, Morocco.

Joe cooking chorizo paella, wild camping, overlooking the City of Chinchilla de Monte-Aragón, Spain.

Picnic lunch in Monaco (we had breakfast in France and dinner in Italy that day!)

Exploring the quaint streets and bridges of Chioggia (also known as Little Venice).

Enjoying the serenity in the evening sunshine, camping by Lake Bohinj, Slovenia

Wine gifted after a tasting session at Azienda Agricola La Lastra, just outside Sienna.

Perfect for stargazing - glass roofed mountain huts, La AleGra farmstay, Lusevera, Italy.

Two Bugs on Bikes

Joe celebrating on reaching the top of a big climb, Cres Island, Croatia.

Posing for a picture with Patrick (The Netherlands) and Jules (France), Pag island, Croatia.

Joe getting route tips from the Serbian bikies at the Bosnia-Montenegro border.

Picnic lunch stop at an unopened restaurant, top of the Kotor Serpentine, Montenegro.

Fox visiting us wild camping near Smolyan Lakes in the Rhodope mountains, Bulgaria.

Celebrating cycling across a whole continent, Bosphorus Strait, Sariyer, Istanbul

JACQUI WEBSTER

PART II
AFRICA

Two Bugs on Bikes

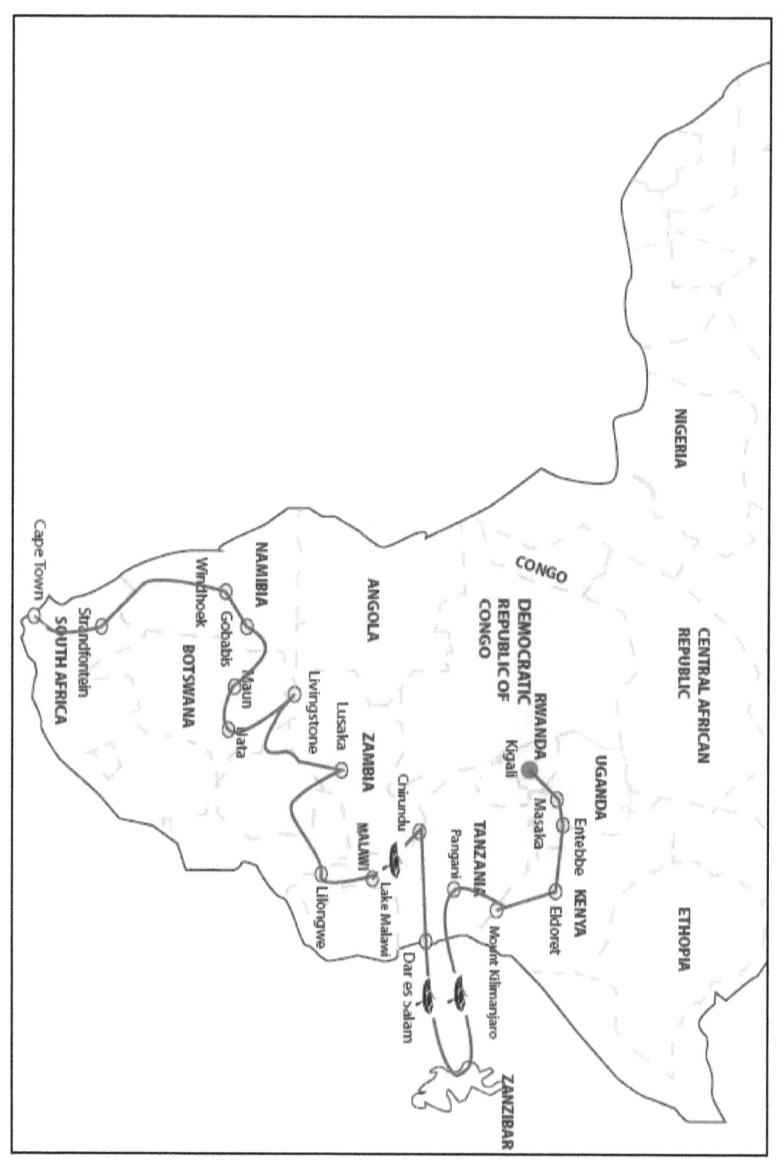

JACQUI WEBSTER

~10~

TWO LEFT SHOES

I was bristling with excitement as we climbed down the steps of the plane into Kigali Airport. The air was warm but not stifling. I could see glimpses of the lush green hills in the distance. We shuffled across the tarmac into the terminal. It was small but relatively modern, with lots of natural light and plants. Local artwork was draped across the walls. Signs were in English and French. The airport staff were dressed smartly, the women wearing bright scarves in the blue, green and yellow of the Rwandan flag.

The immigration official asked lots of questions about our planned bicycle trip. What sorts of bikes did we have, where were we going to go, where would we stay? But apparently it was just out of curiosity. A huge wave of relief crashed over me as our East African Tourist Visa was issued without any problems. We were in Africa!

"Oh no!" Joe exclaimed as he retrieved his bike box from the oversized luggage chute. The box was split open at the top and the bubble wrap was hanging out, revealing wheels and dishevelled bags inside.

"Is anything missing?" I asked, anxiously grabbing my bike box, which was still intact. We had retrieved our bags from the conveyor belt but most of the stuff had been packed with the bikes in the boxes.

Joe rummaged through the box. "The bike seems okay," he said, "but one of the panniers is missing."

He started listing out the contents: "One sleeping bag, one inflatable mattress, one lightweight inflatable pillow" – he paused – "and two left shoes!"

I tried not to laugh. Joe's meticulous nature meant he'd packed one of my shoes and one of his shoes in each front pannier so both sides of the bike were perfectly balanced.

I stifled a giggle, thinking about trying to ride the bike with just one toe cleated in. We had no way of knowing if the bag was lost or had been stolen. I was imagining someone thinking they had snaffled a new pair of shoes only to get home and find they were two left shoes and completely different sizes!

Joe looked around the airport, wondering what to do. We went to customer service and explained. A tall, official-looking man tutted apologetically and asked for our luggage receipt.

"Is this for a bike in a box?" he asked.

Joe nodded, impatient. "But one of the bags from the box is missing," he said.

"Do you have a luggage receipt for the bag that was missing?" asked the man.

"No," replied Joe.

"Then there is little we can do," he said. "You need to file a report with the airline."

For the next ten days Yambi Guesthouse was our home base while we made phone calls, filled in forms, tried to find replacement gear and went on side trips. Tucked away on a dusty red side road in the leafy Gikondo district, Yambi was a tranquil haven from which to explore the bustling city. The food was local, fresh and abundant, and served with a smile. As well as the friendly and attentive staff, we had the company of a constant stream of local and international travellers passing through. Kigali itself is the cleanest city in Africa, partly as a result of Rwanda's 2008 ban on single-use plastic bags, as well as monthly clean-up days instigated by the longstanding president, Paul Kagame.

Despite quickly assembling a solid network of contacts willing to help, it was impossible to find replacement camping gear of the quality we needed in Rwanda. We managed to track down a bike shop and befriended Patrick, who ordered us new shoes and pedals from Kenya. We scoured all the shops and markets in Kigali and put out a request on the Kigali expats Facebook page to find camping gear. We eventually gave up and arranged for one of our friends to buy replacement gear in Sydney and ship it to Kigali.

And then we had to wait. Joe was frustrated, itching to get started on the next step of our adventure. I was secretly relieved. We could be normal for a while. Joe went into planning mode and started mapping out the rest of the trip. We managed to track down a centre where we could get yellow fever jabs and buy enough malaria prevention medication for the next six months in Africa. I tried to absorb myself in the new environment, soaking up the colourful sights, sounds and smells and reading about the history of this small East African country.

A tear spilled from my eye and rolled slowly down my cheek. I wiped it away and stared in shock at the mass grave where the bodies of more than 250,000 people, including children, are interred. It is almost thirty years since an estimated 800,000 people, mainly Tutsis and some moderate Hutus, were killed in 100 days, in the most rapid genocide ever.[viii] We walked in sombre silence, taking in the photographs, personal testimonies, artefacts and written accounts displayed in the museum, which vividly depicted the horrors.

Still waiting for our new gear to arrive, we waved goodbye to the friendly hotel staff, riding our bikes in trainers and with borrowed pedals, as we embarked on a three-day test ride up north to the Sorwathe tea plantation.

A mixture of excitement and trepidation bubbled through me as we left the sanctuary of our new home. Horns beeped and people called out friendly warnings. We dodged cars and motorbikes and were squeezed into the gutter. Buses belched out black smoke as we battled our way up the hill on the main road out of the city. There were literally hundreds of people on bicycles, all men, some just commuting but many transporting goods, including gigantic loads of bananas, doors, live chickens or piles of baskets tied together.

"Are you out of your minds?" A woman's voice rang out, shocking me.

Sweat was dripping down my face. My orange T-shirt was clinging to my body, soaked in perspiration. As I wiped my hand down my leg, I noticed black oil and dust streaked across my damp skin. An immaculate-looking blonde lady, dressed in typical safari attire, was standing too close to me. A small group of similarly dressed tourists were climbing out of an oversized safari car near the roadside cafe where we'd stopped for a drink after a two-hour climb.

"You will die cycling on these roads," the woman proclaimed loudly in an American accent. "My husband had a friend who was killed in France. The roads are worse here. The drivers are crazy. Are you not frightened of getting attacked?"

I held up my hand to stop this uninvited interruption and backed away.

"That was the last thing I needed to hear," I told Joe, who was equally perplexed by the interaction. "I have my fears, but that's none of her business. There are hundreds of locals riding bikes in Rwanda. Is she not worried about *their* safety? Why did she think she had the right to single *me* out?"

Joe put his hand on my shoulder and gave me a comforting smile. "Ignore her, babe. We'll be okay. Let's grab something to eat."

We had been a little nervous setting off for real in Africa, but at least we'd had time to orient ourselves in Kigali. Lots of people had been telling us that Rwanda was like Africa for beginners. Despite its violent past, it's now one of the safest countries in the world, but riding on a road anywhere is still risky, and there were so many unknowns.

I surveyed the delicious looking array of fruit smoothies and sandwiches on offer. "I'm not hungry yet," I said, still rattled by the woman's comments. "Let's just have a coffee."

That was a mistake. Several hours later, we were desperately searching for somewhere to get food. Cycling up hills all day meant we needed to eat almost twice our usual daily intake. It seemed the petrol station cafe was the last commercial food stop outside Kigali. We struggled to find food for the rest of the day, stopping to eat corn on the cob and grabbing a bunch of small, sweet bananas wherever we could.

My calf muscles screamed but I felt elated as we pushed our bikes up the rutted mud road through a small village. Women dressed in brightly coloured kangas (traditional wraparound skirts) walked by balancing baskets of produce on their heads. Kids ran alongside us carrying yellow jerry cans of water. Men passed in the opposite direction, lugging bicycles laden with sacks of corn. Everyone smiled and shouted out "muraho!" (hello). The kids waved and giggled, often wrapping themselves in their mothers' kangas to hide.

The sun dipped behind the Virunga Mountains in the distance and rays of soft light illuminated the lush green landscape. The moderate temperature and rolling hills and fields of crops were a stark contrast to images of hot, dry savannah plains, which was how I had always imagined Africa. We sipped on cold drinks, looking out over the green terraces of the Sorwathe tea plantation, enjoying the serenity after the hard ride. We'd only cycled fifty kilometres, but the day had started with a tough climb up Mount Jali, Kigali's highest peak. Then, after passing through a series of small villages with spectacular views over banana plantations, there was a lengthy descent on rusty-red roads, before a final big climb up to Sorwathe, just outside Kinihira. The route we'd taken had been inspired by The Slow Cyclist, a company that organises cycle tours of Rwanda, but we later discovered these tours are on electric mountain bikes!

Sorwathe was the first private tea estate in Rwanda, opened in 1975. It was founded by a US tea trader, Joe Wertheim, and is now run by his son, Andrew. It's the biggest tea producer in Rwanda, employing 2,500 people and producing 3.5 million tonnes of tea each year. The guesthouse is at the back of the factory, and we were the only guests there. Frederick looked after us and served us a hearty dinner on the terrace overlooking the plantation.

"Where are you from?" he asked.

"Sydney, Australia," we replied.

"Ah, kangaroos," he laughed.

He asked us about football. It turned out that, like many Rwandans, he supported Manchester United.

The next morning, dressed in white coats and wearing hair nets, we toured the factory, learning how the leaves are graded and how different types of tea are made. "Orthodox" is the traditional method where the leaves are left whole, whereas "crush-tear-curl" (CTC) uses a machine to macerate the leaves. We learnt that Taylors of Harrogate in Yorkshire purchases leaves from Sorwathe for some of its tea.

"Can you believe she's from Yorkshire but doesn't drink tea?" Joe laughed with our guide, Catherine, as I screwed up my face during the tastings.

We learnt that tea pickers tend to be women, and often have young children. The work is gruelling, and in many places, tea pickers are paid less than a dollar a day. Sorwathe has been working with UNICEF to improve the situation for its workers, including increasing wages and providing a creche. The workers are happier and crop production has increased.

Later that evening in Gicumbi, we met Hussain, a young hotel manager at Urumuli Hotel, who spoke passionately about his country.

"It's improving," he said, "but it's still hard to get out of poverty."

Due to rapid economic growth that's lifted more than a million people out of poverty since 2000, Rwanda is often referred to as the "miracle of Africa" based on economic progress since the genocide. Yet around 50 percent of people still live in poverty and only 57 percent have access to clean drinking water within thirty minutes of their home, according to UNICEF.[ix]

I later posted a picture of myself pushing my bike with a young kid balancing his yellow water carrier on the bike. We are both laughing.

My caption was *Who's helping who?*

"Yes, but who owns the bike?" Hussain commented, reminding us that while struggling with our bikes brought us closer to the people of Rwanda, there was still a huge imbalance.

"I love this!" I shout to Joe over the music as I grab his hand to pull him closer. We move to the beat, a blend of Rwandan sounds and reggae rhythms.

We had been eating our dinner of local fish and salad when the band wandered into the bar to set up. The small room was soon full of locals: men in colourful shirts wearing funky hats and women in jeans with long braided hair, all laughing and drinking beer.

We learnt that Gicumbi is home to a university and several hospitals employing lots of young people, and we'd stumbled into their Friday night hangout. Several beers later, Joe was beaming as we swayed to the lyrics of the Heritage Band. Rwandan reggae reflects the Rwandan people's journey of healing and reconciliation in the thirty years since the tragic genocide, resonating deeply with themes of social justice, peace and unity.

We returned to our rooms, tired and tipsy, just after midnight, thinking the band was about to wrap up. But it was still blasting out at 4 am. I tossed and turned for the rest of night, struggling to sleep. Young Rwandan people certainly know how to party!

Feeling fragile and tired the next morning, we dragged ourselves up and got back on the bikes.

Arriving back at Yambi Guesthouse was like coming home. The staff wanted to know everything about our trip. A couple from Scotland who we'd met prior to our mini adventure entertained us over dinner with tales of their day trip to Akagera National Park. On the way home, their driver was arrested and led away for arguing with a policeman, and they had to negotiate his release.

The camping gear we had ordered from Sydney was due to arrive in four days, but the bike shoes were still stuck at the border en route from Kenya and looked likely to be there for a while. So we hired a car and headed off to Akagera National Park on a self-drive camping safari.

"This way," said a young guy in a high-vis vest, directing us into a car park. We'd stopped at Kigali's city markets to buy some food and supplies for camping. The hire car had arrived late, around 1 pm, and we were feeling stressed and pushed for time, wanting to get to our campsite before it got dark.

"What do you want? I will get for you?" A teenage boy was grabbing my arm, pulling me towards the fruit and veg stalls. I shook him off gently and smiled.

"We're fine, thanks," I told him.

But we weren't fine.

Rickety wooden shacks were piled high with colourful fruits and vegetables while people ran backwards and forwards carrying supplies. We had no idea what anything was worth, and our bags were being filled with eggs, tomatoes, onions, eggplants and sweet potatoes. When we thought we had everything we needed, the young guy got his phone out and started adding up all the goods. I was trying to keep up but couldn't tell what he was putting into the phone. Eventually he announced an outrageous number for the total.

"Can you add it up again please?" I asked him, determined to pay attention this time. It came to about half the price, but it was still too expensive. I said I'd pay half again and he looked hurt and shook his head. I started walking away and he chased me and begrudgingly accepted my final offer.

In the car later, we realised we'd paid the equivalent of around fifteen Australian dollars. It was a similar price to what we would pay in Sydney, but way too high for Rwanda. We laughed, knowing we had probably doubled someone's daily income and committing to trying to get a better understanding of what things were worth.

Back in the car we felt strangely uncomfortable driving along the dusty red roads through the villages, looking down at the children playing in the streets. We missed the closeness that came from being at the same level on the bikes and interacting with people as we cycled along.

"Oh wow, look, giraffes!" We had just entered the Akagera National Park and were on the way to the park office. We were still a bit bemused by the fact that we could do a self-drive safari after all the stories we'd heard about guided tours. Joe cut the engine and we watched in wonder as the majestic animals lolloped across the road, looking down on us with their big, curious eyes, their beautiful orange, brown and tan coats shimmering in the evening sunshine.

I held my breath.

Joe started the engine and crawled slowly past them.

"Shh, look," Joe said, pointing to the other side of the road, where a herd of African buffalo were staring, their implacable dark eyes boring into us. The large bull at the front lowered his head and pawed the ground.

"Whoa," I said. "He looks angry."

We continued slowly forward, and a group of antelope bounced across the road in front of us.

"This is incredible!" I gasped. I'd imagined searching for hours to spot animals, not seeing them as soon as we entered the park. It was exhilarating.

Setting up camp that night, we felt acutely aware of our proximity to the animals. The electric fence didn't look like much of a deterrent for an elephant or lion. Our lightweight camping tent looked flimsy, to say the least. There was no one else there. We contemplated using one of the reinforced safari tents that were already set up rather than our own lightweight camping tent, but thought they may be for other people. We collected wood for the barbecue and watched as the sun sank over the savannah.

Later that evening, other people arrived with guides who seemed hopelessly ill-equipped. We helped them start the fire and gave them herbs and spices for their Rwandan stew. The evening ended with dancing around the fire with a lovely French family.

We slept soundly in our tent, listening to the grunting of hippos in the lake outside the camp.

The next day we saw zebras, more antelope and even a sleepy lion resting under a tree. We took a boat safari on the river, marvelling at an African fish eagle and other bird life. Awaking early early on the last morning, we set out in search of the elusive elephant before dawn.

"Stop!" I shouted as we turned a sharp corner. Four huge rhinoceros were standing in the road. They stared at us. We stared back at them, then looked at each other. There was nothing to do but wait.

Back at Yambi Guesthouse, there were more delays. We learnt our new shoes were still stuck at the border, but Patrick encouraged us to set off and promised he would get them to us on the road somewhere.

We finally set off for real, waved off by a big group of people who we'd come to know like family and already feeling at home in this part of Africa.

JACQUI WEBSTER

~11~

LAND OF A THOUSAND HILLS

Joe sat on a low bench, beaming kids on each side looking up at him in admiration. I stood against a tree, holding a baby. Immaculately dressed children in school uniforms were dancing and singing as part of a community event raising awareness of drug and alcohol issues. We were near the end of our long, gruelling ride from Kigali heading south-west along the RN1, the main national road in Rwanda. We'd stopped cycling to listen to the music and one of the school teachers had gestured for us to join. People made space and welcomed us. The event was in the local language Kinyarwanda, and everyone seemed to be genuinely uplifted. We immersed ourselves for about an hour, resting and enjoying a deep sense of unity and inclusion with this small community.

"Where are you going?" asked a young man as we stood up to leave. Whereas many of the older people in Rwanda spoke French as their second language, most younger people spoke English which had become the main language in schools since 2008. "Do you need somewhere to stay?" He introduced himself as David, a teacher from the local school, and recommended a small local guesthouse, which he said was about ten US dollars a night, in the nearby town of Muhanga, above a restaurant where we could get food.

We pushed our bikes up a metal ramp outside a three-storey brick building in the centre of town. A young Muslim woman wearing a pink headscarf led us up the stairs to a balcony and from there, up another flight of narrow stairs to a basic small room with a double bed. She spoke little English but welcomed us with a wide smile. She brought us towels and indicated to the bathroom, which was just a basic shower over a drop toilet.

We explored the town looking for supplies. It was a mixture of 1960s brick buildings with all manner of things – carpets, plastic buckets – spilling over the sides of balconies. At street level, wooden shacks sold food or supplies. We waited, people watching, while a cobbler, his face tired and lined, fixed my leather thongs (that's Australian for flip-flops for UK English speakers!) while sitting on an upside-down bucket on the roadside.

After a simple dinner of local beef stew and rice, we retired to bed, exhausted. Joe fell asleep immediately, oblivious to the ruckus of young people shouting and cheering while watching the local football game.

I lay awake, overexcited as the day's experiences – the challenging climbs, the bustling towns, the kids chasing us up the hills, laughing and shouting – ran through my mind. It was great to be back on the road again. The riding was tough and the accommodation far from luxurious, but I felt vividly alive cycling in Africa.

"I can't believe you're riding a bike across Africa at your age!" exclaimed Pierre. He was seventy-two and had just introduced us to his beautiful young daughter, Kimi.

"I can't believe you're the father of a seven-year-old girl at your age!" I quipped, leaning my bike against the wall and smiling.

Pierre showed us to our comfortable ensuite guest room, a lovely bright space with blue-and-white bed covers and dark mahogany furniture, on the ground floor of the Rwanda African Art Museum in Nyanza.

We'd spent the day on a motorbike excursion to the King's Palace, a reconstruction of the distinctive beehive architectural style of the Rwandan monarchy in the country's former capital. We stroked the royal cows with their huge horns and listened to stories about the last kings of Rwanda, who had ruled until 1962 when the Belgians abolished the monarchy and Rwanda became a republic.

Later that evening after dinner, Pierre told us a little about his life.

"I was working as Professor of Organisational Psychology in the University of Toronto in Canada when the 1994 genocide happened," he said, looking down at his plate. "I felt completely helpless. There was no way to contact my family. It was impossible to know what was going on. Every single one of my family was killed."

I gulped and tried to hold back tears as I realised Pierre would have been the same age I was now when the genocide happened. I tried to imagine suddenly discovering that all my family were dead and felt a knot in my stomach.

Pierre returned to his family home in Nyanza ten years ago, where he set up the Rwanda African Art Museum, dedicated to promoting and preserving the cultural heritage of the community. On a personal tour of his museum, he explained how his collection of artefacts, including traditional masks, sculptures and paintings from all over Africa, depicted timeless traditions honouring the ongoing connection between the living and the dead. Most poignant for me was the Japanese-inspired Zen garden, sitting somewhat forebodingly outside our room. On chairs neatly arranged in rows on a sandy quadrant, individual masked effigies were seated, each an ancestral representation of a member of Pierre's family killed in the genocide.

We learnt that despite the positive changes in Rwanda, many people are still healing. "It's a process," Pierre said. "It will probably take a few more generations for people to move on from the trauma."

Two Bugs on Bikes

"It's just a short cut to the other road," Joe said, when I mentioned that the route was supposed to be all tarmac that day. He was so wrong – again!

Two hours later we emerged, exhausted and filthy and, in Joe's case, covered in cuts and bruises, out of the bushes and onto the main road heading towards Nyamagabe. The dirt road had taken us through villages, along the edge of the hillsides, past banana plantations and villagers harvesting sorghum, along almost impossible sections of rough gravel, over broken bridges, and through rice paddies where people were working. We had to push our bikes a lot and several times the villagers had to help us. Joe was really struggling. He was breathing hard and his voice sounded strained. I made a note to myself that I needed to keep an eye on him. Maybe we were eating enough for me, but not for him.

Over the next few days the riding got easier and Joe seemed to be feeling better. We'd stopped taking the malaria prevention medication as Joe was having side effects, including headaches, feeling like his heart was racing, and being overly sensitive to the sun. We would just need to take extra care not to get bitten by mosquitoes, but we were at quite high altitude, which reduced the risk. We always made sure we had enough food, including stopping at the side of the road whenever anyone was selling avocados, bananas or nuts; enjoying big lunches of up to five portions of carbohydrates (pasta, rice, cassava, sweet potatoes, Irish potatoes, beans and meat in sauce) in the workers' cafes for a couple of dollars; and seeking local foods such as brochettes (meat skewers), matoke (green bananas fried with onions and spices) akabenzi (pan-fried pork) and agatogo (plantains with meat and spices). Food was much easier to come by now we knew what to look for.

Sipping hot tea, we drank in the view of terraced tea plantations clinging to the hillsides from our camp at Kitabi Eco Center at the top of Mount Kitabi. After another long day in the saddle, we'd showered and washed our clothes in a bucket before relaxing and reflecting on the journey ahead, staring across the deep green canopy of the Nyungwe Forest National Park before us.

The next morning, our serenity was a distant memory.

We'd just entered the gates of the national park, where we were greeted by an extended family of baboons sitting quietly, grooming themselves and nursing their babies. The babies were adorable, their dark round faces with big eyes staring out at us. We'd slowed down and I was filming them on my phone, which, it turns out, was a mistake.

"Watch out!" I'd yelled, as the large male started running in Joe's direction, leaping through the air towards him and lashing out with his claws.

"Maybe this wasn't such a good idea!" Joe shook as he pedalled furiously, trying to put some distance between his bike and the male baboon who'd made a lunge for him. Joe was visibly shaken as he skirted past the rest of the troop, who sat and stared stonily, protecting their habitat.

Nyungwe Forest National Park is the oldest conserved rainforest in Africa and home to thirteen different species of monkeys, amounting to 20 percent of the primates in Africa. We had about sixty or seventy kilometres to ride, so this didn't feel like a good start.

"Let's hope this group was just guarding the gate and they don't chase us through the rest of the park," I said, trying to reassure him.

Fortunately, this turned out to be true. The rest of the ride through the jungle was absolutely breathtaking. We broke up the long climbs by stopping to sit on walls and stare across the lush expanse of rainforest. Towering trees with dark, dense leaves formed an almost-impenetrable roof over the forest floor, which was thick with ferns and other flora.

We flew downhill, our eyes fixated on the trees, trying to spot different varieties of monkeys.

Nyungwe National Park is on the border of Rwanda, with Burundi to the south and the Democratic Republic of the Congo to the west. Armed soldiers – male and female, many barely out of their teens – patrol the roadside every few kilometres. Dressed in camouflage gear and holding rifles, they were strategically positioned to make visitors like us feel safe after reports of rebels attacking people in 2017 devastated the tourism industry. Initially their presence felt intimidating, but most of them smiled and shouted out words of encouragement, which reassured us.

That night we camped alone under a shelter on a wooden platform at the Uwinka Visitors Centre. We drifted to sleep listening to the electrifying chorus of croaking frogs, the pulsating rhythm of the crickets and cicadas and the haunting call of owls. Packing up our tent the next morning, we watched as a troop of black-and-white colobus monkeys swung through the trees, glancing nervously in our direction and calling out to each other as they advanced through the jungle on their morning ritual.

The next few days' rides were spectacular, on smooth tarmac roads towards Lake Kivu then along the Kivu Belt Road. Once, we'd set out early anticipating a long tough day with seventy kilometres and 1,700 metres climbing. But the hills just melted under our pedals and the kilometres disappeared behind the incredible views. Stops for food and water were made memorable by the locals, who joined us for many parts of the ride, playing music or trying to race with us.

"Maybe we should try wild camping here?" pondered Joe as we looked at the map, trying to find somewhere to stay near Lake Kivu. We'd arrived at an eco-lodge in Kibuye, where we'd planned to stay for a few days to rest before attempting the Congo Nile Trail. We were camping on the lawn, but there were no views and the place seemed a bit drab and dreary, so we were looking for somewhere to camp by the lake the next evening.

"But there are so many people," I said.

Rwanda is the most densely populated country in mainland Africa, with a rapidly increasing population – currently about 13 million – squeezed into 26,000 square kilometres. In contrast, Australia has twice as many people spread out on a land mass more than 300 times the size.

"We'd never find a place to pitch our tent without being surrounded by kids," I continued. "I love the kids here, but I need my space to relax after a long ride."

"I know but you said you wanted me to be more adventurous" Joe replied, laughing.

Allured by the intrepid tales of more seasoned bikepackers, we were constantly debating the pros and cons of wild camping versus staying at campsites or in guesthouses. So far, our experiences of wild camping hadn't been that great. And we were in Africa now, so we had the added fear of wild animals lurking in the shadows. Real ones, as opposed to the rabbit that frightened me in Bulgaria.

Lake Kivu is one of the African Great Lakes and is situated in the Albertine Rift. Approximately forty-two kilometres long and fifty kilometres wide, it is a continuation of the natural border with the Congo and is surrounded by majestic mountains. Lake Kivu is one of the three lakes in the world known to experience limnic eruptions caused by carbon dioxide trapped under the water. Even deeper under the lake is a big layer of methane, which scientists say could potentially cause a huge eruption one day, releasing the carbon dioxide into the atmosphere and threatening the lives of over 2 million people (about one-seventh of the Rwandan population).[x]

In 2016, commercial methane extraction began with a view to both reducing the risk of an eruption and generating an energy supply, but some people say the extractive process itself could lead to the eruption it's trying to prevent.

We pitched our tent at the side of the lake in front of the fire pit on the lawns of a cosy, calm resort with eight beach bungalows and space for a few tents.

We'd arrived without warning and the husband of the couple who owned the place had to leave for Kigali, but not before welcoming us and introducing us to a friend and fellow cyclist over FaceTime. His wife then took us out for dinner to a nearby hotel in her huge old Land Rover. Later that evening, sitting around the camp fire, we listened in shock as she shared the harrowing story of her experiences in the genocide. She'd been nineteen when her whole family was murdered in front of her.

"I tried to hide under the bed and shield my eyes," she told us. "I was dragged away and beaten and threatened. I barely escaped with my life. There isn't a single day when I don't feel the twisted knot of guilt in my stomach, knowing that they all died." Survivor's guilt is common for many people in Rwanda.

She was only the second person – Pierre was the first – to discuss their personal experiences of the genocide. It was unusual for Rwandans to open up about this. Most guarded their grief behind their big smiles, deflecting the violent past and speaking with passion about their country.

The memorial museum had given us a much better understanding of how things had unfolded in 1994, but the personal reflections made us realise it was still impossible to comprehend why, even for those who'd lived through it.

The next morning we noticed the woman getting up from one of the tents on the nearby deck. "Why are you sleeping outside?" Joe asked her. She looked shy.

"I don't like sleeping on my own in the house when my husband is not here," she said, smiling sadly. "I get frightened. I prefer to be outside near other people."

"Where are you from?" A small kid in jeans and a red T-shirt was running alongside me, trying to make conversation. I was struggling to stay upright, bouncing over boulder-sized rocks on a dirt track, my knuckles white on the handlebars.

"Australia," I replied breathlessly.

"Ah, kangaroos!" He beamed.

Joe was just ahead of me. Two other kids were trailing him. They had been running alongside us for several kilometres now.

"Holy shit!" cried Joe, screeching to a halt. Ahead of us, a huge river, about three hundred metres wide loomed, its water rushing.

"Ah, crap." A wave of despondency flooded through me.

"No worry, I carry bike!" the kid in the red T-shirt said. "You follow me."

It all made sense now. I reluctantly let go of my bike, grabbing my phone from the mount on the handlebars. The kid hoisted the heavy beast over his shoulder and set off towards the water. Kicking off my shoes, I stumbled into the river behind him, balancing precariously on the rocks as the water gushed between my legs.

Joe followed behind us carrying his own bike, too proud to let the kids help.

When we reached the riverbank safely, we sat down to share a pineapple with the kids, but they looked at us in disbelief until we gave them some change. Then they ran away laughing.

We sat looking at each other anxiously. We were exhausted.

It was day one of our three-day off-road route on the Congo Nile Trail, a 257-kilometre stretch of dirt roads and single-track trails starting along the coastline of Lake Kivu and continuing up through the divide that separates the Nile and the Congo rivers and into Nyungwe Forest. Originally opened in 2011, the beginning and the end of the original route are now paved, leaving only about 100 kilometres of dirt tracks.

Bikepacking.com[xi] had rated it as "perhaps the best bikepacking route in East Africa", with "primitive dirt roads and single trails winding through verdant jungle and farmland, exuberant children cheering and chasing you as if you were riding for Team Rwanda", so we felt we had to do it. The fact that it was rated as a difficult mountain bike ride should have been a clue that it was probably going to be impossible on fully loaded touring bikes. We'd spent a long time reading other cyclist's reviews and blogs and discussing the idea, but eventually ignored everything we'd read, jokingly chanting, "Why take the easy way when you can take the hard way?!"

Two Bugs on Bikes

We were nine kilometres in and already it seemed way too hard. The first part had been rideable, but then the long downhill section had been almost impossible. And then there was the sand! But the worst was still to come. Ahead of us was a treacherously steep 300-metre climb to Musasa. We could barely push our bikes. Seeing us struggling, some young kids abandoned the goats they were herding and helped us.

Having previously denounced the idea of giving money to children as it encouraged them to skip school and pester travellers, I now embraced this form of child labour whole-heartedly. The kids were the only thing that made the Congo Nile Trail possible (and sometimes even fun!) for us.

"There's no one here!" I moaned, pulling up at Musasa Homestay, the only place to stay for miles, and finding the gates locked. A young man came across to say hello and went to fetch the caretaker, who let us in and showed us a room at the back of the dark concrete building where we could lock up our bikes. A wooden table and two dilapidated chairs sat abandoned on the porch. The caretaker gestured for us to sit and rest.

"I'm starving," I said. "Is it possible to get any food around here?"

"Come with me," said the caretaker.

We swapped our cycling shoes for trainers and followed the caretaker back up the road we'd just cycled down towards the town. We'd looked out for food when we'd passed through but hadn't seen any options.

"Here," said the caretaker, leading us into a dimly lit bar where men were gathered, drinking beer and watching football. The TV was hanging precariously from the wall, wires sprouting out from all sides. The picture flickered and went blank. Everyone groaned. The barman gave it a nudge and it came on again and everyone cheered.

"You buy me beer?" asked the caretaker, pulling up a stool at the bar.

Joe looked at me with one eyebrow raised as if to say *here we go again*.

"Can we get food here?" I asked, not holding out much hope.

"You drink beer, they bring food," said the caretaker, smiling and revealing a few missing teeth. The other patrons were looking at him curiously and he was obviously feeling proud of having foreign friends.

"I guess we should be celebrating surviving today," I said to Joe, who grinned and ordered three beers.

We were given some stale chapatis, which we washed down with the beer, chatting to the barman and other locals about Australia and trying to explain why we were cycling across Africa. The men shook their heads, tutting in disbelief and returned their gaze to the game.

Afterwards we wandered around the town but could only find doughnuts, which turned out to be stale. Even the kids wouldn't eat them when we tried to share them the next day.

Musasa Homestay was basic but comfortable. The landlady was there to welcome us when we returned and showed us to a room with three bunk beds. Chickens and pigs wandered freely across the stone courtyard leading to a communal bathroom with a bucket and a twenty-litre yellow jerry can of water for the two of us to share for showering and washing our clothes.

"I feel amazing!" I declared as I emerged from the bathroom, washed and with clean clothes ready to hang outside in the afternoon sunshine. It was surprising how good you could feel after washing in a bucket.

Later that evening we enjoyed a simple but nourishing hot dinner of Rwandan beef stew, beans and greens with three hikers from Israel, exchanging stories of our travels before collapsing into bed for a solid night's sleep.

The next day's ride was just twenty-eight kilometres with only 500 metres of climbing (compared to 1,023 the day before). The scenery was stunning but much of the route was still unrideable. At times we weren't sure we were going to be able to make it.

Ahmed, the young Muslim guy who'd showed us to the guesthouse the day before, was walking to his village at the same time. He and some young girls helped us for a while, but we told them to go ahead as we didn't want to make them late for the mosque.

Some other young kids started following, running alongside us as we bumped down the rutted track. We knew what was coming this time. The ground crumbled away in front of us, revealing a three-metre drop to the river below. Looking to the right we could see the remnants of a collapsed old bridge, broken in half in the middle and separated from the banks. There was nowhere to cross. Unclipping our bags, we shared them out among the kids and followed them down a precarious path along the river where there was a shallow part for crossing, then up the other side. When we reached the top of the hill, we caught up with Ahmed and gave him a 5,000 Rwandan franc note to share among the children. They all seemed happy.

We didn't find any food on the route that day and hadn't been able to pick up snacks the day before, so we were ravenous when we arrived at our next stop. Solene, the young woman running the guesthouse, served us some rice, beans and cabbage left over from their dinner the night before. I swear it was the best food I've ever eaten. But even this restorative meal was eclipsed the next day.

"Look, what are they cooking?" I gestured to where some women were sitting on upside-down crates, tending a sizzling hotplate over a fire, with what looked like tiny fish with onions and tomatoes bubbling away.

We stopped at the edge of the road and leaned our bikes against a small wall. We were immediately surrounded by local villagers. One of the women looked up and caught my eye.

"Sambaza – tacos!" she said. She picked up a chapati, which we learnt was made with sweet potato flour, from another hotplate and delicately spooned in some of the fish mix, adding a few chillies and a squeeze of lemon.

We agreed on four tacos and practised our Kinyarwanda with the locals while we waited, looking out over the lush green valleys.

"Muraho, amakuru?" (hello, how are you?), we said. "Nitwa Jacqui; nitwa Joe." (I'm Jacqui; I'm Joe.)

We devoured the four tacos, two each, having negotiated a fair price. They were the most delicious thing I'd tasted in weeks.

After such gruelling days on challenging terrain, it was a huge relief to suddenly emerge from the jungle onto tarmac in Gisenyi. We stopped at the first bar we saw and had the most amazing banana smoothie before rolling down the hill to Paradise Malahide, the modest resort hotel by the lake we'd booked for a night to recover.

"I'm loving being in Africa," I told Joe later, after a relaxing afternoon reading. The difficulty of the last few days' riding was already fading, leaving only sun-soaked memories of happy kids and dramatic scenery. "I think a little bit of my heart has always been here."

Joe smiled and nodded. "Yes," he agreed, "but I can definitely see why it's called the Land of a Thousand Hills!"

~12~

OLIVIER

"**K**aribu! (Welcome!) Where are you from? How can I help you? Did you ride far? Where are you going?"

Olivier, an enthusiastic young tourism intern, was bombarding us with questions as he showed us to our room at the Africa Rising Cycling Center (ARCC) near Musanze. We had booked to stay at the home of the Rwandan cycling team for a couple of days. It was our last few days in Rwanda. We wanted to get the bikes serviced and cleaned and stock up on supplies before crossing the border into Uganda. Musanze was also the base for the Volcanoes National Park, which made it a touristy spot for people who wanted to come and see the mountain gorillas.

"Thank you. We are from Australia. We rode today from Gisenyi – eighty kilometres. We're tired now," I said, exhausted, as Olivier wheeled my bike into the room and showed us around, pointing out the bathroom (yay for running water!) and the little kitchenette where we could prepare our own food if we didn't want to eat in the restaurant.

We were ready to collapse after another huge day's riding, starting with a crazy thirty-kilometre category 1 climb (one of the most difficult ratings, according to the Tour de France classification system) out of Gisenyi, followed by thirteen kilometres downhill, then a relatively flat stretch before going off road for twenty kilometres, including a fifteen-kilometre climb and a five-kilometre descent. The last ten kilometres took us into Musanze on glorious smooth tarmac.

Early on, halfway up the big climb out of Gisenyi, we stopped at the side of the steep road to have a breather and eat a banana. A stream of men, straining to push bikes heavily laden with milk urns or huge bunches of bananas, paraded past us. Some of those bunches must have weighed sixty-five kilograms, which would be like pushing me up the hill on a bike! Even with our loads, we realised that our pain was nothing compared to what these guys were doing – especially when we had chosen to do this for fun! We shared the rest of our bananas and water with the workers, who shook our hands gratefully and continued up the hill.

Turning off the main road was a mistake. Some gravel roads are delightful but others are brutal, with corrugations causing constant jarring from the handlebars to rattle into our shoulders.

We stopped to rest at the side of the road by a sign for the University of Global Health Equity near Butaro and were immediately surrounded by children.

"How are you? I'm fine. Give me money," they all chanted, giggling.

These were often the only English words the children knew. Sometimes we wondered whether they even understood what "give me money" meant or if they had just been told to say that. Smiling and dressed in an assortment of colourful clothes, looking like a Vinnies fashion parade, the kids prodded each other, daring their friends to get closer and ask for something.

I took a packet of biscuits from my top pouch, thinking there were enough to share. Immediately the kids surged forwards, their hands outstretched. More kids appeared from nowhere. I desperately tried to give them all something, breaking the biscuits in two, but they were shouting and grabbing. I felt anxious, trying to be kind but having to say no.

"Buretse!" A stern-looking, well-built woman wearing traditional clothes and carrying a basket of mangoes shouted at the children to stop and waved them away. All but the bold ones dashed off. The others stood waiting. The lady walked away, tutting and shaking her head. She seemed ashamed of the children but also angry with us.

This was an ongoing dilemma in Africa: whether to give money and share food, knowing that this would be welcome in the short term, but in the long run could contribute to a culture of begging and harassment, and even lead to children skipping school. Or to just look after ourselves, stopping for snacks on long rides and ignoring the puppy-dog eyes of the hungry children by our sides. Making this decision a hundred times a day was exhausting. In the end we tended to share food when we could if we knew we would be able to get more.

After such a stressful, long day, the Africa Rising Cycling Center felt like a sanctuary. Opened in 2015 following the 2014 win of the Tour du Rwanda by Team Rwanda, it's known for its role in developing cycling talent and promoting the sport across the continent. It has sixteen houses dispersed throughout well-kept gardens, as well as a restaurant with a top chef, a training room, and a well-equipped bike garage with a mechanic to service bikes.

Sadly, Team Rwanda was nowhere to be seen during our stay. We later learnt that the ARCC was undergoing management struggles. The secretary general of the Rwandan Cycling Federation that funded the centre, Benoît Munyakindi, was in jail on corruption charges and the federation president, Abdallah Murenzi, was facing charges of being an accomplice.[xii]

But at the time we weren't aware of this, and no one mentioned it. Everyone we met at the centre reflected the idea that the centre was dedicated to improving lives through sport.

Eric, the bike mechanic, shared his own story while he was looking over our bikes.

"I grew up in a small village where cycling was part of the fabric of life," he told us. "My father was a bike mechanic. I learnt everything I knew from him. I wanted to be a professional cyclist so I could escape from the village life and earn lots of money to send back to my family. I trained hard but never quite reached the standard. Landing this job here, working with the pros, was like a dream come true. I still often ride out with the teams so I can be there to fix the bikes if anything goes wrong."

Eric showed us the team bikes hanging on the walls and explained how he taught bike maintenance and repairs to young cyclists who were training at the centre so that they could look after their bikes when they went home (there are very few bike shops in Rwanda outside Kigali). He showed us pictures of the current team, pointing out Joseph Areruya, who won the 2017 Tour du Rwanda, making him a source of inspiration for many young cyclists.

That night we tucked into a delicious dinner of beef stew with green beans, tomato and avocado, plantains, rice and potatoes. It was a meal fit for any athlete.

The next day we went on a guided tour of the area with Olivier.

"Come look," he said, gesturing for us to follow him towards a group of women working in the fields, carrying wicker baskets and dressed in the traditional kanga skirt with cotton blouses or a T-shirt on top. Most had their hair covered with bright coloured material.

I had been asking Olivier about the fields of white flowers on the flat lands at the base of the Volcanoes National Park, where we were walking.

"These flowers are used as a natural insecticide, pyrethrum, which is a good source of income for the local villagers. They farm in cooperatives," Olivier explained, digging his hand into the wicker basket of one of the women, who were now all standing still and watching us.

We learnt that pyrethrum is a plant-based insecticide extracted from the heads of dried chrysanthemum flowers. Increased crop production was supported by a US Agency for International Development (USAID)-funded partnership in 2007, with the goal of improving incomes and standards of living for farmers by improving the quality of the flowers that they farmed. The partnership helped the farmers establish cooperatives to improve farming and transportation practices, reorganise to remove middlemen, get rid of corruption and improve financial management. It also provided crank-powered radios to remote farming communities to ensure they could receive farming news, best practice information on seed harvesting, market insights and health and wellbeing information.

By the time the partnership had wrapped up in 2015, production had increased by 371 percent, and many of the workers were now financially independent and able to pay their children's school fees.

Walking back towards the town of Kinigi, we chatted to Olivier about his life.

"What are you planning to do after your internship?" I asked him.

"I need to finish school," he said. "But at the moment it isn't possible as my mum doesn't have money to pay the school fees."

He explained that his father had left when he was small and that his mother had hurt her back and wasn't able to work. He had two brothers and a sister, who he needed to support. When he wasn't at the cycling centre he worked for his neighbour, who was building a house.

"I work one whole day sifting soil and making bricks," he said. "My neighbour gives me food while I work, then at the end of the day he gives me some money, usually about a thousand Rwandan francs."

"That's just over one US dollar," I commented.

He nodded. "With this money my mum can buy maize for the family for the week," he explained. "But then I have to work another day so we can buy eggs."

Looking at the menu outside the touristy cafe where Olivier suggested we eat lunch, I realised that most meals cost about eight dollars. Joe and I were used to eating at the local restaurants where we would pay less than a dollar for a huge meal.

"Come here for a second," I called to Joe, who was chatting with Olivier. Turning away so Olivier couldn't see, I continued, "It doesn't seem right to go for lunch here with Olivier when it will end up costing twenty times what he gets paid in a day."

Joe nodded in agreement.

We walked over to where he was standing.

"This restaurant looks really nice, thanks, Olivier," Joe said, "but we'd prefer to eat in the local restaurant like we normally do when we're on our bikes. It will cost a lot less, and then we can give you the extra money. What do you think?"

Olivier was very happy with this idea. We squeezed together on a child-sized bench at a wooden table, enjoying a simple soup with a tiny chunk of beef and a plate of potatoes and kidney beans. It was tasty and filling and Olivier seemed completely content.

"I'll pay double if I can drive." Joe was negotiating a ride home with one of the local bicycle taxis. Olivier and I waved and shouted out for him to be careful as he set off, wobbling along the cobbled road. The driver was perched on the back, grinning, and all the other bike taxi drivers were laughing and shouting as the crazy foreigner disappeared.

"I'm nervous," I said to Olivier as we followed on foot. "He always goes too fast and the brakes on those bikes are so bad he won't be able to slow down for the speed bumps."

It seemed an eternity before we saw the bicycle taxi driver who had gone with Joe coming back up the hill towards us. I felt a rush of relief and the guy stopped to tell us how much fun it had been and how fast they'd gone down the hill.

Olivier and I wandered back through the back streets of the local village. A woman was sitting at the side of a pile of rubble, a hammer in her hand.

"What's she doing?" I asked.

"She is making big rocks into little rocks," he said, "to make gravel for the foundation of houses."

This was a common sight in Rwanda and the rest of Africa. We later learnt that a wheelbarrow of gravel took about five hours to make and that for this people were paid less than a dollar.

"I don't think I can do the hike if we don't pay Olivier's school fees," I said to Joe that evening. We were planning to do a walk up to the top of Mt Bisoke. It was going to cost $150 for us to both to do the hike. This was the same as Olivier's school fees for a whole term.

"I was thinking the same thing," Joe replied. "He didn't ask us for money, but I think we should offer to pay at least for the first term until he gets on his feet again."

Mount Bisoke was one of the volcanic mountains in the Virunga National Park on the border with the Democratic Republic of Congo (DRC). We were doing the climb in the hope of seeing gorillas, although we knew it was a long shot. The hike up was through thick, green vegetation over rocky terrain with stunning views back down over the coffee plantations below.

"Come up here?" I shouted back to Joe who was behind. The pace of the group we had joined was too slow, but a few of us got ahead with one of the armed rangers, Francois. He had been assigned to walk with our group, carrying a rifle in case of buffalo or other dangerous animals on the route.

Joe dodged passed the other people in the group to catch us up and we ran together up the hill trying to keep up as Francois sprang over tree roots and ducked under vines, pointing out different birds and monkeys on the way. I was struggling to catch my breath and my eyes were peeled hoping for a glimpse of a gorillas. But there were none.

Reaching the top, I sat down to rest and watched in amusement as Joe tried to join in a traditional dance with a bunch of friendly young zoology students.

Olivier was absolutely beaming with joy, waving his flag and dancing along to the music, as we waited for the VIP guests to arrive at the annual gorilla-naming festival, Kwita Izina, the next morning.

Kwita Izina is one of the biggest community events in Rwanda and it was a complete coincidence that it was on while we were there. Everyone we'd met had said we had to go. The annual festival, where baby gorillas are given their name to ease identification and support conservation, began as a small local tradition modelled off a centuries-old tradition in which Rwandans name their children in the presence of family and friends. But the celebration has gained international recognition and now draws a large crowd of prominent guests, including celebrities, diplomats, conservationists, athletes and academics. The Arsenal legend Sol Campbell and actor Kevin Hart were some of the people naming the twenty-three baby gorillas born that year.

Joe and I protested as we were shepherded into the tent for special guests where all the dignitaries were seated while Olivier was sent to queue with the locals. After sitting in our seats straining to see the famous people going up to the stage, we eventually slipped out of the tented area to join Olivier in dancing with the thousands of local people who had turned out to watch the show on the big screens in the nearby fields.

Pictures of the baby gorillas' faces are unveiled on the gigantic screens as the crowds sing and cheer as each name is revealed.

"I'm going to come back and name a baby gorilla one day," I shouted to Olivier over the noise. "I'm going to call it Hope," I said.

"Icyizere," he corrected me. "That's Kinyarwanda for hope."

The day before we had told him we would pay his school fees, so he was now able to start back at school in two weeks' time. He had cried and hugged us when we gave him the news.

Now, watching him looking so happy, I felt a small tug at my heart.

~13~

CHANCE ENCOUNTERS

"Can you hear that?" asked Joe.

Mist was rising from the dusty red dirt road through the jungle. At an elevation 2,300 metres and climbing, it was hard to hear anything except my own laboured breathing. My wheels were bumping over the rocks on the rough gravel road. I held my breath so I could listen.

"What? I think I can hear sticks banging against trees," I said.

"Stop," said Joe. "Listen."

I put my feet down and rested on my handlebars, grateful for the break. Straining my ears to tune into the loud, pulsing sound of the jungle, punctuated by birdsong, I suddenly became aware of another distinct sound over the background noise.

"I can hear grunting," I said. "Do you think it's gorillas?"

"Let's have a look," Joe said.

We stacked our bikes up against the bank at the side of the road and stood on tiptoes, peering into the tangle of dense foliage.

"Look, I think I can see men, over there," whispered Joe pointing down through the trees to where I could see three figures with their backs to us.

"They must be gorilla trackers," said Joe. "They're heading in our direction. Let's ride a bit further along the road and see if we can see them."

My heart was pounding as I got back on my bike. I couldn't believe we could be so close to gorillas just cycling along a road. We stopped again and could see the men were closer. I could now make out one guy in a red T-shirt and another two men. One was carrying a stick and the others held machetes.

"That definitely sounds like gorillas," I said as I heard a series of low grunts coming from just ahead of the men. "Let's go a bit further along the road. They seem to be heading that way."

"What are you doing here?"

I was suddenly face to face with one of the men we'd been watching.

"Do you realise it's illegal to track gorillas without a permit?" the man continued. He was about my height, wearing an official-looking shirt and a flat cap. One of the other guys was standing behind him, looking at me questioningly. They didn't look unfriendly but still, we were on guard.

"We were just riding past on our bikes and heard noise," said Joe, gesturing towards the bikes laying haphazardly by the road. "We stopped so we could look and see what the noises were."

"Are the gorillas here?" I asked, unable to contain my excitement.

"Yes," replied the man.

We stood there not knowing what to do next. The men looked at each other, then started conversing in their local language.

"Are you planning to see the gorillas while you are here?" asked the man in the red T-shirt.

"No," I answered.

"Yes," replied Joe at the same time.

"We mean, we'd like to but we haven't really decided," I attempted to explain. "We want to see them but it costs a lot of money."

Two Bugs on Bikes

Just that morning we'd been discussing whether we should go and see them while we were here. It was considerably cheaper in Uganda. It was something I'd always wanted to do since reading *Gorillas in the Mist* when I was about fifteen. I thought we might regret it if we didn't go.

"Would you like to see them now?" the man offered.

"Absolutely!" I replied without hesitating.

"You will have to pay," said the man.

"Of course," I agreed.

They suggested a price and I declined, knowing what the official tours cost. I offered them half, which was still one hundred US dollars for each of the three men.

They agreed. Joe and I looked at each other wide-eyed, hardly able to believe our luck.

"We'll need to hide your bikes quickly," said the second man, the one wearing the red T-shirt, now taking control.

We climbed over the bank and down into the jungle with our bikes and stashed them, one on top of the other, behind a large thicket of branches, out of sight of the road. I quickly grabbed my passport and some loose change, and we followed the men into the jungle towards where the other man was waiting near the gorillas.

After five minutes of trudging through the thick vegetation, badly equipped in cycling shoes with cleats that caught on every thistle, I was suddenly on high alert. One of the men was on the phone. We had followed them left and then right deep into the jungle and I realised I was completely lost. I couldn't believe we had followed three men with machetes into the forest. What were we thinking?

"Why is he on the phone?" I asked Joe, starting to panic. "Do you think they're selling our bikes?"

My worst fears about being kidnapped by bandits suddenly felt very real, as though we'd walked straight into the trap. My heart was pounding. I could barely breathe.

Suddenly one of the men turned round and signalled for us to be quiet.

I held my breath, fearing the worst.

"Look, here," whispered the lead man, gesturing just ahead through the branches.

Two big brown eyes met mine and immediately my fear was replaced with awe. A large female gorilla was sitting about five metres away, staring directly at us, her dark brown coat glistening in the damp air. She eyed me curiously for a moment, then looked over to Joe before reaching up into the tree to pull down a clump of leaves and resume munching, looking up every now and again.

It's hard to describe the intensity of the feeling of being so close to such a majestic animal in its natural environment. The noise of the jungle seemed to subside, and we could just hear her steady munching and smell the fresh leaves as she ate.

The men gestured for us to take a photo, and we expected to be whisked away quickly once we had our shots, but they waited patiently, watching us warmly as we gazed at the gorilla in amazement. After several minutes they indicated that we should move further to the right, where they pulled back some of the vegetation to reveal three baby gorillas swinging playfully from the branches, knocking into each other mischievously as they jumped from one vine to the next.

Moments later, one of the men chopped down another large branch to reveal the group's silverback, who eyed us cautiously, seemingly assessing what risk we posed, before turning his back on us and slouching off.

"That was incredible!" I hooted to Joe once we were back on our bikes riding along the dirt track. "I can't believe you didn't even take your passport with you."

"I didn't even think about it!" said Joe, laughing.

"It was just as well you left our money with the bikes as well," I said. "There was no way I wanted to pay them before they'd guided us back out of the jungle."

Riding along, we debated the right and wrong of what we'd done. We realised we'd probably cheated the national parks body out of a few hundred dollars that would have gone towards conservation and running the parks. But by the same account we'd given money that would directly support the families of the three men, probably doubling their monthly income.

I made a commitment with myself to make an annual donation to the Uganda Wildlife Conservation Foundation and we both agreed our experience was far richer as a result of our "unofficial" tour.

As we neared Buhoma later that day, the skies blackened and the rain started to fall. It looked like it was setting in for a few days. We'd planned to camp at a place on the edge of the town, overlooking the jungle. We'd heard reports of another Aussie cyclist camping there and seeing the gorillas from her campsite. But we decided another chance encounter with gorillas was unlikely, so we quickly looked at the map and located a nearby guesthouse.

Several hours later, dry, clean and fed, with everything we owned in the washing machine, we were cuddled up on the sofa with Sione, the daughter of the lovely American couple who were running the guesthouse, feeling like part of the extended family of travellers and medical students who were staying there while working in the adjacent community hospital.

"This reminds me of a work trip to Samoa," I told Joe, describing the lodge where I usually stayed with other development workers and medical students or interns during my visits to work with the Ministry of Health.

Bwindi Guest House is the former home of the hospital's founders, Scott and Carol Kellerman. It began as an outreach clinic under a tree and has grown into a 155-bed hospital providing much needed services to over 100,000 people in Uganda. The guesthouse has hosted hundreds of people over the last twenty years, helping to support the hospital as well as the Uganda College of Health Sciences and the Batwa Development Program. The Batwa are one of the oldest surviving population groups in Africa. The Bwindi Impenetrable National Forest has been their ancestral home for millennia, but in 1991 the establishment of national parks in Uganda led to their displacement, forcing them into a new life.[xiii]

Listening to these stories, I reflected on my first-ever research assignment to Tarun Bharat Sangh in India, where I helped to document the impact the establishment of the Sariska National Park on the "displacement refugees" for Oxfam India. That was also in 1991, in the last year of my bachelor's degree. I was twenty-one and learnt a lot about my own limitations as well as having the privilege of spending time immersed in a different culture.

On a tour of the community hospital the next day, we learnt that malaria and HIV were still the main burden of disease here in Buhoma, followed by malnutrition. Most people nearby are farmers and herders who live on less than a dollar a day, without running water and electricity. They have to walk for hours to collect water and firewood. Diarrhoea, caused by lack of clean drinking water, and an inadequate supply of nutrients including protein are contributing to malnutrition. Despite these challenges the community hospital had led to improvements in health care outcomes – remarkably, 100 percent of babies born to mothers with HIV left the hospital HIV-free, and rates of stunting were reducing.

The brick walls were painted with murals depicting happy, healthy families with messages highlighting the importance of eating fresh fruits and vegetables and promoting breastfeeding.

"What a clever, simple way of making sure everyone that comes into the health centre sees these messages," I commented.

"What it would be good to understand is the causes of increasing rates of hypertension and diabetes," explained Eliad, the communications director, who was showing us around the hospital. "People here do not have access to processed foods and most people don't drink or smoke, so it's unclear what's driving the increasing rates."

Waving goodbye to our hosts Daniel and Rachel and their daughter Sione the next morning, we felt like we were leaving family. A plan had started forming in my mind about coming back to Africa to work one day.

Two Bugs on Bikes

Back on our bikes, for the next few days we rode through the famous Queen Elizabeth National Park.

"Are you sure it's safe to cycle through a national park?" I asked Joe for the hundredth time that day.

"Of course it's safe," he said. "We wouldn't be allowed to do it if it wasn't."

Right on cue, a motorbike sped past us carrying five people; the driver was the only one wearing a helmet. A toddler was balanced on the handlebars in front of the driver and two other kids were crammed between him and their mother, who was perched precariously on the back, holding on to the two kids with one hand and a large basket of produce with the other.

Unlike most national parks in Africa, Queen Elizabeth National Park has a public road running right through the centre as well as villages dotted throughout the park with people living harmoniously (mainly) alongside the wild animals. Balancing the needs of the people, who are predominantly agriculturalists and fishermen, with conservation efforts to protect the natural habitat is a constant challenge for the park authorities.

I'd read everything I could about cycling through the parks, which had confirmed it was permissible and relatively safe (according to Joe, the odds of being attacked by a lion were much lower than being attacked by a shark swimming in the sea at home, and we did that most days) but I was still on high alert.

Eventually my sense of adventure and awe at seeing the animals up close overrode my nerves. Just the day before we had cycled through the Ishasha Sector and I'd had to stop as a whole herd of impalas bounded across the road right in front of me. Joe filmed from behind as I stood watching them. Ishasha is known for its tree-climbing lions, but we'd made sure we weren't out in the evening, which was when you were more likely to see them.

Getting hungry, we turned off the main road down a side street towards the little fishing village of Kisenyi on the edge of

Lake Edward. The street was lined with market stalls and wooden shops with music blaring out and kids playing games on the side of the road.

"What are they cooking on that fire?" I said to Joe, pointing to a group of young lads. We worked out they were fried cassava strips and agreed to try them. The teenagers laughed and asked our names as we negotiated a price for a paper bag full.

Rows of brightly painted fishing canoes with handmade outriggers and black nets lined the shore of the lake. Fishermen, old and young, wearing jeans and colourful T-shirts and wide-brimmed hats, looked curiously at us as we walked past with our bikes, looking for somewhere to sit and eat our lunch. With no obvious place to rest, we perched on the side of one of the boats.

"There's some picnic tables over there." An old man with a wrinkled face and a walking stick gestured back towards a cluster of white painted houses that stood out from the wooden shacks and mud huts. We wheeled our bikes over to what seemed to be an abandoned tourist lodge and found a table under a bamboo shade, where we set up for lunch.

"Look, there's a family of warthogs!" Joe pointed to behind one of the houses.

I jumped up in joy and scrambled to get a closer look. "How cute are the babies!" I cried. Seven piglets were running alongside the mother, looking so proud with their noses held high in the air.

Joe sang "Hakuna Matata" from *The Lion King* for the rest of the day.

"Can you please stop singing that!" I said, laughing at him as we were cycling back through the village towards the main road.

"I'm trying to soak up the ambience. I love the fact that all the shops are playing music, competing with each other for air space."

Just then we passed a street food vendor selling chapattis. He was blasting reggae music from the local radio. "This is Africa!" the DJ shouted out as the song came to an end.

Two Bugs on Bikes

Goosebumps formed all over my skin and a rush of adrenaline surged through me as I absorbed the sensations – the smell of fried flour and fresh fish, the sight of the wooden shacks lining the roadside and the pulsating sounds of the reggae music.

"Whoa!" said Joe, suddenly putting out his arm to stop me.

At the other side of the road, no more than ten metres away, stood an elephant, flapping its ears and trumpeting.

"Shit!" I unclipped from my pedals and tried to back up but nearly stacked.

"Stay still," Joe said, his voice low and serious.

This wasn't what I'd had in mind for my first encounter with an elephant. My heart was thumping.

"Let's back away slowly," I said to Joe, who nodded. We took a few steps back, getting out of the elephant's danger zone.

Just then a motorbike came past with three men. We shouted and flagged them down to warn them about the elephant.

"You'll be fine. Follow us!" they said. One jumped off and grabbed a big stick and then they sped off before we could get started again.

We watched as the elephant started flapping its ears and shaking its head up and down, threatening to run at the men. Instead, the three men jumped off the bike and ran towards the elephant with their arms raised in the air, shaking their sticks, and the elephant turned and jogged away into the bushes.

"Come on, let's go now!" said Joe, jumping back on his bike and pedalling after the men.

"Slow down, will you!" he shouted after me, ten minutes later. I was still riding as fast as I could away from the elephant. "You can't ride like that all day. Relax. It's okay. We just scared that elephant when we came around the corner unexpectedly."

The road through the national park was rough and slightly uphill and seemed to take forever to ride through. There were animals everywhere: impalas, buffalo, zebras. Later in the day we came across two majestic old bull elephants wandering towards the road. I sped past and Joe stopped to look while they meandered across the road behind us.

"Amazing!" Joe said.

He was standing too close for my liking. I kept my distance.

As we reached the tarmac road at the Kazinga Channel – a huge stretch of water that links Lake Edward with Lake George and is home to the biggest concentration of birds, crocodiles and hippos in Africa – I felt my shoulders relax a little and a huge wave of relief rippled over me; we'd made it right across the wild national park. We stayed in a lovely rustic lodge (I learnt that having a tent is a good bargaining tool for negotiating reduced prices).

The sun sank down over the huge expanse of water as we had a cold drink and chatted to a group of German men who were there for a development project providing technology to improve the efficiency of making clay bricks for building houses. We had been wondering what the tall piles of bricks with fires inside had been – it was the traditional way of pressing and drying the bricks. During our time in Uganda, we spent a lot of time discussing how people sat beside the roads smashing up rocks for the foundations of their houses, as I'd seen in Rwanda with Olivier. This was so painful to observe when we know there are machines that could do this.

Later, relaxing on the terrace of our lodge, listening to the sound of the hippos grunting below, we discussed the route for the next few days. We could feel the tug of the Rwenzori Mountains in the north pulling us towards them to explore. But the rain was coming from the north, so it made more sense to start heading back east towards Kenya, before heading south. Joe plotted the route on the Komoot app while I sat writing. Then we looked over the route together, discussing how long each day was going to be, what the road surfaces might be like, and where we could stay. We'd adapted to our different roles but went over every decision together so that we were both responsible if things didn't go to plan.

Several days later, I stood outside watching a large female warthog with eight or nine suckling babies lounging on the edge of the road by the gates to the Lake Mburo National Park. We'd set off early that morning to get here and I was already tired.

Joe was trying to negotiate with the park wardens, who were refusing to let us through.

"We rang the park office, and they said it was okay to ride through the national park without a guide," he explained.

"What do they know?" said the warden. "They are in Kampala."

"But it's the national parks' headquarters," said Joe. "They should know the rules for the national parks."

"I've told you, you can't go through without a ranger," repeated the warden. "It's dangerous. And there is no ranger today. You need to book the ranger and come back tomorrow."

"But we have nowhere to stay and no food," Joe argued. The plan had been to stay at a campsite which had a restaurant just inside the park.

"What about if we just go to the campsite on this truck?" I suggested, pointing to a truck that had just arrived and was about to enter the park to deliver supplies. There was plenty of room in the back for our bikes. I wandered over to the driver and asked if he would take us to the campsite in return for a few dollars. He agreed without hesitating.

"No, it's not allowed," said the warden. "You need to come back tomorrow."

He put his hand up to indicate that the conversation was over and went back to eating his lunch. We were stumped, not to mention starving. The warden's cold rice and beans looked delicious.

"It's so frustrating that I did the research to make sure we were allowed to cycle through the park and now we're being told we can't," Joe grumbled.

"How far is it back to the next town?"

"About thirty kilometres. And I didn't see anywhere to stop for food on the way here."

Half an hour later I was struggling to push my bike up the concrete driveway to a nearby lodge that we'd managed to find on the map.

"It should have been obvious it was going to be pretty high when it's called Eagle's Nest," I commented.

"Wow! Check out this view," Joe said, leaning his bike against the railings of a large wooden deck overlooking a grassy terrace. "What an amazing place. Look down there, you can see the village we rode through to get to the national park. And look, over there is the national park. Can you see those elephants?"

We had climbed so high I could barely make out some tiny grey shapes in the distance.

We were the only ones at the Eagle's Nest Lodge. We ordered a pizza and salad to share before chilling out and reading for the afternoon. We had persuaded the lodge owners to let us camp on the grassy terrace and later that afternoon managed to get a lift back to the park ranger's office to book the ranger for the next day.

"This turned out to be a pretty cool plan in the end," I mused over a candlelit dinner later that evening.

"Let's just hope the ranger turns up tomorrow," Joe replied. We slept soundly that night, snuggled up in the tent listening to the drumming rain.

"This is impossible!" I said the next day, trying to push my heavy bike through thick mud.

"It's just for a short while," said the ranger, stopping to pick up a stick for me to scrape the mud out from my chain ring. It had rained all night and the main road through the national park was closed.

Our ranger was a small, slim, shy-looking guy on a lightweight mountain bike that bounced over the mud. I didn't feel reassured by his presence, doubting his ability to protect us from dangerous animals. The rifle slung over his shoulder looked like a children's toy.

"Look, he's the same height as me!" said Joe, stretching out his hand towards a baby giraffe who was no more than three metres away. Barely a week old, it still had its umbilical cord and looked a little wobbly on its long legs.

Four adult giraffes stood nearby, watching over the baby. They were further away and eyeing us suspiciously.

Our ranger had told us to park our bikes against a bush a few hundred metres away so we could walk closer to the graceful animals. He'd explained how we should walk diagonally so that we could get a bit closer without them getting scared that we were approaching. It was amazing seeing them so close.

"Look at their eyebrows," I cooed. "They are so beautiful."

"Check out that big fellow," said Joe, gesturing towards an old buffalo. He was standing on the other side of a watering hole a safe distance away.

"Stop quickly, jump off your bikes," said the ranger suddenly, his voice tight.

I looked up to see the buffalo had started trotting towards us. My instinct was to ride off as fast as I could, but the ranger put his hand on my handlebars.

"Get off that side," he said, gesturing for me to put my bike between me and the buffalo, which was running faster now with his head down.

Fear rose up into my throat.

The ranger threw down his bike and cocked his gun, pointing it towards the buffalo.

The animal stopped dead in its tracks.

"Now just walk slowly," said the ranger.

I was breathing heavily as I started pushing my bike along, trying not to look at the angry buffalo.

"Okay, you can ride again now, but just go slowly," said the ranger, slinging his gun over his shoulder and getting back on his bike.

"Oh my goodness, I am so glad you were there," I said to the ranger, hugging him as we said goodbye and giving him a good tip on our way out of the park.

Without his guidance I definitely would have tried to run away from the buffalo, and apparently that would have been the worst thing to do.

"I'm happy to be leaving the national parks for a while now," I confessed to Joe on our way out.

"Watch out for those zebras!" he said as a whole herd frolicked across the road in front of me.

~14~

WE ARE THE STARS

Back on the tarmac, my anxiety about wild animals was rapidly replaced by truck anxiety. It was raining steadily and spray from the heavy wheels of the trucks that thundered by splattered over our bikes and bags as we headed east towards Masaka.

"Let's stop here and wash the mud and sand off," said Joe, gesturing to a group of people washing motorbikes at the side of the road.

It was a real family affair. Two kids held each bike while Mum fetched a big bowl of soapy water, then one kid sponged the bikes down while Dad rinsed off with the hose. The kids were meticulous, cleaning the chains and wiping over the bags while we sat at the side of the road watching on and playing with the smaller kids who were hovering curiously nearby, staring at us with huge brown eyes and daring each other to touch us. Joe pretended to be a lion cub and roared, scaring them off for a minute before they descended into giggles and approached again for another go.

The service and experience cost us a couple of dollars. They probably would have taken half of that, but we set off feeling brand new and happy to have contributed to the family income that day.

Like Rwanda, Uganda is a low-income economy which is still paying the costs of relatively recent conflicts. It has a population of just less than 50 million, with almost half the population aged under fifteen. There are kids everywhere! More than half of the population lives in substandard housing, often mud huts with limited access to services, including electricity and running water. One of the most significant events in recent history was the expulsion of the Indian minority by the then-president Idi Amin in 1972, followed by a prolonged civil war, which is why many people still think of violence and bloodshed when they think of Uganda.

We were constantly treated with curiosity and kindness. Stopping to find something to eat at the side of the busy road, we came across a Rasta DJ selling rolexes – not the type that you wear on your wrist, but the type that you eat! It's basically an omelette (often with tomatoes and onions and sometimes cheese) rolled up inside a chapati – excellent cycling food!

"Where have you come from?" said the smiling Rasta, his hair tucked up inside a red woollen knitted hat, despite the humid weather. He had a small charcoal fire on top of the bench in his wooden shack where the chapatis were cooking and he was whisking up eggs in a plastic bowl.

We gave him the short version, describing our trip from Kigali. He looked impressed but slightly incredulous.

"But you look so clean!" he said.

"Ah, that's thanks to the motorcycle wash station," I answered.

"Good idea," he responded, laughing as he poured the egg into the sizzling pan. He asked us what we did for work, if we had children, why we wanted to cycle through Africa. The usual sorts of questions. I commented on the music he was playing and it turned out he had his own music channel. He played me a song while we ate our rolexes. It sounded great, and the rolex tasted amazing. We cycled off with smiling faces and full bellies.

It was these types of encounters that kept us going even when things got tough. We could be feeling completely busted, cycling into a headwind in the rain with trucks flying by. Sometimes you just wanted to get it over, to stop, to never have to ride your bike again. And then the smallest thing would happen. A kid would call out "muzungu!" (white person/traveller); a truck would flash its lights and the driver would wave; we'd suddenly spot a giraffe in the distant plains. And that was it, we were back in the present, in Africa, having an awesome experience, and the pain and enormity of what we'd taken on was forgotten, for a moment at least.

We learnt the importance of staying in the moment, always noticing our environment and constantly trying to absorb as much as we could about the people and places we visited. And for the most part, we felt blissfully content and vividly alive.

"Isn't that where the Masaka Kids live?" I said to Joe as we cycled past the driveway of a large property, after a few days off the bike in the town of Masaka.

"Oh yes!" said Joe.

"Let's go and see them again and say goodbye," I suggested.

We had visited Masaka Kids Africana the day before in a taxi, having made an appointment following recommendations from Paul, a charismatic Irishman we'd met the night before over a drink by the fire in the backpackers where we were staying. Paul was travelling from Cairo to Cape Town (albeit in a slightly haphazard route) overland, making the most of his global network of golf and rugby players.

Paul told us about the Masaka Kids, as well as visiting the Kenyan runners in Iten and climbing Mount Kilimanjaro, which pretty much established our direction for the next few countries.

The Masaka Kids Africana is an orphanage where many of the kids sing and dance and, as a result of their talents, have become a YouTube sensation. Visiting them was a highlight of our trip. When we arrived in the taxi, the kids all ran up to meet us and each one wanted to hug us. Hassan, the director, showed us around and told us his story and his plans to expand and improve the facilities in the future. The thirty kids were aged two and above and had lost either one or both parents due to famine or war. Hassan himself had been a street kid, but was helped by a USAID project and managed to make a living from music, which inspired him to establish a home to support other kids in similar situations.

Joe crouched, holding a toddler, and I filmed as the kids did an impromptu performance of their hit song "Happy Birthday". It was my niece Ella's birthday and so I live streamed the performance to her in the UK. Afterwards we helped serve the children a lunch of rice, beans and vegetables from the garden, and I was asked to provide the volunteer staff (all former Masaka Kids) with some nutrition tips.

"How good would it be to come back and work there?" I said to Joe that evening.

There were currently only thirty orphans living at the home, but the plan was to expand to 200 over the next few years. Joe agreed it would be interesting to come back and maybe help with building the guesthouse or developing other income-generating projects for the children.

Dropping in again the next day we were greeted with an even greater level of enthusiasm, despite being unannounced and on our bikes. The kids crowded around us, wanting their photos taken, and soon after erupted into their version of "We Are the Stars".

It was hard to drag ourselves away from the smiling faces, but the prospect of reaching Lake Victoria – the biggest lake in Africa, which stretches down across Uganda, Kenya and Tanzania – later that day spurred us into action.

The good energy from the children stayed with us for the rest of the ride. We talked more about the idea of coming to live and work in Africa. I'd just been awarded a five-year grant on strengthening food policies in different countries, which could potentially support work in Africa. Joe said he'd be prepared to give up his job and could see himself helping to build accommodation or teach the children sport.

Forty kilometres later we were having our second breakfast, perched on a narrow wooden bench in a shack near the ferry port, drinking steaming-hot coffee out of tin mugs and eating scrambled egg and chapati. We had already bought our tickets and were waiting for the ferry to Buggala Island, the largest island in the archipelago of the Ssese Islands, which consists of eighty-four half inhabited islands in the north-west of Lake Victoria.

The short ferry ride was uneventful. On reaching the island, we cycled another thirty kilometres along red dirt tracks through palm oil plantations to the north of the island, where we spent a frustrating night trying to swat mosquitoes in a run-down lodge on the waterfront. It was a relief when the alarm went off and we could finally get up, but we felt terrible after only two hours of decent sleep.

The highlight of our last night in Uganda was playing with the local kids outside the Harmony Hotel in Bugiri, near the border with Kenya. The kids were super excited to see us when we arrived, so Joe bought popcorn to share and we had fun hanging out, despite having no common language.

As we reflected on our time there, we realised that, overall, Uganda has been just as spectacular as Rwanda. We felt like we'd made strong connections and could see ourselves coming back to work here in a few years – maybe linked to the Bwindi community project or the Masaka Kids project, or possibly both.

It was a cool morning and the road towards the Kenyan border was long and flat. Joe and I were cycling hard, trying to cover as many kilometres as we could before the headwind picked up. I was at the front with my head down. I looked up to see a young man in jeans and a T-shirt riding a bicycle taxi wearing sandals. He gradually pulled up beside me and then sped past me. He sat up and turned back to look at me, giving me that knowing grin. The race was on.

I stepped on the pedals, mustering all my energy to go faster and catch him. Joe was sitting on my wheel in the slipstream, waiting for his turn. Just then three more bicycle taxi riders shot past us laughing and picked up the other rider. Joe overtook me and jumped on one of their wheels, trailing them until he had saved enough energy to get past them. I stuck to him like glue as we made our way past the four riders to the front of the growing peloton. We started pulling away, our relatively expensive, well-oiled touring bikes an obvious advantage over the rusty old cycle taxi bikes that were creaking with every pedal stroke.

The victory was short-lived, as we ran out of steam and the four riders rattled past us again. This went on for twenty kilometres.

We arrived at the Kenyan border exhausted and exhilarated, stopping to buy the winning competitors rolexes and drinks. They thanked us, still laughing as they slapped our backs and hugged us goodbye, sending us off with love from Uganda.

Sharing the load of pushing the bike and carrying water up the hill, Gicumbi, Rwanda.

Jacqui and Joe with Olivier (see Ch 12), National Parks headquarters, Musanze, Rwanda

Small child helping Joe push his bike over a rickety bridge, north of Nyanza, Rwanda.

Feeling the love in a remote mountain village between Nyanza and Huye, Rwanda.

Joe with Francois, National Guard who guided us up Mt Bisoke, Rwanda.

Two Bugs on Bikes

Camping at Kitabi overlooking
Nyungwe Forest National Park,
Rwanda

Joe riding with the locals. You are never alone cycling in Rwanda.

Joe pushing his bike uphill on the Congo Nile Trail, Rwanda

Godfrey, cycling guide from the Slow cyclist, and his son, Kisoro, Uganda.

Kid on bike, Bwindi Impenetrable Forest, Uganda.

Joe watching Bull elephants crossing the road, Queen Elizabeth National Park, Uganda.

Jacqui helping to serve lunch for the
Masaka kids, Masaka, Uganda

Joe and Jacqui Masaka kids, Masaka, Uganda.

Giraffes up close on guided cycle safari through Lake Mburu National Park.

Two Bugs on Bikes

Rasta rolex seller at truck stop near Akagete, on the Mbarara-Masaka Road, Uganda.

Joe and kids in Bugiri on our last evening in Uganda before crossing the border into Kenya.

~15~

RUNNING WITH THE KENYANS

A huge groan reverberated around the room as black lines streaked across the screen, which crackled and turned dark.

"Oh no, not again," someone said, standing to check the power cords and hitting the side of the TV. "The power's off, check the generator. Quick, there's only ten minutes to go!"

Eliud Kipchoge's trainer was sitting on the edge of his seat in the crowded clubhouse. We were in Iten, the home of the Kenyan runners, watching the Berlin marathon, where several Kenyan runners were competing. Kipchoge was currently in the lead.

The power came back on and the screen flickered back to life, just in time for us to watch Kipchoge win the race in 2 hours, 2 minutes and 42 seconds, just seconds slower than the record he'd set the previous year and making him the first person to ever win the event five times in a row. Everyone stood up to cheer, give high fives and hug each other as second place was taken by another Kenyan, Vincent Kipkemoi.

It was a great day for Kenya and a thrill to be watching from Iten, alongside the friends, running mates and trainers of the winning athletes. The women's race was taken by Ethiopian runner Tigst Assefa, who set a remarkable new marathon world record for women, winning the race with a time of 2 hours, 11 minutes and 53 seconds.

We'd learnt some of the secrets of the Kenyan runners the day before during a visit to Brother Colm O'Connell, an Irish missionary turned athletics coach who's known as "the Godfather of Kenyan running". Our Irish friend, Paul, had introduced us to Brother Colm, who'd been happy to meet us. Dressed in a humble green pullover and slacks, with a wide-brimmed hat, he showed us around St Patrick's boarding school, where many of the athletes started out. I noticed that the thin metal bunk beds were crowded into a room with less space than the orphanage at Masaka.

"This is where we prepare the food for the boys," said Brother Colm, pointing to a huge metal pot over a fire where the chef was mixing rice and beans. "We have a nutrition adviser on site who advises us to make sure they are well fed, and we grow as much of the produce as we can."

Inside one of the training rooms, he showed us the plaques with the list of world champions (twenty-five, to be precise!), world record holders, marathon winners and Olympic champions.

"All of these people were from the same school?" I asked incredulously, looking up and down the list of names on the gigantic plaque that covered most of one wall.

"Yes," said Brother Colm. "Here was my first gold medal winner."

He showed us a picture of Peter Rono, who had won the gold medal in the 1,500 metres at the 1988 Olympics. Then he pointed to a photo of Matthew Birir, who won gold in the 3,000 metres at the following Games.

"It's fantastic that you have all of this on record," I said.

Next, he showed us the pictures of Wilson Kipketer and David Rudisha, the two fastest men ever to run 800 metres, Kipketer taking the record in 1997 and holding it until 2012, when Rudisha took it from him. He has held it ever since.

Women's names also covered the board.

"But St Patricks is a boys' school," I said. "Where did all these female champions come from?"

"There is also a girls' school in the town," he said. "In the late 1980s, we set up a training camp for Kenyan women, who have also been very successful. Mary Keitany and Edna Kiplagat were both trained through our camps."

Back inside Brother Colm's modest house, in the grounds of the school where he'd lived and worked for the last forty years, we drank coffee and ate homemade biscuits while he told us his approach to unlocking the secret of the Kenyans' running success. Arriving in 1976 at the age of twenty-eight from County Cork in Ireland, Brother Colm found a basic school with no electricity or running water.

"I didn't come here as an athletics coach," he said. "I came as a young missionary who wanted to teach and support people to get out of poverty. But the school track coach, Peter Foster, brother of the British distance runner Brendan Foster, recruited me as a coach and then after a year he went home and left me to get on with it.

"My approach was based on working out what each personality needed to motivate them, and I built my training philosophy around understanding what the Kenyan runners needed, rather than bringing an approach from outside. Other factors include the food – mainly the ugali, which is the Kenyan name for the maize porridge that's a staple of Kenya and other East African countries – their natural physique, and the fact that many of them have had to run long distances to and from school from an early age. But by far the most important factor driving success is the sheer desperation to succeed for survival, as one of the only ways of lifting themselves and their families out of poverty.

"Interestingly, many of the runners, having achieved their goal of winning the Olympics or another great race, never go on to win again," Brother Colm added. "Once they have the money to support their families and communities and obtain a better life for themselves, even if only temporarily, the motivation to train hard and win is lost."

Back at the training camp the next morning, I woke up and opened the door to find Joe doubled over, a look of acute pain on his face.

"What happened?" I asked.

"I thought I'd go out for a run and was adopted by a couple of the local runners," he said. "I was okay for a while but then we turned off the main road and they picked up the pace and I had to try and hang on, otherwise I was going to be lost. Fortunately, when I was just about to collapse, I recognised the back of the training centre, so I was able to cut through and get back here."

"It looks like they taught you a bit of a lesson," I said, laughing. "Maybe you should go and jump in the pool to cool down."

After watching the marathon the next morning, we said goodbye to the new friends we'd met and jumped back on our bikes. We were feeling refreshed after resting in comfortable accommodation, enjoying a massage and a few swims in the pool, and eating good food.

Back on the road we were struck again by how different Kenya seemed to Rwanda and Uganda. Grass verges lined the road and there was a distinct absence of kids. This was due to the substantially lower birth rate in Kenya, but also the fact that nearly all children go to school.

"I really miss the kids!" said Joe.

"Me too!" I replied. "But the peace and quiet is also nice."

As we climbed up away from Iten along the tared C23 road towards Nyaru, we were rewarded with increasingly spectacular views over the Great Rift Valley. The road was in good condition and there were hardly any cars – just the odd flock of sheep or donkey to navigate around.

Colourfully well-dressed groups of people were wandering back from church or family events or just out walking. The vegetation was lush and green, with huge eucalyptus trees, conifers, and deciduous trees, which didn't really feel like Africa. Even the wooden stalls lining the roadside looked idyllic in their ramshackle style with eggshell-blue painted doors and windows.

"People would pay a fortune to have a shed like that in their backyard at home," I said to Joe.

"You'd pay a fortune!" Joe laughed, mocking my love for shabby chic furniture and old wooden benches.

We arrived unannounced at "Eric's cliff top campsite", which we had read about on iOverlander, an app for people finding places to stay in Africa. As we approached on the road leading to Nyaru, we were met by a group of about eight men who were standing in the yard chatting with Eric. We weren't sure whether to stop, but they beckoned for us to join them.

"Is this the campsite?" I asked, feeling like we'd disturbed a community meeting.

"Yes." They all nodded. "Karibu."

One by one they stepped forward to shake our hands and tell us we were welcome. They asked about our bikes and where we were from. Then just like that they all wandered off and we were left with a beaming Eric, who couldn't wait to show us around the campsite.

As it turned out, it wasn't really a campsite, but a sheep field at the back of the house.

"Here is where you can camp," said Eric, pointing to a flat patch of grass on the edge of a cliff overlooking the Great Rift Valley.

"I can move the sheep," he continued, seeing me glance anxiously at the big ram and three large female sheep guarding the spot.

"It's perfect!" I said, beaming at Joe.

We were up at about 2,400 metres altitude. The view over the valley was mesmerising. Cows grazed in the field to the right with a backdrop of sharp, craggy cliffs slanting down to the sweeping valley that stretched out to the left as far as the eye could see. The vast plains of the valley below were a patchwork of green and brown textures dotted with small villages.

"I'm sorry about the lack of facilities. We haven't had anyone come to camp since before COVID," Eric said.

"It's lovely!" I replied. "I'm not sure I've ever stayed in a more spectacular camp spot."

After helping Eric move the sheep to a nearby field, we pitched our tent and stowed our bikes in a work shed next to the house. Eric showed us to a small shower room in the entrance to his house, which he shared with his wife, Mary, and told us we could wash and change there and use the bathroom whenever we needed to.

Later that evening, when we were cooking outside in the small garden on the camp stove and it started to rain, they invited us inside and pointed to a narrow kitchen. It had a dust floor and mud walls, with a fire in one corner and a concrete slab that served as a workbench along one side of the room. A few pots and pans, salt and some lemons from the garden were scattered around the empty room. I sat on a rickety chair and Joe perched on an overturned bucket as we cooked our pasta and vegetables, chatting contentedly, pleased to be out of the rain and feeling looked after.

"Where would you like to eat?" asked Eric, peering at us through the material that was draped between the kitchen and the living area.

"Maybe we could join you?" I asked cautiously, not wanting to take advantage of their hospitality.

"We would love that," said Eric. "Some people like to have their privacy, but we love to get to know our visitors. We are just about to have our dinner now. Please come through."

We dished up our pasta and moved through to the small living room where Eric cleared a few old armchairs for us to sit on and put placemats on the coffee table for our metal camping bowls. Eric sat opposite on a sofa and Mary brought in steaming bowls of fluffy ugali with greens and a clear soup with a tiny lump of meat.

"Karibu," said Mary. "If we'd known you were coming, we would have cooked for you too. May I say grace?"

"Yes, please do," we said, bowing our heads.

It was cosy in the small living room, listening to the sound of the rain as the now-familiar smell of the local food wafted across the room. Joe looked at me and smiled. The wooden stove was still burning and Eric moved it closer to us so we could feel the heat. The room was bare except for a large map on the wall and some wrinkled photos with no frames.

"Are these your children?" I asked them, pointing to the photos.

Eric nodded and they told us about their family, one son working on the mines near Nairobi, one daughter in the north of Kenya with her husband and two grandchildren. They said the grandchildren visited whenever they could, but it was hard for the family to find time.

"We brought up the family in this house," said Eric, "but there is no work here, except for on the land, and that's hard and doesn't make enough money for everyone."

"But who were all the children in the yard when we arrived?" I asked, thinking of the young boy that was clinging to Eric as if he were family.

"The young boy is our neighbour, and the other two kids are my brothers' children," he answered. "My brother lives across the valley, but the children like to walk across and hang out here."

"We enjoy having all the children around," said Mary, as she poured us hot ginger tea after the meal.

It was dark when we stumbled back along the rickety fence and through the gate to our tent in the sheep field. But the moon lit up the steep rockface, and we could sense the vastness of the valley stretching out before us.

"Where do you think that is?" I asked Joe, pointing to the twinkling lights at the other side, as we were brushing our teeth outside the tent.

"It's Kabarnet on the other side of the Rift Valley," he replied. "We will be cycling over there to Eldama Ravine tomorrow."

"So, we'll have to go all the way down and then back up again?" I sighed. "It's been cool staying up so high for so many days. The air feels so fresh up here."

We slept well that night, snuggled up in our sleeping bags, soothed by the big hug of unexpected close connections. The next morning Eric made us avocado toast on the wooden stove before proudly revealing his grand plans for a mega-campsite, with ten pitches for tents or campervans, each with their own path and solar lighting, a modern amenities block with running water, and a big car park.

"It sounds incredible," I said, not wanting to curb his enthusiasm, "but it's perfect for me exactly how it is now."

Eric said they didn't want any money, that we were now family, and it was enough that we'd spent time with them. He was happy that we'd showed him how to make an entry on Google Maps and left a glowing review so other people could find him. Joe gave him 2,000 shillings, about twenty US dollars, saying it could be a gift for the grandchildren. They hugged us like we were their children and told us to stay safe and keep in touch.

"I'm scared. I don't think I'll be able to sleep," I whispered to Joe several nights later as we lay in our tent outside the aptly named Windy Ridge Motel on the edge of a steep hill.

It was almost 8.30 pm and we could still hear trucks thundering by, making it impossible to forget that we were going to face an extremely busy road with no shoulder the next morning. Partly due to bad planning and partly because there wasn't really any other option from Iten, we'd ended up having to cycle twenty kilometres up out of the Great Rift Valley on the notorious East African Highway, the main transportation route for trucks carrying cargo between Sudan and Ethiopia to the Port of Mombasa.

"We'll go early. It'll be okay," said Joe, although I could tell he was nervous as well.

The next morning was as bad as I had feared.

"I'm walking," I said, jumping off my bike and positioning it between me and the side of the road where the trucks were screeching past, often blasting their horns, never slowing down. "This is a complete death trap. They must think we're crazy."

I was too hot. My legs were shaky and my heart was threatening to jump out of my chest, partly from the exertion of trying to stay on my bike in a narrow gutter with lots of rocks while cycling up a steep hill and partly from fear of imminent death as the trucks thundered past.

"Just keep going slowly. We haven't got too far to go now," said Joe. He was trying hard to encourage me, but he looked tired and pale.

"Let's stop here for a rest," I said, pointing to a sign for the Great Rift Valley with spectacular views beyond. I posed for a photo, which we later posted on Instagram – it looked like the most idyllic place in the world!

When we reached the turn-off after ten kilometres battling a mud track at the side of the road, I could have collapsed with relief. "That was the worst two hours of the trip so far," I declared.

It couldn't have been more different from our experience in Kiserian, on the edge of the Ngong Hills, an area made famous by the 1985 film *Out of Africa*. There we shopped at a well-stocked supermarket and attended a seventy-fifth birthday party for a charmingly eccentric British-born Kenyan woman Susan, or Wamucii as she has been named by the local Kikuyu people, who let us camp on her lawn.

Just as the Ngong Hills conjured up memories of what we'd imagined Africa to be like from the famous film, the next few days riding were iconic Africa –dusty red sweeping plains stretching out to the mountains as far as the eye could see; acacia trees, with upside-down nests for the weaver birds; groups of cattle crowding each other for shade; an occasional donkey crossing the road. The tarmac road was the only sign of human life for kilometres. The towns were few and far between. We stopped at one for water and found a small shack housing a few shelves of products behind iron bars. Later that day we reached Mashuru, where we found piala (rice and meat), beans and corn for a couple of dollars. Basic, but more than enough and served with kindness.

We were getting close to the border with Tanzania now and for our last day in Kenya, we planned to do a one-day safari in Amboseli National Park. Here, Mount Kilimanjaro is the backdrop, the majestic snow-capped peaks providing an impressive setting for photos of giraffes and elephants wandering across the plains.

We arrived at Amboseli Eco Camp tired and hungry. Although I'd called ahead to let them know we were coming, the place was completely closed and seemed deserted. After discarding our bikes at the entrance and roaming around for a while we eventually found a security guard, but he couldn't speak any English. He put his hand up to indicate for us to wait and made a phone call to someone, then pointed up the hill to a nearby house and indicated someone would come.

A few minutes later we heard the low engine of a motorbike and watched as it bounced over the rough ground towards the lodge. A young man wearing jeans and a T-shirt dismounted from the bike and shook our hands.

"I'm John," he said. "I'm the neighbour. The owner thought you were coming tomorrow, but he's told me to give you a key and you can make yourself at home and have a shower. Someone will come later."

"Thank you," I said. "We were hoping to book a safari for tomorrow. Do you know how we can do this?"

"They'll tell you when they arrive," he said.

But no one came. Two hours later we were sitting on the balcony in our private wooden lodge, showered and rested, watching the sun setting behind the peaks of Mount Kili in the distance. The setting was magical, but I couldn't enjoy it.

"I'm starving!" I said to Joe eventually. "It's getting dark. No one is coming. Maybe we should just set up the stove and cook the emergency camping meal."

"I think you're right." Joe stood up to get the stove while I rummaged in the food bag and pulled out two crumpled packets of dehydrated chicken korma.

As we were going to bed I sent one last text to the owner.

Hi. We've had our own food for dinner and are comfortable, thanks. We're going to sleep now but are still keen to do a safari tomorrow. Great if you can confirm if this will be possible and what time we will need to start.

I didn't hear back so we went to sleep thinking it wouldn't happen.

Just before 7 am we woke to a knock on the door.

"Your breakfast is ready! Your driver will be here in twenty minutes!" a woman said.

"What? Really? Wow!" I rubbed my eyes and tried to wake up.

"They called me last night," explained Maria, the safari lodge worker, when we wandered into the kitchen. She was whipping up scrambled eggs for our breakfast. "But it was dark and there is a cheetah that lives around here. I couldn't risk coming in the dark."

Wilson, our driver, arrived while we were finishing our breakfast of beans, cassava and eggs with toast and avocado. At seven feet tall, he towered over the table and his beaming smile lit up the whole room.

"Let's go!" he said, clapping us on the shoulders as we were finishing our coffee. "It's an hour's drive to the gates and we want to get there before the crowds."

"This is just for us?" I said, pointing at the long-wheel Land Rover safari car parked outside.

"Yes," he replied. "This is my car, and today, just for you."

"Wow!" I said. "I love it!" Based on what we'd paid, I hadn't been expecting a private tour – and definitely not in a safari truck with an open top like you see on all the flash brochures.

"Only the best for my friends," said Wilson, beaming.

Over the next few hours, we learnt that Wilson was from the Maasai tribe and had forty-two brothers and sisters.

"My father has seven wives," he said. "He is a cattle herder and still lives off the land, so it is okay to have lots of wives. But I live differently. I don't grow my own food. I have to work for money, so I can't afford to have more than one wife. My children are also embracing the more modern way of life. One is in Nairobi studying to be an accountant and the other is married but lives out of town. Times are changing," he added. "It's getting harder and harder for the Maasai to live their traditional ways of life."

He asked us if we were planning to go and visit the Maasai Mara and we said no. We had to decide which way to go a few weeks ago. It was a hard decision not to visit such an iconic part of Africa, but you couldn't get all the way on bikes. It was the end of the great migration, and we would probably not be able to see the huge herds of wildebeest and buffalo jumping across the dry rivers. Plus, there was something wrong to me about the fact that one of the most famous and frequently visited ancient tribal peoples were still experiencing so much poverty. I hated the fact that governments exploited such groups for tourism without using enough of the money they made to support these communities.

"Quiet, look here." Wilson had stopped the truck and was pointing towards a pile of branches at the side of the road. After staring for a while, I noticed a cheetah lounging in the sunshine at the side of the woodpile. I gasped. We'd only just gone through the gates of the national park. We drove on. Clouds obscured the iconic views of Kilimanjaro, but the light was amazing. Throughout the day we saw hyenas, giraffes, elephants, lions, buffalo, wildebeest, fish eagles, herons, flamingos, impalas, water buck, warthogs, geese, goats, zebras and roller birds. The large expanse of water, savannah, palm trees and hills were the ideal settings for the animals to parade themselves.

"What a difference twenty-four hours can make!" I said to Joe that evening as we watched the sunset over Mount Kili from our balcony.

"So true!" Joe replied. "Last night we went to bed tired and hungry, thinking we weren't going on safari, and we couldn't have imagined a better day."

"Wilson was the best guide we've had on this trip so far," I said. "He just seemed to know where all the animals were going to be and was completely in tune with what we wanted."

"Yes, and what a truly beautiful man, so generous in sharing his stories," said Joe. "And I'll never forget that smile! It's crazy to think that people pay thousands of dollars for those sorts of experiences in a big group and we just paid two hundred bucks for both of us for our own private tour."

"Yes, but remember how stressed we were last night?" I said. "That's the payoff."

We laughed, holding hands and looking out over the spectacular view as the sun tossed its last rays over the majestic mountain. Tomorrow, we would cross the border into Tanzania.

Joe began chatting about our next days' route, but my mind was far away, imagining when and how I might come back to Africa.

~16~

SCALING THE SUMMITS

I drew in heavy, ragged breaths, looking down at my feet illuminated by my headlamp, as I put one foot in front of the other on the steep rock, sweat starting to soak through my six layers of clothing. Glancing up ahead I could see two rows of lights snaking up the dark mountain. It was just before one in the morning and we were one of the last groups to set off on the six-hour climb, aiming to reach the Mount Kilimanjaro summit at daybreak.

"You are fit and fast. You will pass all the other groups on the way up. Take it slowly. Just put one foot in front of the other. Stay behind me," said Armani, one of our guides from Solo Adventures.

I wasn't feeling so confident. Having spent the last few months at altitudes of over 2,000 metres on our bikes, we had been persuaded to take the six-day Umbwe route, the fastest and hardest route up the mountain. The four-day hike up to the base camp had been easy for us. The first two days we hiked through lush green rainforest and didn't meet any other climbers. We had a good rapport with our guides, who constantly slowed us down by stopping to share information about the flora and fauna. Burnt blackened trees stood out starkly against the white rocky ground, which was patched with shiny orange moss and green succulents. As we emerged from the rainforest, the view opened up and we could see glimpses of the peak of Kilimanjaro. She looked majestic, crowned in a halo of white clouds.

On the second night, we joined the hordes of other people at the Barranco Camp who were going to attempt to summit the mountain over the next few days. We arrived too early, and our crew were still setting up camp as the sun was setting over the mountain, now towering above us. It was humbling how much food and equipment they carried up the mountain for us. As well as our two-man tent, there was another two-man tent for the guides, the cooking tent where all the meals were prepared and where the cook and porters slept, a dining room tent with a table and three chairs (one of the guides joined us for each meal) and our portable toilet tent.

We took a walk around to try to soak up the atmosphere and enjoy the scenery. There was an air of nervous excitement around the place as everyone arrived from the different routes and the porters set up camp and started cooking.

"Look at that guy!" I said to Joe, watching in shock as a male hiker with an American accent stood chatting on his phone, one knee bent and his booted foot resting on a rock while one of his porters cleaned his boot.

Joe and I were struggling with the guides and porters thinking they had to do everything for us. We had chosen the company based on a recommendation from our Irish mate Paul, as well as doing our own research to satisfy ourselves that they were a small business committed to making a difference to the environment and the lives of the porters. The crew all seemed happy, which meant a lot to us. But we had been shocked when the bus arrived to pick us up from our hostel in Moshi and we realised that there were fourteen people – two guides, a cook and eleven porters – just for us! We felt uncomfortable after spending the last half year making do with whatever we could carry on our bikes.

After two more easy days walking through changing terrain, we reached the Barafu camp at 4,673 metres, still full of energy. There was no water, so the porters set up camp then walked back five kilometres to a nearby river to collect water for washing, cooking and drinking. I wanted to go with them to help, but our guide said we needed to rest. We sat in the dining room tent while Shabani checked our pulse rate and oxygen levels. We were then served another incredible nutritious lunch of vegetable soup followed by thick beef stew and potatoes and sliced pineapple.

It was hard to get any sleep the night before the summit, knowing we were going to be woken before midnight to start the climb. The high altitude made it worse. I could feel my heart pounding in my chest. We were cold, even though we were wearing everything we had and cuddling up to each other with a hot water bottle.

"I'm scared it's going to be too cold up there," said Joe. "I hope the gear we've hired is good enough."

"We'll be fine. Let's try and get some sleep," I said, pulling him closer.

"Time to wake up! Here are your drinks. Breakfast will be ready in twenty minutes." It was just before midnight and Shabani had left steaming mugs of tea and coffee outside the tent. We packed and sipped the hot drinks before pulling on our layers of clothing and trying to force down some food.

Nothing could have prepared me for how hard the climb to the summit was going to be.

After the first steep scramble up the rocks, the gradient evened out and we just followed in a line: Shabani, Francis, the assistant cook, Joe, me, the youngest porter, Jafar, and then Armani. We only needed two guides, but Francis and Jafar had joined because they wanted to share the experience with us, plus it would get them one step closer to promotion to be a guide.

After about an hour the temperature started to drop. After two hours I started to feel lightheaded. We still had four hours of climbing ahead of us.

Unlike the other groups, we had strict rules about when we could stop to rest, which was about every ninety minutes. We'd rest on a rock and one of the crew would open our daypacks and our water bottles for us to drink.

The last three hours were surreal. Every step was harder than the last and getting to the top seemed impossible. We spiralled through sensations, both physical and emotional.

I cried at the sight of a female porter helping a young woman to stand up.

Joe told me how much he loved me and how lucky he felt that he had me to share these sorts of adventures with. I felt flooded with emotion and had to fight back more tears.

The night was interminably long and dark, and brutally cold. Sometimes we walked in silence, just listening to the sound of our breath and the crunching of our feet on the frozen ground. Sometimes the guides would sing to us or shout out words of encouragement.

"You've got this!" said Armani. "You guys are tough. You will be our first clients to summit from the Umbwe route. Make us proud."

I wasn't sure I was going to make anyone proud. I felt nauseous and disassociated. Twice now, I had stumbled onto my hands and knees and struggled to get up.

"I can't feel my hands or feet," said Joe. He looked white and panicked.

I tried to smile but could feel my lip quivering and had to look away. This was too much. What were we thinking? Mount Kilimanjaro is the highest mountain in Africa. We hadn't trained for this. This was by far the hardest thing I'd ever done.

At first light we reached the crater and could see the glaciers before us. Relief flooded me and I cried again. We still had to make the summit, but it was not much higher now. The last hour was skirting around the crater. I knew we were going to make it.

The sun was just starting to creep over the mountains in the distance as we reached the summit, exactly as planned. We posed for a few photos with the glaciers in the background. We had made it. But there was no time to celebrate. After a few weak high fives with the one group ahead of us, we had to get out of the way so other people could get their photos at the famous summit sign.

Then we had to get down as quickly as possible, reducing the time for potential altitude sickness to affect us.

We descended via a different route back to base camp, sliding down the shale as quickly as we could, until it was warm enough to stop and drink hot ginger tea. Now that the mountains were flooded with light, the enormity of what we'd done started to sink in.

"Jambo, jambo bwana," sang the guides as we sank down the mountain. Originally a Kenyan Swahili greeting song, it has been adapted as a motivational song to include words of encouragement and trekking advice for people climbing Mt Kilimanjaro.

This was the song the crew had sung to us on the bus and then on our arrival at the Umbwe gate before we started our trip. It was a song Joe and I would continue to sing on the bike for the rest of our time in Tanzania and beyond.

Back at Mkoani Homestay, where we planned to spend the next few days recovering, we collected our certificates and said goodbye to our crew. It had been a bit stressful for us to learn that what they were paid was below minimum wage and we were expected to make up for that with tips. We'd read about tipping and tried to understand how much we would need to take before we set off, but hadn't realised we would be just two people with fourteen crew. We dug deep to give them as much as we could, but it wasn't as much as the guides had asked for. It was frustrating that companies couldn't be more transparent about what was expected so we could have come prepared. They tried to argue that if they paid the porters more, then they would get taxed, so it was in everyone's interests to pay them less and have this supplemented by tips, but we still didn't think the system was fair.

It was hard to see how that situation was going to get better in the near future.

Some things were improving, though. One of the reasons why there were so many people in each group was that the porters were only allowed to carry twenty kilos each and they were weighed in at the start of each trek. Plus, there were strict rules in place about not leaving litter at the sites or on the trail. But this didn't seem to apply to toilet waste. While the camps had drop toilets and most of the groups had their own portable toilets, there were no toilets on the trail and if you did need to stop it was always clear that you weren't the only one there. It couldn't be that hard to ask hikers to carry a trowel and a ziplock bag rather than leave toilet paper and tissues strewn along the trail.

"Would you recommend climbing Mount Kili to any of our friends?" I asked Joe over dinner in the guesthouse's garden that evening.

"I'm not sure," he replied honestly. "I'm glad we did it. It's an incredible experience to climb that high and to have that sense of achieving something harder than you could imagine ..."

"But the long-term social and environmental implications are a bit of a worry," I said.

"I know," he agreed. "I have no complaints about Solo Adventures other than the lack of transparency over the tips for the porters, which seems to be the same for all companies. But the toilet waste situation was horrific. The image of that guide blatantly emptying the Portaloo over the side of the mountain in front of where everyone was camping is stuck in my head."

"Maybe we should write and give feedback," I suggested. "I'm sure we won't be the first ones, but at least it will hopefully give them some ammunition if they're committed to doing more to change things."

~17~

THE MEDICINE MAN

"**A**h, that feels so good!" I said, sinking into the cool water and swimming over to the waterfall to let the water cascade onto my shoulders, pounding my tired muscles. I threw my head back, letting the water rush through my hair. The sun was filtering through the trees, warming my face and casting light onto the rippling water.

Joe took a few strong strokes out towards me under the waterfall and emerged glistening and smiling.

"It's so refreshing," he said. "Exactly what I needed after that brutal ride."

We washed and rinsed out our cycling clothes, changing into our shorts and T-shirts and towelling our hair.

"You are good? Ready to head back?" our host, John, asked us.

"Sure! Thank you. That was incredible. I feel brand new," I replied, collecting my things and getting ready for the walk back.

We were camping at Yefuka Farm in the eastern plains of the North Pare Mountains. The campsite is run by John, a local traditional doctor, and his wife, Lily. On the way back, John, who was wearing a smart blazer over a polo shirt and a colourful bucket hat, told us about the farm, which he bought in 1986. He had planted crops and nurtured the trees to make a small income from selling food and medicine.

"This is the Tamarind tree – *Tamarindus indica*" he said, pointing to a tall tree with a thick trunk and feather-like leaves. "It can be used for tummy pain, diarrhoea and dysentery. It is also good for healing wounds and for inflammation."

He pointed out an evergreen tree with thick, dark-green leaves and plum-like fruits. "This is the *Pygeum africanum,* or African cherry tree," he said. "It can be used to prevent or cure lots of different illnesses, including urinary tract infections and prostate cancers."

"And this is *Moringa oleifera*, which can also be used to boost the immune system and even to prevent cancer. I have a client who flies all the way from Canada to get his treatment from me," he added.

I was curious to learn more about the potential medicinal benefits of the different plants.

Later, sitting in the small hut that served as a dispensary, sheltering from the rain, I looked around at the different powders in plastic containers covered with dust on the table and wondered who actually came here. We were miles away from anywhere and hadn't seen anybody since we turned off the main road about forty kilometres ago. It had been a hard ride for us to get there. We'd had a critical decision to make about sixteen kilometres from the start that morning. We could either stay on the main road or turn off and go around the mountains, which would be longer and harder but potentially more interesting.

We had both been completely smashed after climbing Mount Kilimanjaro, but whereas I'd bounced back after a few days, Joe hadn't regained his energy.

"We should stay on the road," he said. There's hardly any traffic and it will be much quicker that way.

"But it's always much more interesting going off road through the small villages," I said. "We can't just ride all the way to Cape Town on the main road."

Several hours later, as we were bumping over rough corrugations, passing miles and miles of nothing on the gravel road, I regretted this. Joe said nothing for a long time. But as we climbed higher, the scenery transformed into a tropical paradise with banana plants, coconut trees and enormous mango trees lining the roadsides and mountains looming majestically in front of us.

Now, lying by our tent in the evening sunshine after an afternoon exploring the farm and learning about traditional medicine, we were both glad we'd taken the hard option.

"I can only give you plantain stew and chapati," John said.

"That sounds perfect," I said. "Can we come and give you a hand?"

"That would be lovely," replied John. "Lily will be back from the market soon. Come this way."

We followed him up the dirt track to his house, an old stone building on a raised ledge overlooking the valley.

"Karibu, come in," he said, ushering us into a small living room that was also used for cooking. John moved a few clothes off an old sofa, and we sat down while he peeled plantains on the floor.

I looked around me, taking stock of the humble set-up. The stove was just a gas bottle with a ring on top. There was a selection of big aluminium pots for cooking but no place for preparing food, just a wooden cabinet with some crockery and cutlery and a small table for eating. There was a small TV in the cabinet but John said they rarely watched it as there was no mains electricity, only limited solar power.

John went outside to the yard for more water while I took over peeling the plantains.

Some time later Lily arrived, looking hot and tired, carrying baskets of produce from the market. After a brief embarrassed hello, she disappeared to the room next door, emerging looking completely resplendent in a bright orange kanga (a large piece of fabric which is wrapped around the body in different styles, such as a skirt or dress) and matching headscarf.

Lily immediately ushered me out of the way and took over the cooking, bending over the pot from her hips with straight legs, adding onion and carrots to the boiling water and then ripping apart and oiling pieces of chicken, which were also added to the pot. The result was delicious and nutritious, authentic food fresh from the market, shared with John and Lily, who entertained us with stories of their children growing up and living in different parts of the country. Dessert was a fresh orange and a big mug of steaming-hot spiced ginger tea, which filled me with warmth.

"That definitely trumped kebabs and chips with all the truck drivers on the main road," I said to Joe.

"Sure did," he replied with a smile, already drifting off to sleep.

Several days later, after getting back on the relatively quiet main road and staying in hostels in the roadside towns of Same and Hedaru, we headed up into the Usambara Mountains. Leaving the tarmac was always a tough decision and again we debated whether it was the right thing to do.

Joe was still low on energy, but I wasn't keen on spending more nights in bland guesthouses. Hot showers were nice, but I didn't want to spend my afternoons looking at four walls with the sound of traffic rumbling by. I preferred being in the mountains. Joe had identified a couple of places where we could camp that sounded spectacular, but there was no easy way to get there.

The gravel road we turned into was badly corrugated and there were large patches of soft ground, making it impossible to ride. We kept sliding off the road and having to push our bikes.

"I don't think I can do this!" said Joe, putting down his feet to look at the map on his phone. "It's another three kilometres along here until the turn-off and it's not clear what sort of road that will be. And then there's a really big climb."

"It isn't much fun," I agreed. "But I don't want to go back to the main road. We can't just give up and take the easy route every time things get a bit hard."

We pushed on, Joe muttering that it was my decision and that I'd better not be complaining later.

Two hours later I was the one wanting to turn around.

"Ouch!" I said, skidding over into a thorny bush and finding my face just inches from a big pile of animal dung.

"What's this?" I asked, pointing it out to Joe. "What could have done this?"

"Looks like either a rhino or an elephant by the size of it," said Joe. "There's a game reserve over to the right there."

We had turned off the gravel road about an hour ago onto a single dirt track over a wide plain that stretched seemingly forever towards the distant mountains.

"There are no fences?" I started to panic. "I really don't fancy coming across a rhino out here. I'm not sure this is even a road. I think we should turn back."

Joe checked his phone. "Komoot shows a road here and it looks like it joins back up with another gravel road further ahead. Let's just keep going for a bit longer and see what happens."

I swung my leg back over my bike and kept pedalling along the red dirt into the dry heat, feeling the sweat mixing with the dust around my neck. There was hardly any vegetation except for prickly bushes and the occasional thorny acacia tree. Alongside the track was a wide ridge of open ground.

"Looks like the start of a new rift valley," I said. "Maybe that's where the road was at one time?"

After what seemed like hours but was probably only forty minutes, we heard engines coming up behind us, and then two motorbikes bounced past, each carrying a passenger, through the bushes.

The drivers waved hello and smiled, as if our presence here was nothing unusual.

"You see! It is a road!" said Joe. "We must be getting close to where it joins the other road up to the town now."

I relaxed a little, comforted by the fact that we weren't the only people out here in the African bush. Finally back on what looked like a road, we started the big climb. Joe was nervous again. "I think this might be too much for us," he said as we were resting at the side of the road, having just completed the first 200 metres of the 1,200-metre climb.

"It's tough, but we can do it." I tried to encourage him the way he had supported me in the early days of our trip. "We can just take it easy and stop every couple of hundred metres. We have plenty of time and we have food."

Another hour later, we were pushing our bikes up the gravel road. The road was so steep we had to push, then squeeze the brakes and take a big step to catch up with the bike. Joe was carrying 20 kilograms more than me, which evened us out in terms of strength when we were cycling on the flat road. But this meant he was unfairly disadvantaged when we were pushing. I soon got ahead of him, so after resting for a while, I left my bike at the side of the road and went down to help him push his.

"It's too far to continue like this in this heat," he said, looking defeated.

"Let's just stop and eat something and enjoy the views for a while." I replied. "Maybe a truck will pass by. Then we can get a lift up the hill."

We were about halfway now. I was okay and enjoying the challenge, but Joe was finding it almost impossible, and it was getting harder to keep his spirits up. When we set out on the trip, we both thought that he would be the one pushing me to go further and higher than I was comfortable with. But he often seemed to be the one that was holding us back. We both knew this wasn't right (he was fitter and should be stronger than me). We had tried changing the weight each of us carried on the bikes, but it didn't seem to make any difference and so again I had the nagging feeling that something was wrong. He was too slow to recover from tough days or getting sick. I couldn't help thinking again that this change had started after he'd had COVID so could be a form of long COVID. I was worried we could be making it worse by the constant exertion. I even wondered whether any of John's medicines could have helped.

No cars or trucks came by. We climbed back on our bikes and pedalled a bit further.

"Check out these views," I said, looking back over the plains. "You can see the track that we came along way over there. And is that the little hamlet where we turned off the gravel road?"

"That must be nearly thirty kilometres away now," Joe replied.

Two Bugs on Bikes

We were nearly at the top of the hill. I was exhausted, but the blood was pummelling through my veins and pulsing in my head. I looked at Joe and he grinned; I felt relief that he looked better and the now-familiar adrenaline rush that comes from realising that we had done what we thought was impossible was starting to kick in.

The road flattened out as we approached a town and rode along a lively market street that had people selling every type of fruit and vegetable from the backs of old cars and colourfully painted vans. The smell of hot ginger tea wafted through the air. Women dressed in their bright kangas sat at the side of the road in front of piles of tomatoes. Men pushed bicycles laden with milk urns or huge bundles of greens. Children ran from one stall to another, helping to carry supplies.

An old woman looked up from her pile of bananas and held a bunch out to me. "Jambo (hello), karibu (welcome)," she said. "You buy?" Her beautiful brown eyes had the mischievous twinkle of the child she might have once been, in contrast to the lines of her wrinkled face. I nodded and grabbed some notes out of my top pouch, offering them in place of the bananas. She fumbled in the folds inside her kanga to give me some change but I held up my hand indicating she could keep it. She beamed, placing her hand on her heart and bowing her head in thanks.

At the other side of the market, the road continued out of the town. Steep terraces rose from the roadside, dotted with hundreds of mud brick houses with thatched roofs clinging precariously to the edges. Dark silhouettes of children wandering home from school through the fields emerged in the afternoon sunlight and as they saw us a chorus of "muzungus! Muzungus! Bye-bye, muzungus!" erupted from the hillside. More children appeared on the other side and the chant started there too, so that it felt like we were in an echo chamber, laughing at the chaotic shouting bouncing off the hillsides as we pedalled past children jumping up and down and waving.

The next day we rolled down to the town of Lushoto, which was decorated with purple jacaranda trees. After another lovely healthy lunch we began a last long climb up to the Shewai campsite, high in the west Usambara Mountains.

"I could stay here forever!" I sighed, gazing at the distant mountains from a wooden bench next to our tent, which was pitched at the edge of a grassy patch at the front of the camp. A few low-key glamping tents were occupied by a group of young German hikers who were resting after their hike with Elly, the owner and manager of the camp. Later that evening we walked over to a nearby lookout for sunset drinks and marvelled at the pink streaks of light filtering through the layers of cloud that were settling on the mountain peaks.

Back at the camp, Happy and Name, two young Rasta girls, were in the kitchen prepping dinner from fresh ingredients grown in the camp gardens or sourced from the nearby markets. The place had a relaxed hippie vibe. There was only solar electricity in the camp (just enough to charge phones) and no running water. A concrete room with a wooden door on a latch and a wide, shoulder-height window contained a drop toilet, which doubled as a bucket shower room. If you were prepared to wait, the girls would heat a bucket of water for you to wash with.

"What was the best thing about your day?" I overheard one of the German hikers asking her friends.

"Definitely the shower!" responded the young guy. "After the long walk, standing looking out over those views and pouring warm water over my head felt simply amazing!"

I chuckled, completely understanding, but at the same time thinking how impossible it would seem to people back home that washing from a plastic bucket over a drop toilet could be so amazing.

"It's raining!" I said to Joe excitedly the next morning as we lay in our tent, just starting to wake from our heavy slumber. The rain was like music to my ears. The night before, Joe and I had come to a stand-off, arguing about whether to stay and rest for a day or just keep going. As always, I wanted to stay and rest but he felt we needed to push on. We agreed to let the weather decide for us, as it wouldn't be safe to try and ride down the steep hills in the rain. I now had the whole day ahead of me to rest and relax, to write and reflect on our journey so far. And rest was likely exactly the medicine Joe needed to get his strength back – even though he wouldn't admit it.

"You win!" said Joe, rolling over and smiling at me. We snuggled up in our sleeping bags, warm and safe, listening to the rain from inside the comforting cocoon of our tent.

"Is there anywhere you'd rather be?" I asked later that morning, as we were sipping hot coffee from our metal camp mugs, looking out over the view.

"Nope," he replied. "Even that brutal ride up the hill yesterday was worth it, just so you could have this view. But I'm looking forward to riding downhill tomorrow!"

JACQUI WEBSTER

~18~

THE SPICE ISLANDS

"**D**o you realise there's nothing except the ocean between us and Australia for about 8,000 kilometres?" asked Joe, lying back and submerging his head as we bathed in the warm water. We had reached the Indian Ocean and were on the east coast of Tanzania near Pangani. It was the end of three long days riding on a mixture of tarmac and gravel, roads past endless fields of sisal plants (the oldest commercial cash crop, smuggled into Tanzania from Mexico by a German in 1893 – the fibres of the plant are used to make textiles, paper and plastic) and through remote villages along the coastline. It had been flat, but it was the end of October and it was getting ridiculously hot.

"It's also about 8,000 kilometres between here and the UK, where we started out this trip visiting your family," Joe continued.

"And we've cycled 10,000 kilometres to get here," I said, shaking my head in disbelief. "In some ways that makes the world feel pretty small. Yet, despite travelling so far and traversing two continents, we've only seen such a tiny part of it."

"Let's hope we can get a boat to Zanzibar," said Joe. "It's still a long way to Dar es Salaam if we need to keep cycling and get a boat from there."

While the main tourist boats to get to Zanzibar went from Dar, we'd read online in another cyclist's blog that you could get a small speedboat from Pangani, but we hadn't been able to verify this through more recent information. Joe headed off to ask the locals for advice.

Lying in the tent watching the sun come up and listening to the waves lap against the shore, I was brimming with excitement. Zanzibar had been on my bucket list for decades following a sliding doors moment when I nearly went to work there after completing my masters degree in development studies in 1993. Between my honours degree in sociology at Durham University and my masters at the University of Leeds, I took a year out and went to Spain so I could learn Spanish while teaching English. When I finished my masters in development, I assumed that because my parents had invested so heavily in my four years of tertiary education, the world owed me a living and it would be easy to get a job.

But the world had other ideas. I struggled to find the sort of work I was interested in. Exhausting every opportunity for getting a paid role while working in soul-destroying telemarketing jobs in London to pay the rent, I applied for a position with Voluntary Service Overseas (VSO). Based on the combination of my English teaching experience in Spain and my education in development, I was offered a dream role coordinating English instruction for the community health workers at the Ministry of Health in Zanzibar. This seemed like a great stepping stone into development, and I had everything lined up to go. Then at the last minute, VSO downgraded the job to an English teacher, and I was less excited. I didn't need more English teaching experience. At the same time, I was offered a role as a project officer coordinating a food poverty network for what later became Sustain: the alliance for better food and farming. I took that role, thinking I'd stay for just six months until I found a job in Africa. But I loved the work and the people and stayed much longer than I'd originally planned, before being recruited to work on food poverty for the UK government's Food Standard Agency. That role led to a broader role in consumer engagement in policy making and then to a different role coordinating the UK government's salt reduction strategy.

Now, looking out over the Indian Ocean, I couldn't help wondering how things may have turned out if I had taken the role in Zanzibar. Thirty years earlier, when I was twenty-three, the idea of working on an island that had been a centre for trade in spices and slaves, blending African and Arabic influences with the European influences of the Portuguese colonists, had seemed so exotic. Maybe I would have ended up living and working in Africa, which is what I thought I wanted to do. Instead, I'd worked on salt reduction in the UK for a few years before moving to Australia and working mainly in Australia and the Pacific Islands. Apart from a few short trips to Cape Town and a previous holiday in Morocco, this was the first time I'd spent any time on the African continent.

It's interesting where life takes you. My life didn't feel very planned. I never set out to move to Australia. An opportunity to spend a few weeks working in Sydney had coincided with the abrupt end of a long-term relationship. I suddenly had no reason to go back to Amsterdam, where we had been living, or London, where I had been before that. So I never went home. It was hard living away from my friends and family in the UK, but I had no regrets. Australia had been good to me, and I wouldn't have met Joe or been on this adventure if I hadn't stayed in Sydney.

I couldn't imagine my life without Joe.

He returned triumphant, shouting as he ran towards me, jolting me out of my reverie.

"There's a boat that departs tomorrow morning around nine. It's quite small but they said it would be fine to take the bikes. There are a few other locals and another muzungu family booked on."

Carrying our bikes on our shoulders through the sea to put them on the little ten-passenger speedboat for the one-hour trip across to Zanzibar couldn't have felt less like commercial tourism. Unsurprisingly, we were running several hours late due to waiting for the Dutch family who had been driving from Pangani town. It turned out they were living here in Tanzania and were heading to Zanzibar to get the plane to Amsterdam for a visit back to the

Netherlands. The other people on the boat were all locals heading over to the island for work. We were the only tourists. No one seemed in the least bit concerned that our bikes were taking up half the boat.

The wind was picking up and I was feeling nervous about the ocean crossing on such a small boat.

"Please put on your life jackets," said the driver as he fastened his own and took the anchor from one of the guys on the beach. And with no further instructions or information we were off, slicing through the calm waters, the ocean spray splashing over the bikes on the deck and cooling our faces.

"Look, dolphins!" I shouted, pointing towards the east of the boat where a pod of eight or nine dolphins was leaping in and out of the water. They darted over towards us and dived underneath the boat, emerging at the stern and dancing in the wake.

"Amazing!" said one of the young Dutch girls.

"Look at the colour of the ocean!" said Joe.

In the fifty minutes that we'd traversed the ocean from the mainland to within sight of Zanzibar, the water had turned from a murky brown to bright aqua spotted with patches of lighter colours. The soft yellow hues of the sandy island fringed with green palm trees were coming into focus in the distance, giving us a glimpse of the paradise before us.

As we approached the beach at Kendwa Rocks, we saw it was lined with bars and tall hotel blocks towering over the sand. Confident, scantily clad girls posed for photos alongside young Maasai, whose red rectangular cloth seemed to be draped in a deliberately provocative off-the-shoulder style. Dragging our bikes over the sand, we saw huge signs advertising a full moon party and realised it was that day.

We looked at each other. "We can't miss the full moon party!" I said.

After resting at our guesthouse in Nungwi, we walked three kilometres back up the beach to join the other tourists watching the African dancers on stage, trying the food – a blend of American and African cuisines – and drinking fancy cocktails. Dressed in our best clothes, pulled from the bottom of our cycling bags – Joe in a white tropical-print shirt and shorts and me in a black singlet with a colourful wraparound miniskirt – we kicked off our thongs and immersed ourselves in the party atmosphere.

Musicians and dancers from different neighbouring African countries took turns to come up on to the stage. Dressed in their traditional tribal attire, bare-chested warriors beat drums as dancers paraded their talents across the floor. The crowd was a mix of foreign tourists, including quite a lot of families, as well as Tanzanians who'd come on the boat from Dar for the night. We mingled, keen to meet people but struggling to connect over the loud music. As the cocktails started to kick in, we found ourselves dancing to the uplifting African beats, despite feeling inadequate compared to the adept African dancers.

"It's probably time to get out of here," I said to Joe at around 2 am. I'd suddenly realised the demographics had changed and we were now among a small minority of remaining tourists dancing with locals to hardcore drum and bass. Joe was sweating and bleary eyed from too many beers.

We paid at least triple the usual price for a taxi back to our guesthouse, where we immediately collapsed into bed.

The next morning, I explored Nungwi while Joe was still sleeping. The short walk from where we were staying to the beach threaded through streets lined with stalls selling all kinds of tourist treasures – beautiful local arts and crafts as well as typical island clothing. I resisted the calls of the salespeople, mumbling that I was travelling by bicycle and couldn't carry anything.

Reaching the waterfront, I smiled at the sight of a traditional fishing boat bobbing in the calm, azure sea. But the guesthouses and cafe bars were crammed together on the beach, making it hard to find a patch of sand. Western music blared from the bars, where tourists sat in bikinis or board shorts, ordering bacon sandwiches to soak up the alcohol from the night before. This was a far cry from the exotic spice island I'd imagined. Thankfully, we'd decided to only stay one night in Nungwi and were planning to jump back on our bikes and explore the island later that day.

The ride south from Nungwi was relatively short and flat. Away from the coast, the island was completely different. Women wearing traditional clothes walked along the streets carrying bundles of wood on their heads. Bicycles were parked at the side of the road, their riders at work in the rice fields, trousers rolled up to their knees. Stalls sold tropical fruits and nuts at the side of the road. Children in blue-and-white uniforms walked home from school hand in hand. Some of the girls had their hair covered. Muslims mixed with Christians, Africans with Arabs. Much more like the Zanzibar I'd imagined thirty years ago.

Back on the coast at Kiwengwa, we wandered the backstreets to find somewhere to stay. We'd read that Kiwengwa was one of the best beaches on the island, with long stretches of pristine white sand.

"This place has good reviews," said Joe. It was an Airbnb one street back from the beach. "Why don't you go and have a look while I wait with the bikes."

I knocked on the door and was greeted by an elegant, well-dressed European lady who invited me in and showed me around. The place was newly renovated and immaculate, and I felt conspicuously grubby in my sweaty cycling clothes.

"What do you think?" asked Joe as I came out ten minutes later.

It was a beautiful house and the rooms were lovely, but it could have been in France. I was keen to find somewhere with more of a local vibe to spend the next couple of days.

"What's this place?"

Across the road was a big doorway. It looked like it could be a guesthouse but there was no signage. We leaned the bikes against the wall and went inside, where we found a kind-faced young man dressed in Maasai clothing and holding a baby. A quick glance around revealed it was a small guesthouse.

"I'm Walter," said the young man. "Come and look around." He gestured towards the ocean.

This feels more like it, I thought.

My shoulders noticeably dropped as I wandered out towards the beach where a few handmade sun loungers decked out with lime-green cushions were neatly arranged on the sand, giving the small place a shabby chic feel that appealed to me.

A wooden sign emblazoned with the words MAMBO MAZURI, which is Swahili for good things, hung from ropes, creating a natural frame for the traditional boat on the waterfront.

"How much are the rooms?" I asked. "We'd like to stay two nights."

"Take a seat here," said Walter, gesturing to a wooden bench near the reception area. "I'll check availability."

There were just six rooms in total: four facing the sea and two garden rooms. There didn't seem to be too many people around, so I was hopeful. I really wanted a room facing the sea.

"This is Elisa, the manager," said Walter, introducing a European woman. So, it's not locally run after all, I thought.

"You are in luck," said Elisa. "We have this room available for two nights." She pointed to the last room on the front facing the sea. "However, I need to let you know there is a party in the restaurant next door tonight. It doesn't usually go on until too late, but it could be noisy for a while."

We laughed. So much for our quiet time. Joe said it was fine and that we could always go to the party. We negotiated a price that would be outrageous in most parts of Africa, but seemed reasonable for Zanzibar on the waterfront. The room was quite small but had everything we needed. We showered and washed our clothes then went out to find lunch.

Later, chatting with Elisa, who was Italian and married to Walter, we learnt that things had been challenging for the small tour operators since COVID, with fewer independent travellers like us visiting the island. And it seemed it was only going to get worse as the government was planning on introducing a new rule that guesthouses had to have at least ten rooms.

"This will push out all of the small businesses," Elisa said. "It is already hard for locals to compete and with the new laws it will be impossible. The large international chains will just take over.

The benefits of tourism have not spilled over into the local community as promised, and this will just make things worse."

"Such a shame," I replied. "The president of Tanzania is from Zanzibar. I would have thought she might want to do something to protect the cultural heritage of the island. Surely community-led tourism is a good way to do that?"

Several days later we rode to Kizimkazi, the local village where the country's first female president, Samia Suluhu Hassan, was from. Promotion of the annual Kizimkazi festival, first held in 2015, attracts tourists and locals to a celebration of local culture, and is one of the ways in which the government of Tanzania is trying to foster entrepreneurship and boost tourism, at the same time as empowering women and youth. What started off as a local festival has now been taken over by the national government. In August 2024, the festival was also used to launch the opening of the Salaam Cave – historically used as a ritual site for locals – into a sea turtle conservation site, now promoted as a key attraction for international tourists. Opening the cave, the president asked the locals to avoid land conflicts, reassuring the villagers that they would be provided with alternative burial sites and compensated for any loss of land.

"We should all benefit [from the developments]," Suluhu Hassan had said,[xiv] thanking the bank and the development companies for sponsoring the festivities.

It was quiet when we rode through the narrow, winding streets past coral stone houses with thatched roofs. It was hard to see what the festival had done to improve the lives of the people in the village, many of whom still lack access to electricity or clean drinking water. We were hoping to get some lunch before heading to Karamba, our last stop before the capital Stone Town, from where we would get the boat back to the mainland. According to Google Maps, there was one fancy restaurant on the waterfront, but we kept an eye out for somewhere more low-key.

Three dilapidated looking dhows bobbed on the shoreline. Many other boats were floating aimlessly out at sea. Two fishermen lay asleep under the shade of a palm tree, but otherwise there seemed to be no one around.

Looking behind us, we saw what looked like a small cafe. There was a plastic table and chairs and a round tiled area that looked like it was for washing and cooking fish. As we got closer, a young boy looked up from where he was slouched over a table with his head in his hands. A few telltale traditional metal pots were the only sign that there might be food.

"Jambo," said Joe. "We are looking for something to eat."

The boy stood up reluctantly and shuffled over to the road, pointing towards where we knew the expensive restaurant was.

"The restaurant is round over there," he said.

"But what about here?" asked Joe, pointing to the pots on the stove.

"You want this food?" the boy asked, surprised. "The tourists never eat this food, just the local fishermen."

"Have you got fish?" asked Joe. "And maybe rice or cassava?"

"I can cook fish," he replied, starting to perk up a bit. "You wait here." He pointed to the plastic chairs and ran off towards the boat.

After a delicious meal of fresh fish served with rice, beans and spinach, we stood up to pay and said thanks to the young boy.

Hardly anyone had passed by while we were eating, but two young men were now walking purposefully towards us.

"You want a dhow ride? You go to see dolphins?" they asked, holding out tatty leaflets.

We shook our heads. "No, thank you."

We'd gone on a boat trip to go snorkelling around Mnemba Island from Kiwenga a few days before. We'd had to ask the boat driver to turn around as we were so upset by the sight of thirty boats all jammed full of tourists, jostling for position to cut off the dolphins so they could push the passengers in so that they could say they swam with dolphins.

Chatting to the boys, we discovered that most tourists just arrived on boats from one of the bigger towns and spent an hour zigzagging across the bay to watch the dolphins without disembarking at Kizimkazi. There were around 3,000 people in this small village, and it was hard for them to make a living there.

The reception area at the Karamba Eco Boutique Hotel was tastefully decorated with large sofas for lounging, books about local history, and local artefacts. Chatting with the receptionist, we learnt that the place was owned by a German woman, Gemma. Our guesthouse in Jambiani had also been owned by a German couple, and Mambo Mazuri had been owned by an Italian, Elisa.

"It seems almost impossible to find any locally run guesthouses on this island," I said to Joe. "At least Elisa was married to a local Maasai."

"The Maasai aren't local to Zanzibar," Joe reminded me.

The hordes of young Maasai men wandering the beaches trying to pick up Western women had been a shock to us since arriving in Zanzibar. Kizimkazi seemed like it was remote enough to get away from them, but at Kiwenga or Jambiani, as soon as you stepped outside they were by your side, trying to engage you in conversation so they could persuade you to come to their sisters' craft store.

One time when I was walking alone along the beach, a tall boy with Rasta hair and fake Gucci sunglasses latched on to me and, after asking my name and where I was going, started asking me about my husband, why wasn't he with me, and did I want to go on an outing with them. I tried to engage in meaningful conversation and learn something about his life and why he was in Zanzibar, but he wouldn't be steered off course. Eventually, irritated, I had to be really assertive to get him to leave me alone.

Back at the guesthouse I did some research to try to understand the situation. I found an interesting article in *Nature*[xv] about how the Maasai had been flocking to Zanzibar for years to benefit from the growing tourism industry. It explains how the men "skilfully employ their traditional materiality: red robes, swords, daggers, clubs, beaded sandals and jewellery, as well as their own muscular bodies, so as to construct an extraordinary image, which they use to attract the attention of tourists and promote their businesses. Concomitantly, their use of modern material objects, such as mobile phones and stylish sunglasses, undermines their extraordinary image, making their presence mundane and even disturbing, to the extent of being accused by some Tanzanians and tourists of faking Maasai identity."

It was an interesting article that acknowledged the fact that the Maasai are one of the most famous tribes in the world yet still face a huge amount of discrimination. They hadn't really benefited from the years of tourism that they'd supported and many of them were likely in Zanzibar as a potential way out of poverty back home.

Despite huge strides in terms of economic growth, primarily due to tourism, more than 25 percent of people in Zanzibar were still living in poverty. While poverty had reduced, the reduction was about a third of the rate that could be expected, and there were still huge differences between urban and rural areas. According to the World Bank, over 80 percent of the requirements for tourism (labour, food and drink, building materials) were currently sourced from outside Zanzibar, bringing no benefit to the local economy. The World Bank recommends making tourism more inclusive by diversifying tourism projects and involving communities, at the same time as supporting local employment and agricultural production.[xvi] But this seems a far cry from what we saw and learnt on our trip around the island.

After seven days cruising around the island, we headed into Stone Town, a UNESCO World Heritage Site known for its role in slavery. Zanzibar was one of the largest slave trading centres in East Africa, with hundreds of thousands of slaves passing through in the eighteenth and nineteenth centuries when the island was a hub for the Arab traders. Although the slave trade took place over the whole island, Stone Town was one of the most brutal slave markets, where most of the inhumane transactions took place. I ducked my head as we walked into one of the cells that had housed the slaves while they were waiting to be sent to market. Concrete slab shelves on either side of the cramped room would have served as beds. Most of the cells were standing room only, with chains and shackles on the ground for feet and on the walls for hands.

The Anglican cathedral across the square was built in 1903 on the former site of the slave auctions. Now, a scruffy monument outside depicts slaves in chains looking up from a pit. I shuddered at the thought of how frightened the men and women must have been, tired and malnourished from the journey and stripped of their identities, as they awaited their fate in the markets. Wandering around the museum to shelter from the rain, we learnt about the British anti-slavery protestors who helped end the slave trade (ironically, nothing was mentioned about the African people who fought so long and hard and risked their lives to end slavery).

One hundred and fifty years have passed since the abolition of slavery, yet I couldn't help thinking that things hadn't progressed enough.

~19~

TWO BUGS

Dar es Salaam sapped my soul. After Istanbul we thought we were ready for anything, but it turned out that this city was no place for bikes.

"I think this is one way!" I said to Joe, frantically trying to follow him weaving between the five lanes of traffic going in the other direction.

We were stressed and tired after getting up early to catch the ferry from Stone Town and having to detach our bags from our bikes to go through the security scanners at each end.

"Can't we just wheel the bikes through the scanners?" I'd asked again, as we'd been instructed to stand aside.

It was raining heavily as we got off the ferry, and vehicles were jammed into the narrow streets going in all directions, making it difficult to pass as Joe navigated his way through the back alleys of Dar to find a bike shop. I needed some new cycling pants, and we needed some spare inner tubes for the long ride south-west on the T1 towards Mbeya, from where we would drop down south and cross the border into Malawi.

What was supposed to be a shop turned out to be a market stall and its owner, Beta, whose Facebook page had been advertising bike gear, turned out to be selling an impressive array of electrical goods. There wasn't a bike in sight. After stacking our bikes at the back of a stall selling plastic buckets we were ushered into a little room where we were given mint tea, and I was presented with some second-hand men's cycling shorts.

"These are good for you?" asked Beta, smiling. "You take?"

I shook my head. I was already starting to feel daggy and dirty, my few clothes faded and worn. I wasn't going to spend the rest of the journey in oversized men's shorts.

"I used to stock lots of cycling gear," Beta explained. "But then COVID and no customers came and so I had to divert to other things."

We left feeling dejected, without new clothes or inner tubes.

I suddenly had a bizarre feeling of cultural disorientation.

Hundreds of tuk tuks (or bajajis, as they are known in Tanzania) were scrambling in every direction, drivers shouting and beeping their horns, bouncing over the rain-filled potholes and showering us with mud.

"It feels like India!" I shouted to Joe as we tried to wheel through the traffic jam, dodging between the tuk tuks, cars and pedestrians. I hadn't associated tuk tuks with Africa, but later learnt that the Tanzanian government had imported hundreds from India to ease traffic congestion.

It didn't seem to be working. We weaved backwards and forwards through the hectic streets, trying to find somewhere to eat. We settled for some sort of fast-food restaurant just off the main market route and ate rice and peas. We hadn't decided on anywhere to stay that night and Joe was keen to head straight out of town, knowing how far we had to travel to get out of Tanzania.

"But there are so many things to see and do in Dar es Salaam," I said, not at all excited about trying to battle the traffic to get out of the city. But I wasn't really excited about staying, either.

We skirted through the town and found another bike shop on the outskirts, but it only seemed to stock kids' sports gear.

"I'm so over this!" I said. We were standing at the side of the road outside the bike shop while I changed from the casual shorts and T-shirt I'd worn on the ferry into my old, padded cycling pants with holes in them. "I feel dirty and daggy and exhausted!" I gestured to the mud and oil that was splattered all over my legs and practically stomped my feet in frustration. "I can't believe we're in the capital of Tanzania and we can't find any new cycling gear," I ranted. "I'm tired. I need new clothes. I need to dye my hair. I need new glasses. I need a spa hotel!"

"Calm down!" said Joe, smirking. "You were the one who wanted to come to Africa!"

I glared at him.

"Let's just keep riding," he said. "It'll get better once we get out of the city."

But it didn't get better. Over the next two weeks we covered 900 kilometres, sleeping in budget guesthouses at truck stops at the side of the T1.

The T1 is the main highway between Tanzania and Zambia. To say there were lots of trucks would be a gross understatement. For the most part there was a shoulder where it was possible to ride the bikes, but there were lots of potholes and in some places where they'd re-tarred the roads there were big ridges of tar between the edge of the road and the shoulder, which were extremely dangerous to navigate when huge trucks were thundering alongside us.

In the small city of Morogoro we met up with Jonny, a fellow English guy travelling in the same direction. We'd connected on the Cairo to Cape Town WhatsApp group and agreed that it would be good to ride together through the Mikumi National Park. Safety in numbers, we'd all agreed, knowing there were wild animals, including elephants and lions, in the park.

Morogoro is famous for Gambian pouched rats, known colloquially as hero rats, as they are trained to sniff out landmines and tuberculosis. The city is also known for the controversial Mindu Dam. Situated on the Ngerengere River, it's the primary source of water in the region, meeting 80 percent of the city's water needs. However, from its inception in 1978 there was a surge in bilharzia infection rates and the city's water supply was polluted from mercury run-off from the nearby gold mining activities. More recently the impacts of climate change, deforestation and changing land use continue to impact water quality.

Wandering around the humid, wet streets of the city later that day, I bought myself new transition glasses, surprised to find the technology to check my prescription from my old glasses and make a new pair in a few hours. I had only had sunglasses since Spain and it was a relief to finally be able to see again once the sun had gone down.

Sharing stories over dinner in Mama Pierna's guesthouse, a crumbling colonial-style garden retreat on the outskirts of Morogoro, we learnt that Jonny was a self-confessed introvert and IT geek who had never left his hometown. He had shocked friends and family by abruptly giving up his job and announcing he was going to cycle to Africa. He didn't know what had made him do it. Cycling from his home in Peterborough to London, he took the train to Paris and cycled through Spain and across to Morocco before getting stuck in the Western Sahara and deciding to fly to Kenya and start again from there.

Hats off to Jonny for being so brave.

Travelling alone, he survived mainly on jam sandwiches, buying supplies in the evenings so he didn't have to stop on the road.

The next day, having ridden past an elephant loitering by a bridge and gawped at giraffes running alongside the road, we stopped at a truck stop to try to find somewhere to eat. We found a typical-looking wooden shack serving food. Leaning our bikes against the wall outside the cafe, we washed our hands with soap and water from the plastic barrel container with a plastic tap and a bucket underneath. Inside the shack, we sat down on the wooden benches.

"What's this?" asked Jonny as a young lady served us small plastic plates with three sections: one containing ugali, one kisamvu (cassava leaves in peanut sauce) and one filled with soup with two small chunks of meat.

Joe and I tucked in hungrily, rolling the ugali into balls with our hands and using it to scoop up the meat and vegetables.

Jonny looked at the food reluctantly and eventually I found him a spoon.

Two hours later, Joe and I were standing at the side of the road holding the three bikes.

Jonny was squatting behind a tree. I was scanning the fields behind him anxiously for lions, no longer sure about safety in numbers. Over the course of the rest of the day we saw buffalo, wildebeest, warthogs, impalas and zebras, but no lions.

Jonny cycled much slower than us and it was a relief to get out of the national park and off the main road to a lodge, where we camped for the night.

"Look at me," said Joe. We were sitting around the campfire relaxing after a tasty meal of Tanzanian beef stew and rice in the lodge.

"You look like a pirate!" Joe said. "Pass me your glasses." I took them off and gave them to him and he laughed. It turned out that only one lens had transitioned back to clear; the other had stayed dark from the sunshine. So much for the technology.

For the next week, the three of us travelled together. Although Joe and I cycled faster than Jonny, we stopped more often, and for longer. We'd be sitting at the side of the road or at a cafe having food and Jonny would roll up. We'd discuss where to stay for the evening and invariably end up eating together.

It was fine at first. Jonny was easy company and it was good to have someone else to exchange stories with. But after the first few days, I missed my closeness with Joe and the interactions with locals we had together, which seemed to dry up when there were three of us.

On day seven of travelling with Jonny, we reached our planned destination at lunchtime. There had been some nightmarish sections where there was no hard shoulder going uphill and the road surface was all broken up, so we were constantly dodging death with the trucks. But we decided to just keep pedalling, clocking up a total of 140 kilometres that day and leaving Jonny behind us. We were sorry not to say goodbye in person, but let him know once we arrived.

Two Bugs on Bikes

Resting outside the shop at a petrol station about fifteen kilometres from our destination, we were sharing a cold drink and staring at a metal container, watching as two bugs traversed the edge. We were transfixed. Every time the lead bug turned the other one followed, even when it went right over the edge into the danger zone. Then the one behind scrambled past the lead bug and forced him to change direction so they went back to safety.

"Those two bugs are just like us!" said Joe, chuckling.

"I was just thinking the same thing!" I replied, resting my head on his chest and smiling. It was good to feel that strong sense of togetherness again.

The next day was another long slog of over 100 kilometres. It was hot and we were tired. Parts of the road were treacherous, with trucks flying past up the hill and either no cycle lane or one so full of potholes it was dangerous to ride in. Stopping on a bridge to rest part way up the steep climb, we were mobbed by aggressive kids asking for money.

Further up the road, a line of locals carrying machetes were walking down the road. There wasn't enough space between them and the road. I had to jump off my bike to get past them, narrowly missing the trucks. It was raining and I could feel sobs rising in my throat.

"I can't do this anymore!" I said to Joe, bowing my head in defeat. "I don't want to be here. Everything seems ugly."

"Come on," said Joe. "It's not much further to the top of the hill now. You've done harder stuff before. You can do it. We'll be there before you know it."

I got back on my bike.

When we finally turned off the dreaded T1 after the town of Mbeya at 1,800 metres altitude, my spirits lifted. That was one road I never wanted to travel on again.

The next day we headed south and climbed up to 2,300 metres altitude into the spectacular southern highlands, which were cooler and greener, the ridges covered in coffee and banana plantations.

"The last couple of weeks have been really tough," I said. "In hindsight, maybe we should have taken a bus or a train."

We were sitting on the terrace in the lovely, air-conditioned restaurant of an eco-lodge on an avocado farm, the cool breeze a welcome relief after the relentless heat of the road.

"But then we'd never have met Jonny!" said Joe. "Or seen all the giraffes in the national park. Or tasted all the street foods at the truck stops."

"Or tasted the grit and tar in our teeth for days on end!" I quipped back. But as I said it, the exhaustion and frustration of the last couple of weeks started to melt away. The hardships were already fading into the background and what was left were the memories: the funny moments with Jonny, the unexpected encounters with wildlife, the quest to find decent food in the truck stops, the friendships struck up with strangers, and the things that we'd discovered about ourselves along the way.

"You're right," I said smiling. "The toughest challenges always lead to the best stories."

~20~

NOT YOUR REGULAR CRUISE

"**B**y bicycle, from Rwanda, aaaaaaaay?" The large, round-faced official behind the counter at the Songwe border crossing between Tanzania and Malawi was holding my passport and looking at me in disbelief. She turned to the two uniformed men sitting chatting at the back of the office.

"These two have travelled from Rwanda by bicycle. Can you believe that?"

"By bicycle?" repeated one of the men, shaking his head. "Aaaaaaaay!"

The woman asked us more questions. Where we were going. Where we were going to stay. How long we travelled each day. If we liked Africa. And of course, why we were travelling by bicycle and not in a car.

By now a small team of officials had gathered behind the metal bars at the customs booth, eager to join in the conversation and check out our bikes. A long queue of people was growing restless behind us.

Eventually stamping our passports and handing them back, the friendly official wished us well on our journey and told us to be careful once we got to Zambia, as the people there were not as honest as the people of Malawi. Such was our experience at most border crossings in Africa: the officials were intrigued and interested in our journey and always warned us about the people in the neighbouring countries.

Border crossing days were always interesting. Sometimes the differences between countries were subtle and it took a while to notice the shift. Other times the changes were immediate. Crossing from Tanzania to Malawi we were struck by the differences.

Back on our bikes after a quick lunch of chicken in tomato sauce with rice and greens, eaten from plastic bowls in a shack at the side of the road, we immediately noticed how many other people were on bikes, including women, which was something we hadn't seen before in Africa.

Malawi is known as the Warm Heart of Africa in reference to the kindness of its people, and we were not disappointed. Groups of kids immaculately dressed in blue-and-white uniforms burst into a happy chorus of "Muzungus, muzungus! How are you? Bye-bye, muzungus!" as we cycled past.

Malawi is one of the most densely populated countries in Africa, and also one of the poorest countries in the world. There were very few trucks or buses. The only cars seemed to be tiny Ford Fiestas or similar small cars, all completely packed full of boxes or baskets of produce, with more tied to the roof with rope.

A group of women wandered along the side of the road, elegant in their traditional long kanga skirts, one arm reaching up to support the baskets balanced on the top of their heads.

The landscape was flat and dry, the fields empty, waiting for the rice to be planted at the start of the wet season the next month, in December. The scene was a stark contrast to the morning's spectacular ride in Tanzania where we'd flown down rolling hills through the lush green banana farms and tea plantations of Mount Rungwe, before descending further through miles and miles of barely inhabited forested land on the way to the border.

Lake Malawi is one of the Great Lakes of Africa, and the fourth-largest freshwater lake in the world by volume. At around 584 kilometres long and 80 kilometres wide, it takes up one-fifth of the surface area of Malawi.

"What's that smoke over there?" I said to Joe pointing over to the other side of the lake where two large plumes of smoke, each hundreds of metres high, were moving over the water.

We were just setting up camp in a lovely shady, grassy field at the side of the lake near the town of Ngara. Joe looked up from where he was pushing pegs into the ground to secure the tent.

"It looks like something must have caught on fire," he said, "but I can't see anything."

"It seems to be moving in our direction," I said. "I hope it's not toxic."

We watched as the smoke plumed towards us, moving faster as the wind picked up and holding our breath as it engulfed us.

"It's little flies!" I shrieked. Tiny midge-like insects were crawling all over Joe's skin. As he wiped them off more landed. "Yuck! They're stuck all over your face."

"Yours too!" said Joe. "Look, they're everywhere!" He wiped his hand across the tent to remove them, only to see the green tent's fly sheet filling up again.

"What are we going to do?" I said. "We can't camp here, it'll be awful. You can't even see the lake now."

The flies were so thick it looked as though we were surrounded by fog.

But as quickly as they'd come, the flies were gone, whisked away in the strong wind. We brushed the remainder from the tent and washed our faces. Joe finished setting up camp and then, still not feeling well, collapsed and fell asleep on a hammock strung between two trees.

I sat on a wooden bench and watched as a young couple bathed in the lake after washing their clothes and leaving them to dry on the fence. Moments later a herd of cows wandered past, their bells rattling as they picked up their hooves over the logs scattered along the water's edge. A young boy, no more than eight, wearing just a pair of shorts, no shoes or shirt, walked behind the cows with a stick. Another kid was out on the water, paddling an old canoe as the sun set behind him. This was life on the lake. It was peaceful here.

I picked up my phone to see if I could find any information about the swarms of flies. I soon learnt that the fascinating spectacle we had just witnessed only happened once or twice a year, usually just before the wet season. Apparently, the larvae of these lake flies can survive deep in the bottom of Lake Malawi where there is hardly any oxygen and where few other species survive. When they hatch, they hang out in the water until the conditions are right, when they float to the surface and transform into insects.

"Look, babe, this is amazing!" I said to Joe, who was stirring in the hammock. I clicked on a YouTube video, and we watched, seeing images of what we had just witnessed over the lake, but then even more amazingly pictures of Malawians, adults and children, laughing and shouting as the lake flies swarmed towards them, swooping them up in baskets or frying pans, ready to cook or eat.

"Can you believe they make fly burgers?" I said. I later learnt that the flies contain 67 percent protein and are a good source of minerals, making them an important nutritious treat for the local people, who call the burgers kunga cakes.

With 70 percent of the population living under the international poverty line on less than two US dollars a day, it's important to be resourceful. But a phenomenon like this happening twice a year isn't enough to prevent malnutrition. While the Global Hunger Index score for Malawi has almost halved since 2000, nearly 20 percent of the population is malnourished and 35 percent of children under five are stunted.[xvii]

Talking to Andreas, the Dutch manager of the Floja Malawi Foundation and campsite where we were staying, we learnt how the organisation provides education, nutritious meals and health care services for children, their parents and other community members who need it.

"Every day around ninety children come to the school here and are given breakfast and lunch as well as a chance to play and learn," Andreas said as he poured us freshly made coffee from a cafeteria. He told us that the Floja Foundation had been set up by another Dutch couple, but he'd seen an advert and applied to take it over, with his wife. They'd come here eight years ago but divorced four years ago. It wasn't an easy place to live.

"I wanted to make a big difference," he said. "I realised that whatever magic the nursery achieved for the kids, it made no difference if they just went on to the local primary school where there are 1,200 kids and hardly any teachers or facilities. So I set out to raise money from donors to build new classroom blocks. The deal was that the locals contributed bricks and labour and the project did the rest. But after the first few blocks were completed the workers stopped turning up because they had other priorities."

He was disappointed that he hadn't achieved more but said it was hard to change the culture.

"One of the main problems is young girls falling pregnant at fourteen or fifteen, dropping out of school and going on to have six or seven kids," he said. "I thought I'd found a solution when I found out you could have a contraception injection that lasted for four years, but then I learnt that this was already available but the girls either didn't want them or weren't allowed to have them. The main fear was that they would become infertile, but there was also an expectation that the girls were there to reproduce and didn't need an education, as well as fear that they would be rejected if they didn't produce children."

The fertility rate in Malawi is less than four, which is relatively low compared to much of Africa, but still way above the 2.1 rate required to stabilise population growth.

"It's hard to stay motivated," Andreas confessed. "I'm handing over to another couple and heading back home to the Netherlands soon."

Cycling past the small fishing town of Ngara later that morning, we glanced back to see rows of trestle tables covered with fresh fish stretching out towards the shore of the glimmering lake. Fish stocks are a critical source of food for the people in Malawi, providing 70 percent of animal protein consumed, but the fish stocks are declining due to overfishing.[xviii]

We struggled to find enough food for ourselves that day. After stopping at a small town where women were sitting selling tomatoes and eggs on the roadside and being told there was nowhere for us to eat, we pushed on until we saw groups of kids selling mangoes at the side of the road.

Malawi is famous for mangoes. The kids were excited to see us, but couldn't speak any English. An old woman, who we assumed was their grandma, came out to help make the sale. They wanted 1,500 kwacha, about AU$1.50, for the whole bucket. We laughed pointing at our bikes and picked out four, giving them a 1,000 kwacha note. The whole family sat watching as we ate our mangoes African style, ripping off the skin with our teeth and then chewing into the juicy flesh. They looked happy. This was probably the only money they'd make all day.

Forty kilometres later, bumping over the gravel road into Chilumba, we saw a sign saying Ebenezer Chef's Hut. We were still hungry. Something about the way the hut was painted duck-egg blue and red, the wooden menu sign hanging from the wall, and the smiling face of the man who turned out to be the chef and was called Ovid, made me want to eat there. Ovid cooked us the most delicious meal of barbecued beef and capsicum with rice and beans and fresh tomato sauce. He also agreed to prepare samosas and bottled water for us to collect at midnight, when we would pass by on our way to board the *MV Ilala*, which was scheduled to depart at two in the morning.

"This wasn't a great idea. I can't see anything!" I said to Joe as we were cycling from the lodge on the outskirts of town to the port later that evening. We'd wanted to sleep for a few hours in the afternoon before we got on the boat, but hadn't realised how hard it would be cycling back in the dark on the sandy tracks. Now back on the tarmac, I had to shield my eyes from the oncoming car lights.

"This way! Follow me quickly. I told you to come back early," snapped the port manager, Justice, who we'd popped down to meet after lunch to try to understand what was going on.

It was absolute chaos at the port now, with people heading in all directions carrying goods and hundreds of people laying around, women sitting on baskets, babies and small children sleeping. It was impossible to know what the system was.

We followed Justice, pushing past the line of people and climbing over bags of rice and cement and baskets of fruit with our bikes onto the boat, which was already crammed full of people and cargo.

"You need to put your bikes up there," instructed Justice, pointing to vertical metal steps up to the top of the engine tower.

"That's going to be impossible!" I said quietly. We'd never get past all the people.

Somehow, miraculously, the people parted and, after watching me struggle to lift my bike, a passenger took it from me and lifted it onto his shoulder, climbing up to where Joe was at the top with his bike, waiting to secure them.

MV Ilala is a ship that has transported passengers and freight between the mainland and the islands along the length of Lake Malawi since 1951. Every week she crosses the lake from Chilumba in the north and travels about 480 kilometres to Monkey Bay in the south, calling at major towns and islands. We'd decided to take the boat because we'd read that it was an unforgettable experience, but also because it would cut out a big chunk of riding and save us a bit of time.

Laying in our cabin later that night, I was questioning this decision. The ship was old. The metalwork was rusty. The decking boards were splintered and broken in places. Everywhere was dirty and there was an unfamiliar acrid smell that got into the back of my throat. And the boat seemed overcrowded. We were fortunate to have a cabin, but it was small and stuffy. It had two bunks, a sink with a shelf for toiletries, a bench for the bags and a fan. But the fan didn't rotate and there was just a small vent for air.

Sweat pooled on my back as I tossed and turned on the thin mattress, wondering how I'd survive the journey in this heat and imagining what it must be like for most of the other passengers on the ship.

The ship had three decks. Downstairs was the cargo deck where the economy people were crushed in, sitting on benches or mats on the floor where they could find space between the baskets of dried sardines or other goods piled high. Looking down from the relative comfort of the cabin deck, you could see arms hanging over the side of the boat as people pushed their faces up to the bars, trying to get air. It reminded me of pictures of slave ships, and I shuddered at the image. The middle deck had five cabins for guests and two for the captains, as well as the saloon for dining and the kitchen. Upstairs was supposed to be first class but there were hardly any seats or shade, so people had to sit in the sun all day and sleep on the rough decking boards.

The cabin had only been available for the first and the third nights, so we were going to have to sleep on the deck on the middle night. I tried to console myself that it would be cooler at night in the open air, but I felt nervous.

I must have dozed off in the hot cabin at some stage. When I woke the boat wasn't moving and I could hear a commotion outside. I jumped up and went out to the deck to see what was happening. We were at the first stop, Mlowe. There was no jetty, so the boat was anchored 500 metres offshore and people were boarding the ship from the lifeboats or local ferry boats. The small boats were sitting dangerously low in the water, too full of people. Everyone was carrying a crazy amount of cargo, including live chickens and other animals. Mothers balanced baskets on their heads and babies on their backs while climbing up the metal steps as the small boats bobbed up and down, bouncing off the side of the ship. The mood was frantic, but everyone was kind, the ship crew helping the old ladies, everyone waiting their turn patiently and passing cargo up to people on the boat.

It was still early in the morning. We spent the long day chatting to other people on the boat, or eating in the saloon, which was by far the nicest place on the ship, taking time to enjoy the simple meals of chicken or fish with ugali or rice, which were unaffordable for most of the passengers. Later, we lay in the cabin reading or sat on the deck writing. There were two bathrooms on the cabin deck. We often needed to queue for a long time to use the loo or take a shower. The latter was a humbling experience, standing on a slimy wooden floor surrounded by rusting metal pipes, a towel draped over the round window facing the deck for privacy, as I tried to soap and rinse myself under an inadequate trickle of barely warm water. People travelling on the lower or top deck didn't have this luxury.

Our night on the deck was interminably long and hot and I hardly slept. We'd been advised by the manager to put up our tent so we had somewhere safe to keep our bags. But hundreds of people had boarded the boat at Nkhata Bay. When we returned to our tent after a drink at the bar, it was almost impossible to reach it. People were lying side by side and head to toe, and crammed up against the side of the tent. They moved away, allowing us to climb inside, but I lay there feeling like a guilty coloniser who had taken too much space. I was happy to wake at dawn to find that four people had managed to crawl under the tent's fly sheet into the vestibules, two on each side. At least we had shared our space.

Back down on the cabin deck, a young mother was lying on a hessian mat outside our room, cradling a tiny baby.

"That baby can't be more than a week old!" said Joe as we were arranging things back in the cabin.

She'd started getting up to move as we came back, but Joe gestured for her to stay. I searched through my bag for some biscuits and a banana to give to her.

"How old is your baby?" I said, crouching down beside her as she gratefully accepted the food.

"One day old," she said, explaining she'd had the baby in the hospital at Nkhata Bay and was now travelling home to Likoma Island.

"Good to know you can rest up here with your baby," I said, thinking how dangerous it would be getting on and off the boat or being crammed in the economy class downstairs.

At seven o'clock there was a knock on our door and we were greeted by Pablo, a local guide who the ship's captain had sent to give us a tour of Likoma Island. We were tired but knew it would do us good to escape the ship for a few hours. We climbed onto one of the small boats ferrying people and cargo from the ship to the shore and jumped out at the beach, where hundreds of passengers were waiting with piles of goods and kids to get on the ship.

"Surely there must be a more efficient way of getting the people around?" I asked Pablo.

"There used to be another ship as well," he said, "but it was decommissioned. It crashed into the jetty, destroying it, and it has never been rebuilt"

Likoma Island is a popular tourist destination in Malawi thanks to its sandy beaches, clear waters and recreational activities like scuba diving and snorkelling. The main tourist attraction is St Peter's Anglican Cathedral, built between 1903 and 1911.

The cathedral door was unlocked by a local guide, who seemed much more interested in what money we were going to put in the donation box than any information he could share with us. The architecture was impressive, but I walked around stunned that anyone could think that a small island with a total population of around 10,000 could need a massive cathedral with capacity for 4,000 people.

"This must cost a fortune just to maintain," I said to Pablo, who seemed to know much more than the local guide. "Surely it would make more sense investing in education or health care?"

Likoma Island was close to the shores of Mozambique, and it turned out that the British had built the cathedral so they could lay claim to the island as part of Malawi rather than Mozambique, which was colonised by the Portuguese.

We slept well on the third and last night on the *MV Ilala*, tired from the previous two restless nights and the tour of the island. We had mixed feelings about leaving the boat the next day. We'd become accustomed to the hot, stale air of the cabin, the acrid smell of the deck (from the sardines, it turned out) and the familiar food in the saloon. I'd got to know the ship's captain, Harold, who'd been interested in our cycle tour and told us about the history of the ship and the culture of the people of Malawi. Harold was from the Chewa tribe, which is the most prominent tribe. Other main tribes include the Tumbuka in the north and the Yao along the central and southern shore of the lake. Most groups are thought to have originated from the Bantus. The main language is Chichewa and, since the country was colonised by the British, the main religion is Christianity, although around 14 percent of the population are Muslim, a religion which arrived with the Arab slave traders at the start of the fifteenth century.

Malawians are very proud of their ship, which is the lifeline for the people living in otherwise hard-to-access places. While we weren't expecting a luxurious cruise, I'm not sure we were quite prepared for how chaotic and crowded it would be. We survived the seventy-hour trip. Looking back, it was a privilege to share this journey with the beautiful people of Malawi.

For most, making the regular journey in these tough conditions with either little shade or little air is essential for economic survival. Many of the women we saw were with babies or small children. Amazingly, most passengers seemed to approach the experience with gusto, chatting and laughing, and hardly complaining. It was clear that the weekly voyage was an essential part of life on the lake, and the conditions were accepted by the people. I disembarked from the boat feeling inspired by their resilience, humbled by the positivity of the people in the face of such hardships.

But maybe a priority for development in Malawi should be buying another boat and building more jetties.

~21~

THE LONG ROAD TO LUSAKA

"Come play!" called the young boys. We were taking a pre-dinner walk around the small village of Mganja, south-west of Monkey Bay where we'd disembarked the ship. Boys and girls were playing football on a dirt pitch with upside-down buckets for goalposts. The sun was slipping down behind the mountains. We'd climbed 500 metres at the end of the eighty-kilometre ride and the air was fresh and crisp.

We shook our heads, smiling, and wandered on through the village.

"Are you staying with Sister Josefa?" asked a kind-looking man, who we learnt was Tomas and used to work for Nazareth Guest House.

"Yes," we replied. Sister Josefa ran the guesthouse and foundation that we'd read about online. It had two beautiful bedrooms and space for camping, and all the proceeds went to the school and local community. We'd arrived early and had a lovely homemade lunch of cherry tomato pie with salad. Ineke, who had done her anthropological studies in Malawi and later established the Nazareth Foundation, joined us for lunch and talked to us about the project and life in Malawi. She said we'd meet Sister Josefa over dinner that evening.

Tomas introduced us to his family, who wanted to pose for a photo. His wife, Eva, was wearing a school uniform and couldn't have been more than sixteen. Child marriage is a widespread problem in Malawi, with 42 percent of girls married before they are eighteen and 9 percent before the age of fifteen.[xix] Poverty and food insecurity are associated with higher rates of child marriage as families try to ease the burden of feeding the family.

Wandering back through the village we were greeted by shouts of *hello* and *muli bwanji?* (how are you?) as we passed young women lighting the coals on their charcoal fires.

Sister Josefa greeted us with a welcoming smile and a warm embrace. Over a dinner of more delicious locally grown food, we learnt about the foundation's efforts to support the local nursery, the primary school, a secondary school and a school for deaf children as well as the Mua Mission Hospital, which provides care to around 130,000 people. At sixty for men and sixty-six for women, Malawi's life expectancy is low, even for Africa. This can be largely attributed to HIV/AIDS, respiratory diseases, malaria and chronic malnutrition. These health issues are compounded by substandard health services and inadequate access to safe drinking water and proper sanitation.[xx]

"We are working closely with the local community to try and better understand their needs and support them to overcome some of these issues," explained Sister Josefa. "When we complete projects, they are handed back to the community to lead. In this way we estimate that we are helping more than 2,000 children and community members each year."

We left the Nazareth Foundation the next morning well rested and with full stomachs, feeling inspired by the work of the mission and ready for the big climb up to the Mozambique border.

The climb was on a gradient of fourteen degrees which is pretty steep on a fully loaded touring bike. There were pinches of seventeen degrees in places, meaning we had to jump off to push our bikes. We kept stopping to take a breath and gaze at Lake Malawi fading away into the distance.

A colourful truck climbed past us, belching out smoke as it chugged up the steep road, barely travelling faster than us. On the back of the truck were white hessian bags of black charcoal, three or four bags deep, roped down under a big tarp. Five bodies were perched on top of the charcoal bags, smiling and waving for my camera.

Illegal charcoal production and distribution is rife in Malawi as it is in much of East Africa, with 97 percent of households relying on charcoal for cooking and heating. This increasing demand is resulting in rapid deforestation, undermining agricultural productivity and food and water security. Efforts to stamp out illegal charcoal production and distribution have been derailed as demand is increasing and so many people's livelihoods depend on producing charcoal.[xxi]

"Mozambique, Malawi, Mozambique, Malawi, Mozambique, Malawi!"

We had reached the top of the thousand-metre climb that morning and were now snaking along the border which was marked out by the road between Mozambique and Malawi. Mozambique stretched out to the left of the road; Malawi on the right. At the top of the hill we stopped and bought a drink from a shop in Mozambique. I had a cuddle with a gorgeous chubby-faced baby, while chatting to the shop's owners, before continuing along the road in Malawi.

Instead of travelling through Mozambique, we had decided to head down and cross into Zambia, where we would meet a friend to canoe down the Zambezi River just before Christmas. We didn't have too long left to get there and had an important decision to make about whether to cycle through the South Luangwa National Park, which is known for its abundant wildlife and unspoiled vegetation. The road we would need to take was unpaved and there were few places to stay. Other cycle tourists had reported seeing lions on the route. The safer way would be to stick to the T4, the main arterial road linking Lilongwe in Malawi with Lusaka in Zambia, but that lacked beauty and adventure. We were both torn.

"Let's make that decision when we get to Zambia," said Joe. "If there's rain then the road through the park will probably be too hard to ride."

Two Bugs on Bikes

Lilongwe is the largest city and capital of Malawi, with a population of just under a million. We spent our days visiting the markets buying chitenje, the traditional cloth that women use for dresses and skirts, and getting some new bike clothes at the bike shop, which turned out to be the best we'd found in Africa.

Crossing the bridge over the Lilongwe River we were funnelled together with crowds of people bustling to and fro, selling supplies. What looked like slums on the side of the river turned out to be the Tsoka flea market. Black plastic sheets tied to bits of wood formed the shelters, smoke pouring from charcoal fires over which aluminium pots bubbled, people fixing shoes, selling second-hand clothes and plastic bags of radioactive-looking drinks or water. Rubbish was strewn along the river banks where people were washing their clothes in filthy water. We pushed our way through, trying to ignore the many people begging and all the things we could buy.

Back on the road on our last day in Malawi, a constant flow of men cycled in the other direction, their bikes loaded high with bags of charcoal – sometimes as many as six bags on one bike, piled on a wooden frame fixed behind the seat of the bicycle. The men were lean and sweating from the exertion. They had to concentrate hard as one slip and the bike would unbalance, which could lead to injury or even death. The men are paid a punitive price for such backbreaking, dangerous work but it's still three times what the women who carry the huge bundles of wood on their heads to make charcoal are paid. When it is cash-in-hand work and there are no other local employment options there are really no choices but to take on this work.[xxii]

Crossing the border into Zambia at Chipata the next day, we were naively expecting things to get better. Malawi is among the ten poorest countries in the world, depending on which classification system is used. Zambia, by contrast, is a lower middle-income country. However, it turns out this is largely due to its copper and cobalt exports, and the wealth is not distributed throughout the population. The vast majority of Zambians are employed in agriculture, with incomes substantially below the poverty line.

It was 600 kilometres west on the Great East Highway (the dreaded T4) to reach Lusaka. We were running out of time, so decided to press on and skip the national park. For the next week, the landscape we passed was largely the same: endless kilometres of dry savannah with the occasional acacia trees; villages, consisting of a mix of rectangular brick houses and traditional circular houses with thatched roofs, set back from the dusty roadside; the occasional shop, often with amusing names like White Man's Grocery or Broke But Hope Shop. Aside from a few potholes, the road surface was reasonable and there was a cycle lane.

"What are those kids selling?" I asked Joe, looking up ahead to the side of the road where three young boys were holding out what looked like meat skewers.

"It looks like mice," I continued.

"It is mice," said Joe.

We later learnt that mice are eaten as a delicacy by some people in Zambia, including the Tumbuka people in the east. Mice are strung on sticks and cooked, salted or dried. Other common forms of protein are caterpillars, or mopane worms, which are soaked in hot water and then fried with onions, tomatoes, and spices. With other animal protein sources in short supply and expensive, it is not surprising that people in different African countries are so resourceful. We'd already witnessed the remarkable spectacle of the lake flies in Malawi. In a small town in Kenya, we'd watched curiously as women and children had crowded around a mound of dirt, catching termites, plucking off the wings and popping them straight into their mouths.

We cycled on, declining the offers of roasted mice even though our stomachs were growling.

Just outside Katete we stopped at the Tikondane Community Centre. Tikondane means "let's be there for each other", and in that spirit, the centre is run by the people of Katete for the people of Katete. Pulling up on our bikes at the beautiful gazebo-style dining area, we were met by Rachael, the local office manager, who guided us through well-kept gardens to a little cottage with four rooms off a communal kitchen area.

"The centre director, Elke, is from Woolloomooloo in Sydney," Rachael said. "I'm sure she will want to meet you later this afternoon."

We discovered that food and nutrition are a big part of the centre's economic development program. Matthew showed us around the Tikondane food projects, including goats, chickens and rabbits that are raised for meat, guava, lemon and banana trees in the orchard, and the worm farm.

"We are increasingly growing moringa as a nutritional supplement superfood," he explained. "This is where we blend it with ground nuts, milk powder and chocolate. There are many malnourished children in Katete. Moringa is proving to be a good solution and is also a source of income for the Tikondane Community Centre."

Portable grow bags with wooden structures for netting were also being used as affordable and sustainable ways of growing vegetables, and compost piles were dotted across the property as part of the eighteen-day composting program to support increased growth of the gardens.

"Tiko uses much of the food that it produces," Matthew told us. "But we also sell some products. This is where we grind the nuts to make peanut butter. We also sell lemon juice from the trees and the dried moringa in bags."

He pointed out some clay ovens, explaining that the centre is trying to tackle unsustainable charcoal use. "Clay ovens use firewood and retain the heat longer so they require much less wood. This is much more efficient."

"We've seen all the men transporting bags of charcoal on bikes," I said.

"Yes, it's a big problem in this country," he said. "Illegal charcoal production and distribution is leading to deforestation, which is bad for the environment and agricultural production. By supporting the schoolgirls to grow saplings as an income-generating project and helping families to build kitchens with clay ovens that use energy efficiently based on the firewood from the trees they have grown, we are addressing poverty, health and climate change in one project."

Chatting to Elke, the Australian who established the centre, over a glass of South African white wine before dinner, we learnt that the local cultural beliefs are another barrier to improving nutrition.

"People don't understand the concept of healthy eating and the importance of consuming fruits and vegetables," she explained. "Maize is considered to be the only possible food. That's one of the reasons why the people of Katete experience such shocking levels of malnutrition."

She went on to tell us about the 19 Steps out of Poverty program, education and training to help local community members to look after their families' health through better nutrition and diverse livelihood strategies building on sustainable farming practices.

"It's working," she said. "Families are increasingly able to afford school fees and better food."

Elke explained how she'd retrained as a nurse and come out to work in Africa after her husband died of lung cancer. She'd dedicated her life to establishing and running the Tikondane Community Centre and was now ready to retire.

It was one of only a handful of times on the trip when I talked about my work and the parallels with some of the projects I was working on with Indigenous communities in Australia and the Pacific Islands. I was mentally documenting similarities and differences and opportunities for exchanging experiences.

"Please come back and work here," Elke said the next day as she hugged us goodbye. I made a mental note to add it to my growing list of projects to consider coming back to.

The skies were black as we left Tikondane to head towards Petauke.

"Just as well we made the decision not to ride through the South Luangwa National park," I said to Joe.

Two Bugs on Bikes

The next few days we prayed for rain, but it didn't come. Instead, it seemed to get hotter and hotter as we slugged out the kilometres along the T4.

The landscape was unspectacular, just a long tarmac road stretching into the heat shimmer in the distance. Villages lined the roads every few kilometres. Most were little hamlets with a few brick houses and the traditional round houses with thatched roofs. Many of the brick houses looked half-built with the windows bricked up. Pigs and goats were roaming around, picking over piles of rubbish looking for food.

Kids were everywhere. When they saw us they exploded into a chant of *How are you? How are you? How are you?* shouting as loud and as fast as they could until they ran out of breath and erupted into giggles. Even when we were feeling completely busted it was impossible not to smile.

"I'm not sure I can stay here?" I hissed at Joe. We were wheeling our bikes over sandbags down some steps through the back of a disused bar into the Riverside Guest House in Kacholola, a popular truck stop on the T4.

"There's nowhere else for miles," he replied, grimacing. We'd already ridden 110 kilometres that day and needed to rest.

I reluctantly followed him, wondering why it was called the Riverside Guest House when there was no river nearby. At the back of the bar there were two rows of rooms on each side of a stone verandah. A woman was sitting on the floor, nursing her baby. She looked up as we entered and called out some names.

A young girl appeared from a room where the whole family seemed to be staying and went inside one of the other rooms. There didn't seem to be any other guests.

"You can go here and take your bikes in." She gestured for us to go inside.

The small room had green painted walls and a concrete floor. The only furniture was a double bed with a sheet and one grey-looking towel. A small window let in a bit of light, but it had cracked glass and wouldn't close.

"Do you have a mosquito net?" I asked the girl.

She nodded and left us to settle in the room.

We could hear booming music from one of the bars next door as well as the trucks rushing by along the highway.

"This is going to be a fun night!" I said.

Three hours later, I was standing at the side of a crowded hut, beaming with pride as Joe took on the next contender in what had become the Kacholola pool tournament of the century. It seemed like every single street kid in the village had turned up to watch the muzungu pool shark take on the locals one by one.

Wandering around the small town that evening, we'd stopped to chat to two men who turned out to be the local teachers and invited us to their bar for a drink. After a couple of beers, Joe said he fancied a game of pool and one of the teachers said he would arrange it for us. After our meal we headed over to the pool table, which was under an open roof outside another bar. The teacher played first; we watched as he lost the game and then invited Joe to take on the winner.

"They've set him up with the local pool hustler!" said the guy standing next to me. The atmosphere grew tense and people clamoured to watch as it became apparent that Joe was going to win the game. A huge roar went up and all the kids started shouting "Muzungu!" Muzungu!" and clapping with joy when Joe won. After that, everyone wanted to have a go and I had to drag Joe away when he started to lose after a few too many beers.

"That was so much fun!" he said as we stumbled back to our room, falling into bed and fighting over the mosquito net, which wasn't big enough to fit over both of us.

We awoke hot and sweaty with dry mouths and covered in mosquito bites.

"Give me a coldie one!" I said to the shop assistant at Luangwa Bridge later that day.

"Beer?" he asked, looking surprised.

"No, just water please!" I said, laughing. I was sweating profusely from the long climb up the hill to the bridge. It was the hottest I remember being on the ride, with no breeze at all. We had run out of water and were dying for a cold drink.

"Give me a coldie one!" was the main lyric from the number one song in Zambia at the time. The uplifting rap song by Vinchenzo M'bale was playing everywhere we went and Joe and I found ourselves frequently singing it on our long hot rides. A quick listen to the lyrics may have you believe that the song is promoting alcohol as a way of dealing with life's troubles. However, if you listen more carefully, you'll find the song demonstrates how alcohol has become a shield for young people who have literally nothing else. It exposes how the current economic and social situation make it almost essential for young people in Zambia to drink, because even if it only makes them happy for a short while, it gives them a reason to live. High and increasing levels of chronic hunger, lack of employment opportunities even for the educated, escalating costs of goods and services and widespread crime and corruption make it hard for the millions of young people in Zambia to survive in the present, let alone have any hope for the future.[xxiii]

The song helped lift our moods against this sobering reality as we cycled along the endless highway day after day.

Arriving in Lusaka three days later, we were struck by the skyscrapers and modern buildings. Flashy four-wheel drives crowded into the entrance of the shopping centre near our backpackers. Inside it was similar to a mall in Sydney, with every type of shop you could imagine and a range of restaurants and fast-food places scattered nearby.

It was hard to get our heads around this, when for the last ten days we'd been cycling past thatched huts and people desperately trying to eke out a living selling charcoal. Around 60 percent of the population of Zambia is experiencing poverty, living on less than two dollars a day. Yet if you walk around Lusaka, you could be in LA.

JACQUI WEBSTER

~22~

HIPPO DODGING ON THE ZAMBEZI

The dull thud of the paddle banging on the side of the canoe reverberated down the river. Our guide, CB, was banging his boat to make a noise. Otherwise the river was silent; all we could hear was the swish of the water as we glided along, holding our breath, scanning the surface for the ominous dark heads that could launch from the water at any stage.

We knew there were hippos in the Zambezi, but we hadn't realised how many there were going to be or how dangerous it would feel. The first day was particularly intense.

"Hippos to the right and another pod over there to the left," I called to the guide from our canoe, which Joe was steering from the back.

We were paddling hard, trying to keep an even distance just behind the guide, following in a straight line as instructed.

Earlier that day during the briefing CB (short for Cathberg Nyamunda) had said there were four things we needed to be alert to: floating tree stumps, wind, currents and dangerous animals. He then listed at least four types of dangerous animals.

"Stay behind me," CB had said. "If the hippos get stuck between the boats, they are likely to panic and might charge." We'd also been told not to trap them near the land.

Two Bugs on Bikes

"They need to have an escape route to deep water, otherwise they feel threatened," warned CB, still banging his oar on the side of the canoe to scare them off.

"I'm really scared!" I said out loud, wondering why we'd agreed to go on this trip. Hippos are among the deadliest animals in the world, killing about 500 people each year.

"Me too," replied CB, which didn't help. "The river is shallower than usual because of the work on the dam, so the hippos seem more concentrated."

My heart was beating rapidly. Every time we passed within a few metres of the hippos I held my breath, knowing that if they decided to charge, we'd be in the water with the crocodiles.

The idea for this trip had come from Ann, a close friend from Sydney who was heading to see her family in Cape Town for Christmas. Ann was a medical doctor and loved travel and adventure but was a meticulous planner and pretty risk-averse. Keen to meet up with her and confident she wouldn't do anything too crazy, Joe and I had agreed to the trip without doing any research.

The 2,574 kilometre Zambezi River starts in north-west Zambia then flows east through Angola, along the north-eastern border of Namibia and the northern border of Botswana, then along the border between Zambia and Zimbabwe to Mozambique, where it crosses the country to empty into the Indian Ocean. Its most famous feature is Victoria Falls, which we were planning to visit the following week. The four-day canoe trip would take us from Chilumba in Zambia to the Mana Pools on the border with Zimbabwe.

There were seven guests on the trip and three guides, so ten people in total, two in each canoe. Ann was with her nineteen-year-old nephew, Sam, who'd just finished his high school exams in Cape Town. Then there was a quiet but charming older French couple, Gerard and Genevieve, and Juliette, a quirky young American girl travelling alone through Africa after teaching in Tanzania for most of the year. The canoes were heavily laden with camping gear, food, including baskets of fresh fruits and vegetables, and drinking water.

After a satisfyingly healthy picnic lunch of sandwiches with ham and salad that we'd all made together on a grassy bank on the Zimbabwe side of the river, we clambered back into the canoes and resumed our trip downstream.

"Look, elephants!" I said, pointing to a big herd walking majestically along the river bank. Among the family group were three mothers with babies.

"Stop, shhhh!" said CB, gesturing for us to pull up on the sand at the side of the river, a safe distance away.

We watched in awe as the matriarchs ushered the babies down the bank into the river, playfully showering them with water from their trunks and nudging them along. The babies frolicked, rolling in the water, their playful antics a joy to watch. After a while, the procession made its way across the river, splashing and trumpeting as they crossed. One by one they clambered clumsily up the bank, sending shimmers of sand into the water.

Pushing off again, we saw an old crocodile lounging on the bank. He raised his eyelids as we paddled past and shimmied down deeper into the sand.

"Are there ever any casualties on these trips?" Asked Joe, eyeing the crocodile nervously.

"Ask me about it when we get back," said CB smiling.

That evening we camped on an island in a fork of the river. After cooling down in the river (the guides were on the lookout for crocodiles), we pitched our tents. The sun was starting to go down and the jungle-like Zambezi forest pulsed around us. Adrenaline was still pumping through my veins, and I felt a strange mixture of exhaustion and exhilaration.

CB and the other two guides, Wallis and Benjamin, who'd come along to take Sam fishing, were preparing our dinner of chicken casserole with rice and vegetables on metal pots over an open fire on the grassy bank overlooking the river. One by one we joined them and sat around, taking stock of the day. Gerard, the French guy – probably the only person who'd been more scared than me on the water – now had a beer and looked like he was starting to relax. Ann poured me a red wine and sat down beside me in silence. Right on cue, just as we were relaxing and the sun was starting to dip behind the trees at the other side of the river, another group of elephants emerged from the jungle. They waded across the water, their impressive bulky frames silhouetted against the sinking sun's spectacular crimson backdrop.

"Can you hear that?" asked Joe. We were lying on top of sleeping bags in the safari tent.

I nodded, my eyes wide. "I think it's lions," I said.

Joe nodded and I snuggled closer, hiding my face in his chest.

The roaring lions were at the other side of the river, but could swim across if they wanted to. As we'd left the comfort of the campfire to go to bed, CB had told us to make sure we zipped up our tents properly.

"If you need to go to the loo in the night, please make sure you look around first and make sure it's safe," he said, "and zip up your tents when you get back. We don't want anyone to go missing."

"I'm not sure I'll be able to sleep," I said to Joe. He was already starting to snore softly. "I can hear hyenas," I said. "Can you hear the hyenas?" I prodded him.

"Shush, go to sleep!" he said, playfully pushing me away.

I lay awake for a while, listening to the hum of the jungle and the river rushing by. After a while, I became aware of the slow, rhythmic sound of munching near my head and realised a huge hippo was eating grass just outside the tent. I shut my eyes and focused on my breathing, knowing I was safe. The hippo wouldn't try and charge the tent, but I was still alert to the intensity of the experience of such a dangerous animal being so close. I never imagined we'd be doing something like this when we set off on our bikes six months ago. Eventually the hippo moved away, and I drifted calmly off to sleep.

The next day we continued our journey down the river, watching as smallholder farmers tended their fields. A group of children were laughing and shouting as they played at the edge of the water while their mothers washed clothes in the river. A flimsy bamboo fence separated the washing area from the main river, an attempt to guard the children and women from the crocodiles. These are estimated to kill around 200 people each year, although many deaths likely go unreported.

But while deaths from crocodiles and hippos are common, by far a bigger killer here is bilharzia, caused by parasitic worms from freshwater snails that lurk in the water, waiting for their next victim. Known colloquially as snail fever, The World Health Organization estimates that 40 million women and girls are infected each year by the parasite, which can lead to liver or kidney damage if acute, and trigger a disease called female genital schistosomiasis in women and girls (FGS).[xxiv] Lack of access to safe water for drinking, cooking or washing clothes and utensils mean people are forced to use the river water. An outbreak declared at a school in Chirundu (which is close to where we started our trip) in June earlier that year had infected at least 150 children.

Up until that point, Joe and I had avoided bathing in fresh water in Africa, even in Lake Malawi, except when Joe had jumped off the top of the ship in the middle of the lake one day, having been told that the parasites can't survive more than 200 metres from the shore.

Lounging in the water later that day to cool off, we discussed the chances of getting bilharzia from the river. Ann advised that it was unlikely but that we should get a blood test a few months after we'd got home just to make sure. We're so lucky to have access to affordable health care and to be able to go to the doctor just to make sure we're not sick.

In Zambia, 6.4 million people – about one-third of the country's total population – have no access to clean water, and more than 2,000 children die every year as a result,[xxv] according to WaterAid, an NGO with a base in Zambia. Bilharzia is just one of the many waterborne diseases in Zambia.

Shortly after we departed Zambia in December, there was another outbreak of cholera in the region, adding to the cumulative total of almost 20,000 cases and 700 deaths between October 2023 and February 2024.

By day three of our river safari we had relaxed into a rhythm, at one with wild nature. We reached Mana Pools, a UNESCO World Heritage Site famous for its stunning natural beauty and rich biodiversity. Mana means four in the local Shona language and refers to the four pools formed by the meandering Zambezi River. The golden sand banks surrounded by bright blue water create a striking contrast to the surrounding dry savannah plains. A pod of hippos peeked at us as we paddled past their bathing site, one of them snorting into the water. I watched calmly, having grown accustomed to the big creatures. Floating past the banks we saw groups of impalas bounding across the savannah. An African eagle eyed us from the branches of an acacia tree. Pied kingfishers darted through the reeds at the side of the water. Rounding the corner into one of the river's tributaries, we stopped, stunned at the sight of several large groups of elephants stretching as far as we could see.

Sitting around the campfire on our last night on the river, I asked CB why he'd become a guide.

"I'm a trained history secondary school teacher – history and geography," he said. "But teaching under Mugabe's regime became too difficult. I did my tour guide apprenticeship in Zimbabwe in 1996 and then left because I was involved in politics and my family was at risk, so I came to Zambia in 1998 to make a new life. Many of my friends and colleagues left behind were killed or their properties destroyed. Politics in my beloved Zimbabwe has been and still is a risk for business.

"Life as a guide in Zambia has been good to me and as well as canoeing, I do game drives and walking safaris. I also train local guides like Wallis and Benji. I love the river and my job but I'm over fifty now and my heart is set on going into the ministry."

CB said he had four daughters, including 23-year-old twins. He hadn't been able to afford to pay for them to go to university but one was a qualified nurse and the other was training to be a teacher.

"The last one is turning ten in January," he continued. "She was not planned. She came as a surprise but she is currently my best friend. Her name is Makanaka which means Lord you are beautiful."

After four days and three nights on the river we had bonded as a group, and it was sad to say goodbye. CB had been a great tour leader, looking out for our safety, keeping us calm, making sure we were well fed, and sharing interesting information about the Zambezi River and the Mana Pools National Park. But most of all, sharing his personal stories, talking about his roots in Zimbabwe, his beloved family, and the struggles of life in Zambia.

I'll always remember his parting words.

"Remember, the river is like life – sometimes calm, sometimes unpredictable but always flowing forward," he said. "Respect the animals, the land and the water. Leave only footprints and take only memories."

"It's been amazing," I said to Ann, hugging her goodbye. "We will never forget our few days on the Zambezi. Have a lovely time in Cape Town with your family."

"Where will you be for Christmas?" she asked us.

"We don't know yet," said Joe.

"We don't even know where we're sleeping tonight!" I added.

~23~

PRECIOUS AND THE CHICKEN

Back on the bikes, riding through Chirundu was a reminder of how exciting the atmosphere can be cycling through small African towns. Music was blasting from stereos in the shops and people were everywhere, smiling at us and shouting hello.

A small, sporty black car pulled up next to us and the driver wound down the windows. Two men peered out at us to say hello. They asked us where we were from and where we were going.

Still riding along beside them as they bumped over the gravel road, we told them we'd cycled from Kigali in Rwanda and were heading to Cape Town.

"By bicycle?" the two men said in unison.

"Yes," Joe replied.

They asked more questions. The usual: how far we rode each day. Where we stayed. If we had had any problems. If we liked the people in Zambia.

It turned out they were from Lusaka Radio. They gave us their contact details and said we should call if we needed anything and to stay in touch about our journey.

"Be careful in Zimbabwe," they told us. "The people there are different."

We laughed at the familiar warning and thanked them for their kindness.

At the supermarket, we bumped into Tim and Denise, the owners of Breezes River Lodge, who had organised the canoe safari for us.

"You are like celebrities here," they laughed. "People here don't see many muzungus, especially travelling by bike."

We were now cycling towards Livingstone so we could see Victoria Falls before heading to Botswana.

Turning off the main road towards Changa, we were struck again by the now-familiar round thatched mud huts that lined the road. The bottom road, as it was called by the locals, was long, flat and dusty. It took us through the heart of Zambia's rural areas, winding through red clay ground so dry and cracked it looked like there were veins running through it.

It was hot. Stopping under a baobab tree for food and a rest, we noticed a group of children watching us, too shy to approach. We ate our tuna sandwiches hungrily then dug into our bags to retrieve a packet of biscuits, opening them discreetly before holding out the packet to offer them to the children. They ran over excitedly and waited their turn, politely watched over by one of the older girls, who seemed to be looking after them.

"What is your name? Where are you from?" the older girl asked in practised English.

"My name is Jacqui and this is Joe," I replied. "We're from Australia. What are your names?"

One by one the children shouted out their names.

We showed them the video of the Masaka Kids dancing in Uganda and they crowded around me, watching, then performed their own dance for us, laughing and singing. I felt uplifted by the energy of the children as we continued cycling through the hot arid landscape towards Changa.

The energy soon dissipated as the heat kicked in and we struggled along the dusty roads against an increasingly strong headwind. We didn't know where we were staying that night and we both felt anxious.

We'd read on the iOverlander app that there was a guesthouse at Changa but we hadn't been able to find any details.

Arriving tired and hungry, we were despondent. We stopped to rest and have a drink at a shop on the edge of the town.

"Is there a guesthouse nearby?" Joe asked the group of guys sitting outside the shop drinking beers. They pointed to a house up the road. We wheeled our bikes in the direction they'd indicated but couldn't find anything. A man was working behind a sewing machine on the verandah of a concrete building.

"We are looking for a guesthouse," said Joe. "Can you help us?"

He called inside for his wife, who gestured for us to follow her. She showed us to another building and told us to wait there.

Eventually a young guy wearing a bright yellow T-shirt and jeans, who introduced himself as CK (having initials as a name seemed to be a thing in Zambia), came over and told us to follow him. He headed across the road and along a dust track past rows and rows of thatched huts to the back of the village, where he introduced us to someone else and told us to wait while they went to find the owner.

"I'm Precious," said the woman when she arrived, smiling. "Welcome to our guesthouse."

She walked over to one of the three rectangular brick buildings arranged around a small yard and gestured for us to follow her inside. There were four rooms, each off a dark corridor. We chose the one on the end that was slightly larger so we would be able to keep our bikes inside. The room was basic to say the least. It had a dusty concrete floor, walls painted a yellowy-cream colour and two windows with blue painted window panes and dirty net curtains. There were no mosquito nets and no fans.

"We'll need to keep the windows closed because of the mosquitoes," I said to Joe. "I hope it's not too hot."

Joe shrugged. It was about seventy kilometres to the next town so we didn't have other options.

The chimbusu (toilet) was outside and shared by several of the village houses. That was a problem for later. Now it was time to shower. Precious brought us a large yellow jerry can of water and showed us to the bathroom at the end of the corridor. The small room had concrete rendered walls and a concrete floor, with a hole at one edge so the water could drain outside the building. There was a large plastic bowl for washing in.

I tipped a small amount of water out of the jerry can into the bowl and stripped off, crouching over the bucket to soap and wash myself with a microfibre cloth, before tipping the remaining water over my head. Then I soaked and soaped my dirty riding clothes and rinsed them off, using as little water as possible so there was enough left for Joe.

Walking back down the corridor wrapped in my towel, I felt incredibly refreshed.

I dressed and went out into the yard to hang my clothes and towel out to dry on the line. Precious came out to help me.

"Do you have any food for dinner?" I asked her hopefully. We had some vegetables and an emergency camping meal but preferred locally cooked food.

"Just ncima," she replied, referring to the ground maize porridge traditional to East Africa.

"Do you have any meat or vegetables?"

She shook her head.

"I have some vegetables I could give you," I offered and went inside to fetch them.

I held out two tomatoes, an onion and a packet of baby zucchini that we'd picked up at the market in Chirundu.

Precious shook her head. "I don't know how to cook these," she said.

"Maybe I can cook them on the camp stove," I offered. "I can show you how to cook them. And you could show me how to cook ncima?"

Precious nodded, looking happy.

Later that evening she returned with her mbaula (small charcoal stove) and the ncima mix. She sat on an upturned bucket and one of the neighbours brought me an old deckchair. Precious showed me how to get the water boiling before pouring in the maize flour and then stirring quickly so that the mixture formed a smooth, bubbling paste, before adding in more flour. It looked like hard work.

"What are you cooking?" asked the neighbour, Sharon, who we later learnt was from Lusaka and was working in Changa in the health centre.

"I have some vegetables," I said, pointing to the tomatoes and onions I'd started chopping up into the pan ready to cook on the camp stove. "And Precious is preparing us ncima." Precious continued to stir quickly, adding more flour into the stiff mixture in the pan.

"Do you want some chicken?" asked Sharon.

"That would be amazing!" I replied, knowing that we really needed more protein after the long hot ride.

"I'll take you over to the teacher's house where you can buy chicken."

I called over to Joe, who had wandered over to a nearby shack to join some of the locals for a game of backgammon. We followed Sharon along the dusty track through the village, past a small insaka, a gathering and meeting place a bit like a gazebo, which can also be used for communal cooking. We approached a bigger two-storey house, with a car and a motorbike parked outside. Sharon called out to a woman, who welcomed us into the house. We left our shoes outside and climbed up a few steps. Immediately, a well-dressed child came over and offered us a cup of water, which we drank gratefully.

We chatted with the woman, who was the local teacher. Sharon spoke to a man, who we assumed was the woman's husband, and they went outside together.

Ten minutes later, the man came back to the house. He was holding a chicken upside-down, tied together by its legs. He held out his arm with the chicken, handing it over to me. The chicken squawked and I stepped back, alarmed.

"It's alive!" I said, recoiling.

Joe laughed. "I thought you were a farmer's daughter," he teased.

"Any chance someone could maybe kill and dress it?" I asked.

The man smiled, looking amused, and said he could have the chicken killed and dressed for another 10 kwacha, which was just over a dollar.

I agreed without hesitating.

That evening we enjoyed a delicious dinner of freshly cooked chicken with ncima, and a spicy zucchini and tomato sauce, which I made on the camp stove.

Over dinner we got to know a bit about Precious. She was twenty-four and had one daughter and was also looking after her sister's daughter. They lived with her mother.

"My father owns our house and this guesthouse," she explained, "but he has four wives so we never know when he is going to come home. Sometimes he stays. Sometimes he just collects the money from the guesthouse."

There was way too much food for the two of us so we suggested Precious take the rest home for her family. A big smile spread across her kind face, lighting up her eyes. There were no fridges in Changa so the only way to eat chicken was to buy a whole live chicken, which was unaffordable for most families here.

"Thank you! The kids will be happy," she said.

The sun was setting over the thatched roofs of the village as we said goodnight to Precious. We planned to head off early the next morning, so probably wouldn't see her again. Joe gave her the cash to cover the cost of the guesthouse and then gave her the equivalent amount for the dinner, even though we'd paid for most of it already.

"Keep this for yourself to buy clothes or schoolbooks for the kids," he said to Precious, who hugged us both.

It was just three days until Christmas. Riding along the dirt roads out of Changa the next morning, we chatted about what our ideal Christmas in Africa would look like: staying with a local community and being able to contribute a few chickens to the festivities.

Two Bugs on Bikes

~24~

A ZAMBIAN CHRISTMAS IN ZIMBA

"**M**erry Christmas!" I said, waking Joe a few days later. "Time to get on our bikes!" We'd found a place we wanted to be for Christmas Day but hadn't been able to make it there on Christmas Eve. So we got up early to ride the last thirty kilometres to get to Zimba in time for church that morning.

It felt surreal riding along the road on Christmas Day. It could have been any other day. We passed a family walking alongside an ox. Mum and Dad were walking by its side and the three kids were walking behind the plough.

"Muli bwange?" (How are you?) they called out.

"Ndili bwino, kaya inu?" (I'm well, and you?) we shouted back.

I thought about my family back on the farm in the UK. On Christmas mornings, after opening our presents, my sisters and I used to dress up the horses in tinsel and go out for a ride to deliver cards or small gifts to the farm workers or other people living in the nearby houses. Later, we'd join up with the extended family and enjoy a huge Christmas lunch of roast goose with all the trimmings (sausages wrapped in bacon, cauliflower in cheese sauce, roast potatoes, mashed potatoes, carrots and peas). This would be followed by trifle and Christmas pudding, which would be drenched in rum and set on fire before being served with white sauce. We'd often stay sitting around the large dining room table for the rest of the day, drinking and chatting or playing card games, until it was time for another meal.

It was different now. My last Christmas on the farm was 2014, the year before Dad died. I stepped off the plane in Manchester after a gruelling twenty-four-hour flight, only to learn he'd been rushed to hospital. He was in the final stages of cancer and no one expected him to make it home for Christmas Day. But Dad, as always, wasn't going to go down without a fight. He sat propped up at the head of the table, cracking jokes like he always had, while the rest of us – including the three young grandchildren – put on brave faces. We were determined to make the most of our time together, trying to ignore the harsh reality that this would be our last Christmas together. In the end Dad defied all expectations, surviving for another six months. But even with all the hardships that followed, that Christmas Day will always stand out, not just as the hardest day, but as one of the most precious days I can remember.

"Merry Christmas!" I shouted out to a group of young children, trying to snap myself out of my melancholy musings. But they walked on without registering.

At the Overflow Guesthouse we were greeted by an American woman, Ashley, who introduced us to her Zambian husband, Andrew. The beautiful house with air-conditioned rooms couldn't be more different from the guesthouse in Changa, and we'd read that the couple did outreach work with the local community.

"We were given some money by a friend and haven't had to spend any money on Christmas presents this year, so we'd like to give a present of a small amount of cash to one or two families. We're wondering if you might be able to connect us to anyone you think this could help," I asked Ashley, who was feeding their two-year old, Theo.

Later that day, after Joe and I had gone to church and sat through the longest mass ever so we could experience the singing and watch as people walked live pigs and flapping chickens up the aisle as part of the Christmas offerings, we followed Andrew through the village to find Memory.

Memory had been left by her husband earlier that year and had nowhere to live and no income to feed her six children. She was squatting in a half-built house courtesy of a kind builder but could be kicked out at any time.

Memory brought out a straw mat and laid it out on the verandah for us to sit on. She was joined by her four children, a girl of around four years old, two boys around four and six and an older daughter who was about thirteen. They sat quietly while Andrew explained where we were from and that we wanted to give them some money for Christmas. Memory's eyes welled up as I gave her the ziplock bag and she counted the money. We knew one hundred and fifty US dollars wasn't a huge amount, but Andrew had said it was enough for her to buy new clothes for the children, cover their school fees and buy a new stove and a bag of maize flour so that she could restart her business selling fritters.

Later that evening we gave a similar amount to another woman who came to the house.

"Sit down, help yourselves, you are part of our family," said Ashley that evening as she placed several huge pots of homemade food on the table to feed the extended family and many of the local workers.

After dinner they gave out gifts to the community from bags of clothing donated by friends in America. Joe and I sat on the sofa, children draped over our knees, soaking up the warmth and kindness. We couldn't imagine finding a better place to spend Christmas. It was hard to tear ourselves away from the family the next day.

"Zimba is an incredibly special community to us," said Ashley as we were leaving the next morning. "But as with many small towns in Africa, it's not without trials and hardships. We are trying to do something to help lessen these hardships. Thanks so much for joining us and for your help for the community this Christmas."

~25~

TOO CLOSE TO THE EDGE

"Shhh, take off your caps and duck down low so no one can see you!" said the driver of the boat as we sped past the waterfront section of the Royal Livingstone Hotel on our way to the Devil's pool, a natural infinity pool at the top of Victoria Falls. We'd got the number for the tour organiser from the backpackers we stayed at in Lusaka. We hadn't realised this was an unofficial trip and completely under the radar. The team (the same guys who work on the official tours) run these tours outside of the regular hours to get a bit more business.

We'd visited the falls from the national park at the Zambian side the previous day and marvelled at the incredible sound of water plummeting over 100 metres and smashing into the river below. It was cloudy and there was lots of spray, limiting visibility, but it was still awe-inspiring. We'd looked down at the tiny orange specks of kayakers queuing up on the edge of the rocks before taking their chances to cross the rapids near the bottom of the falls.

Now, as we approached Livingstone Island and contemplated swimming near the top of the mighty falls, I had no idea why I ever thought this might be a good thing to do. Joe had wanted to go white water rafting but I said I needed a rest and thought bathing in an infinity pool would provide some welcome respite after the long hot dusty days on bikes.

The sun was starting to set, casting a magnificent light over the cascade of white water as we climbed out of the boat. We removed our clothes and shoes at the edge of the Zambezi River and stepped into the water in our cozzies. We were instructed to swim diagonally upstream through the fast-moving deep water. A thin rope was tied between two rocks at the top of the falls but I was doubtful that it would stop anyone from plummeting over the edge if they didn't swim hard enough.

Although we are strong swimmers, Joe and I kept upstream from the guide and swam as if our lives depended on it. However, the Korean woman and two Japanese guys on tour with us weren't good swimmers and were soon sucked up by the current and catapulted towards the edge of the falls. The guide scrambled to grab them. I could feel the adrenaline pulsing through my veins but not in a good way. I felt tense.

Once we reached the shallow rocks, we were instructed to link hands to form a chain and work together to manoeuvre ourselves to a point only a few metres from the edge of the falls. One of the guides then pointed at a pool of water between us and the edge and told us we'd arrived at Devil's Pool.

"I thought *that* was Devil's Pool!" I said, gesturing to where we had just swum.

"No," said our guide. "This is the main pool here."

The body of water before us was three or four metres in diameter, right on the edge of the falls. The enormous volume of water rushing over the edge meant we couldn't see the lip. Clouds of white spray rushed back up and over from the falls below, creating rainbows before the setting sun, but I was too distracted to enjoy the view.

"Climb down here and hold on to the rock," said the guide, showing us the way. "Ignore the fish. They might nibble you but they won't hurt. They are not dangerous."

"Is this for real?" I gasped.

Joe didn't say anything but his face told me he was as anxious as I was.

We edged nervously into the deep water, holding on to the rocks behind us.

"Ouch!" yelped Joe. "Those little buggers are really biting me. I don't like it!"

I laughed and told him to toughen up, but I wasn't feeling particularly comfortable either.

We sat on an underwater ledge at the side of the pool while the Asian tourists went to the edge. They seemed oblivious to the danger as they posed on the edge of the falls above the torrent of water gushing into the river below.

Our boat driver had transformed into a daredevil stuntman, walking along the lip of the falls in knee-deep rushing water. He was holding an iPhone in one hand and a GoPro in the other, filming the tourists as he tiptoed along the ledge. My stomach churned just watching him. One slip meant instant death.

Our turn came. I let go of our rock on the edge to move towards the centre of the pool for our photos. I clung to anything I could find. The water was moving perilously fast and I couldn't see the edge. There was nothing to hold on to and nothing to stop us going over. I had never seen Joe look so scared.

"Smile, put your hands up!" said the guide, tiptoeing along the edge beside us.

I tried to smile for the camera but it was hopeless. I felt vulnerable but also ridiculous realising that we had taken such an unnecessary risk, and that our own and others' lives were at risk for our thrills.

Joe, ashen, managed a weak smile.

We edged ourselves back to the rocks at the side of the pools and climbed out, shaking with fear.

Meanwhile, the Korean girl went back for more, the guide holding on to her ankles so she could do some sort of superwoman pose over the edge of the rock while the boat driver filmed her saying new year's greetings to her family.

All for an Instagram post.

Back on the boat, the driver asked if we'd had a good time.

"Not really. We were pretty scared," I confessed.

"You are right to be. It's too dangerous at this time of year," he said.

"Why do you take such risks?" I asked him.

"Most work was cancelled during COVID, so everyone lost their incomes," he explained. "Things are picking up again, and more tourists are coming back. But the hotels take too big a cut on the official tours, and there is not enough work for everyone, so we have to do these unofficial tours so we can share the money between ourselves to feed our families. Everything is exactly the same as on the official tours."

Later, we learnt that we'd taken the tour right at the end of the season when the waters were getting too high, and that it would now close for the winter.

Crossing the border at Victoria Falls into Zimbabwe the next day, we said goodbye to the great Zambezi. We didn't realise we were leaving behind the Africa that we had grown to know and love and embarking on a new kind of adventure.

"Who would have thought that we'd ride our bikes across Africa and the most scared we'd ever be would be when we took a gimmicky tourist trip to an infinity pool?" I said.

"I know!" Joe replied. "It feels good to be back on our bikes."

~ 26 ~

THE ELEPHANT HIGHWAY

Another truck flashed its lights.

"More elephants," Joe said, pulling to a stop. "Jeez, that's a big group. Let's wait while they cross the road."

We watched in awe as two large female elephants carefully led three baby elephants across the road. They took turns crossing, pausing to turn their heads toward us and flap their ears, ensuring we were at a safe distance and that no cars were nearby. The first mother crossed to the centre of the road, checking both directions for safety. Once she was sure it was clear, she signalled for the babies to start crossing, while the other female elephant brought up the rear, her head swivelling from side to side as she kept a watchful eye out for any danger.

We waited for another truck to come by and then cycled alongside it so there was a barrier between us and the elephants, even though they were now disappearing into the trees on the other side of the road.

It was early – we'd only just set off and had already seen several groups of elephants. We'd crossed the border into Botswana the day before and now had two long days to reach Elephant Sands, a cool camping resort that we were trying to get to for New Year's Eve.

We need to cycle 100 kilometres today and then back up and do another 150 the next day, making it our longest day yet.

Fortunately, Botswana is one of the flattest countries in the world, the roads are all tarred and in excellent condition and, for the most part, we had favourable winds, which made these distances more manageable, despite the heat.

In stark contrast to most countries in East Africa, Botswana is also one of the world's most sparsely populated countries[xxvi] with just 2.5 million people. Botswana suffered less from colonialism than many other African countries, as inclusive pre-colonial institutions were maintained and systems supported. Now an upper middle-income country, with one of the fastest-growing economies in Africa, much of its wealth comes from minerals (especially diamonds) and tourism. But poverty and unemployment remain high, meaning many people have been left behind in relation to clean water, sanitation and food security.

We hardly saw evidence of that from the roadside, though; we saw more elephants than people on our journey through Botswana.

"Are you sure you want to camp here?" said Joe. "Are you not worried about the elephants stepping on the tent? You've changed so much from that person who made me get up in the middle of the night because there was a rabbit outside the tent!"

"The elephants won't come near the tent," I reassured him. "I want to wake up outside on the first day of the new year and be able to watch the elephants, not to be stuck in some overheated cabin."

We were both hot and exhausted after the 150-kilometre ride in the heat. We'd set off at 6 am to beat the heat and try to get some distance down before the headwinds picked up. We even scheduled our food and rest stops so that we didn't lose too much time. It wasn't even lunchtime when we arrived at the resort, so Joe thought we should pay for a cabin so he could relax in the air-conditioning for the afternoon, but I wanted to be outside in nature.

"We can relax in the lodge and by the pool until it cools down," I'd argued.

Right on cue, three majestic grey creatures walked down to the watering hole in front of us. I breathed in their leathery smell and listened to the sound of them spraying water over each other.

"Let's go have lunch so we can have a rest before the new year celebrations begin," said Joe.

As we wandered over to the lodge, we noticed a big Tour d'Afrique (TDA) tourist bus parked at the back of the campsite, so we anticipated other cyclists turning up later.

In the evening we sat at a candlelit table for two and shared a lovely buffet dinner with a bottle of South African white wine. Most of the other people there seemed to be tourists or white Africans.

"Come and join us," said a gentleman from the next table, which seemed to be two families. It turned out they were from the village of Maun. They asked us about our travels and offered to host us where they lived, but our schedules didn't align.

One of the guys I'd spotted coming out of the TDA bus was sitting alone at a table so I went up to say hello and find out where the cyclists were (it was getting dark and no one seemed to have arrived). He said he was the chef and that they were just driving the bus back from Cape Town to meet the cyclists for the start of their tour in Kigali.

"That's where we've come from," I said.

A woman approached and we were introduced to Chantal, the manager of the tour company.

"I cycled from Cairo to Cape Town solo in 2006," she said. "It was a very different ball game then. Hardly any of the roads were paved and you could go for hours without seeing anyone. Now the main problem is too much traffic on many of the roads."

Walking back to our tent after the sun had gone down, we talked about how different it would be doing something like this on an organised tour with someone else planning the routes and being responsible for where you ate and stayed.

"It would take away all the adventure," Joe said. He had done most of the work planning our route.

"But what if you didn't have me to follow you everywhere? Would you rather travel on your own or with a group?" I asked Joe.

"It's hard to say," he said. "I'm just glad I've got you so I don't have to decide."

"You have to stay awake a bit longer. It's New Year's Eve!" I teased him as his eyes started to droop.

"We need to wake up early," he said. "We've only got two months left and more than three thousand kilometres to go if we're going to reach Cape Town."

We were nervous about going through the desert in Namibia. It was getting hot and we'd heard the roads were rough and there could be bad headwinds.

"There's still the option of getting a truck or bus through part of Namibia," I reminded him.

Back on the road in Botswana, we'd left behind the Elephant Highway at Nata and were eating up the kilometres, setting off early and making the most of the tailwinds. The road ran along the edge of the Kalahari Desert, but all we could see were grass verges and trees. Most of the villages seemed to be set back from the roads, so we didn't see many local people. Towns were far apart and there were very few shops, petrol stations or places to stay in between.

"I miss the gritty liveliness of East Africa," I said. "I miss the people, the music, the street food and being able to buy bananas, mangoes, avocados, tomatoes and other fresh foods at the side of the roads."

"I miss all the kids calling out 'Muzungu, muzungu' whenever we ride past," Joe agreed.

As well as the lack of stimulation on the long rides, we missed staying with local communities. If we didn't want to go a long way out of our way and miss out on some of the main sights in the country, we were forced to remain on the tourist trail, where there were only fancy resort-style places to stay.

Planet Baobab was a trendy safari base on our route, 100 kilometres from Nata and 200 kilometres from Maun. It had eighteen self-contained thatched huts, a tastefully decorated bar with big ceiling fans and cowhide seats and a beautiful aqua pool with little cabanas around the side for relaxing. There were also six camping spots with thatched shelters and barbecue spaces at the back of the garden, meaning we could camp and wake up in a natural environment and still have the luxury of the facilities. It was a very pleasant place to rest for a few days, but we were happy to escape the chic safari-clad tourists with a local tour guide.

"Meet me outside the hotel on the corner where the drive meets the gravel road," said Cesar.

Joe had arranged the tour guide through some travellers we'd met along the road. We preferred to contact them directly to avoid most of the fees going to the hotel.

After bouncing along backroads along sandy tracks past traditional villages, through African mangosteen trees, we arrived at a huge, grassy plain that seemed to stretch all the way to the horizon. We were looking for meerkats on the way to the Makgadikgadi Salt Pans, one of the largest salt flats in the world in the middle of the dry savannah.

"Over there!" Cesar pointed to where the two rangers he'd sent out to look for meerkats were waving. We set off, bumping across the rough ground. My eyes scanned the never-ending expanse of dry grass, trying to spot movement.

"Jump out here. Follow the two men," said Cesar, getting out to open the door for me.

I climbed out of the converted Land Rover onto the hot grass, feeling the heat prick my face and sheltering my eyes from the hot sun, which was now low on the horizon, getting ready to retire for the night.

We followed the men for about half a kilometre towards some mounds of earth on the grass and waited quietly. After a few minutes, a head popped out of one of the burrows and a meerkat emerged, immediately standing up on its hind legs and looking around. Its sleek, sandy coat shone in the evening sunshine, its black masked face dominated by big dark eyes that scanned the scene. I gasped in delight and was shushed by one of the men, who smiled and gestured for me to wait.

One by one the other meerkats emerged from their burrows and stood on their hind legs, their tails sticking up into the air behind them, helping them to balance as they watched us nervously for a while, before darting off to find food.

"What do they eat?" I asked one of the guides.

"Insects," he replied. "Mainly beetles, termites and scorpions."

I looked down at my feet in my thongs (flip-flops). I probably should have worn covered shoes.

The meerkats worked as a team, one keeping guard while the others scavenged for food. Gangs of meerkats can live in groups of up to twenty but this group was just four.

Having exhausted our questions about the meerkats, we jumped back in the car and continued across the arid plains towards the Makgadikgadi Salt Pans.

"It feels like being on the moon!" I said to Joe, crunching over the white surface of salt and mineral deposits which were formed between 10,000 and 15,000 years ago when the lakes that were previously here evaporated.

The land was crispy under my bare feet. Dark veins ran across the shimmering white surface where the ground had cracked in the heat. I would have liked to spend a few days travelling across the vast expanse of largely untouched land and camping under the stars. But already the rains had come, starting to soften the surface and making the journey to Kubu Island, which was famous for its ancient baobab trees that created an eerie other-worldly atmosphere, impossible for us.

We posed for photos on the salt pans. "Jump higher!" said Cesar. We laughed and attempted a star jump holding hands but felt like we only managed to get about an inch off the ground.

Walking back to the car, the heat was stifling even though the sun was sinking. Cesar was anxious to get back on the road for the two-hour journey back to the lodge.

On the way back, I fired questions at him and we learnt about the different tribal populations in Botswana.

"The Tswana make up 79 percent of the people of Botswana," he said. "Then there are the Kalanga and the Basarwa (San) and the Kgalagadi. White Africans only make up 3 percent," he said.

"Yet all the lodges seem to be run by white people," I remarked.

"That's right," he said. "The San people used to occupy this area but they have largely moved out."

The San people are one of the oldest population groups in Southern Africa, known for their click language, one of the Khoisan family of languages. The San people have survived as hunter-gatherers for more than 20,000 years, with some estimates indicating the real figure might be as long as 70,000 years (similar to the Aboriginal populations in Australia). Previously their diet included game such as antelope, berries, tubers, and other plants. They are famous for their rock art, which has deep religious and cultural significance, featuring hunting scenes and spiritual symbols and found in caves or on rock faces.

"Why did they move away from here?" I asked.

"They were displaced and marginalised by the European settlers," he explained. "Then later the focus on agricultural development by the newly independent government in the 1960s further forced them from the land."

It didn't stop there. In the 1990s, under the guise of environmental protection, many San people were displaced from the Central Kalahari Game Reserve, leading to long legal battles, with the San people arguing their lifestyles were sustainable and this was unfair. Today the San continue to battle to maintain their cultural identity and get back their ancestral lands, fighting challenges of land rights, social inclusion and political representation made worse by poor access to health and education.

After a day off the bike, we woke early again and embarked on our longest ride yet – 178 kilometres. It felt great to be out on the road with the cool wind blowing through our hair before sunrise, but just as the sun began to peep over the horizon the sky went black and we were pelted with rain. An hour later we were too hot and praying for more rain, which never came.

The road was monotonous. Elephants were now sparse. Rotting carcasses on the edge of the roadside were a stark reminder that there were still lions lurking in the savannah. The partly burnt-out frames of disused cars and trucks cast shadows along the desert, which slowly changed from dry green to sandy yellow as we headed further south.

Maun is a town on the Thamalakane River in northern Botswana and the jumping-off point for the vast inland Okavango Delta, known for its sprawling grassy plains that flood seasonally, becoming a lush animal habitat. The Moremi Game Reserve occupies the east and central areas of the region, where mokoros (dugout canoes), propelled by wooden poles, are used to navigate through the waterways.

With limited time and not wanting to miss this incredible vast inland river delta, using our Christmas gift from Joe's mum and stepdad, we booked a combined helicopter ride and mokoro experience. Stepping out of the helicopter at the mokoro station, we climbed into the canoe for a ride with our guide, who navigated through the narrow inland waterways. These are home to thousands of birds, including the openbill stork, the African marsh harrier, the blacksmith lapwing, reed cormorants, lilac-breasted roller, spur-winged goose and red-eyed dove.

Flying back over the green sprawling waterways, we were stunned by the density of wild animals – huge herds of wildebeest and zebras, giraffes, antelopes (impalas, kudus, steenbok), and elephants and thousands of buffalo roamed the plains before us. It was incredible seeing them all together from above. There were also a few families of warthogs and hundreds of hippos. The helicopter was a great way to see everything and get a taste of this vast expanse of unspoiled wilderness, but it left me hungry for more.

"Can't we stay longer and do an overnight safari?" I pleaded with Joe.

"We don't have time," he replied. "Plus, we've already done every type of safari imaginable on this trip," he pointed out.

He was right. It was time to get back on our bikes. From Maun, it was still 500 kilometres to the Namibian border, with not much more to see. We covered this in four days. It was the longest, hottest, most monotonous part of our ride.

After months in Africa climbing hills, passing through villages, responding to kids shouting out to us, buying mangoes, pineapples, coconuts, peanuts, bananas, water, soft drinks everywhere we went, riding through national parks, watching giraffes and zebras running alongside the road, dodging elephants and constantly scouring the landscape for lions, sleeping with the sound of hyenas in the distance and hippos munching outside the tents, there were suddenly days and days of absolutely nothing! No hills, no dangerous animals, no villages, no people, no kids, hardly any cars or trucks. No shops, no cafes, no street hawkers, no petrol stations. No other cyclists.

Just two bugs on bikes on the empty road.

~27~

SURVIVAL IN THE DESERT

"**T**his is ridiculous," said Joe, getting off his bike. "It's too hard to ride. It's too hot."

We laid our bikes down on the road. We had been riding for seven days since crossing the border at Buitepos into Namibia. We'd been on the Trans-Kalahari Highway to Windhoek, and were now approaching the Namib Desert. The road was gravel, with patches of soft sand and endless corrugations, and the headwind was getting stronger, making it almost impossible to ride.

I sat at the side of the road looking across the red sandy desert to the rocky hills in the distance. I took a big breath, trying to absorb the arid atmosphere of the unlikely landscape. The scene was like something out of a movie – just miles and miles of sandy red dirt stretching towards the mountains.

We had calculated that it was going to take us ten days to cycle through the desert.

"I don't think I can do ten days of this," Joe said.

"Maybe we just need to plan shorter rides," I said. "One hundred and four kilometres of sandy gravel is probably too far."

"But we don't have much time left," countered Joe. "We need to get some distance behind us if we're going to be able to enjoy South Africa."

"We have to just take one day at a time," I reminded him. "There's no point in worrying about where we'll be in a week's time. We just need to get to the campsite for tonight."

As I spoke, a cloud of dust rolled along the road towards us, pulsating with music. "What's that racket?" I said, looking up. People were shouting and beeping the horn.

For a second I thought it was bandits, but then the car screeched to a stop and out jumped a group of friends we'd made at the backpackers in Windhoek.

"Moshe!" I shouted, so pleased to see him.

"We can't believe you've got this far!" said Sarah, Moshe's girlfriend. "We've been driving for hours! Where are you heading? Would you like some food?"

Moshe, Anna, Brendan and Julia (the young American woman we'd met on the Zambezi canoe safari) had been staying at the same backpackers as us in Windhoek and we'd bonded over stories of our travels.

They gave us a cold drink each and insisted we eat their last pie.

"Why don't you jump in the car with us?" they said.

"Nah," said Joe. "It's not far now."

I look at him in disbelief. Just a minute ago he was slumped at the side of the road saying he couldn't go any further, and now he was full of bravado.

"Are you sure?" I asked him. "It's still thirty-five kilometres, which is going to take another three hours in these conditions."

"We'll be fine," he said. "We've come this far, haven't we?"

I nodded and smiled, happy that we weren't going to break our rule of only bikes and boats.

After another round of hugs and backslaps, we were off again, re-energised, riding behind the cloud of dust that was now gaining distance ahead of us.

Thirty minutes later the reality of the long, hard slog ahead took hold. Each turn of the pedal was a herculean effort. We barely spoke to each other as we pushed on, getting off our bikes every few minutes because of the deep sand.

"I am never leaving from here!" I said, staring out over the wide expanse of rocky desert in the afternoon sunshine, from the shady comfort of a bamboo shelter in the Namibgrens Mountain Camp. The camp consisted of twelve spots about 500 metres apart, each with its own outdoor bathroom and covered area for cooking and eating, nestled into the rocks, blending into the natural environment. It was awesome.

"Look at that swimming pool!" I pointed to a stunning natural-looking oasis, sunk into the rocks in the middle of the camping area.

"Let's go and jump in now," said Joe. "There's no one else here!"

That evening we ate a three-course dinner of locally cooked food delivered to our site from the camp farmhouse two kilometres away.

"This place is absolute paradise," I said as we perched on a rock watching the sun go down over the rocky moonscape. "I love the light, the colours, the rock formations, the wind, the birds, the feeling of peace and serenity. Please let's stay another day."

"But there's nothing to do here," said Joe.

"That's the whole point," I said. "We don't need to do anything. Just eat, sleep and swim. We need to relax – and I'd be happy reading and writing."

"Let's see how we feel in the morning," he said. "We have a long way to go still and I might not be able to rest knowing what's ahead of me."

That night we slept like babies in a cool tent under a sheet of stars while the wind whistled over the mountain ridge.

Two Bugs on Bikes

I woke slowly, careful not to disturb Joe as I lit the stove and crawled into the tent's vestibule. Hugging my coffee, I watched as the sky turned crimson over the rocks and the first light started to illuminate the landscape, warming it gradually before the big golden globe rose over the horizon, pulsing in the clear blue sky. I inhaled deeply, relishing the moment of exquisite natural beauty.

I was nervous to wake Joe for fear he would want to keep riding. Eventually he stirred.

"How are you feeling?" I asked.

"My legs are numb with fear," he responded.

"So we have to rest!"

"I guess," said Joe, still sleepy.

My heart lifted. I grabbed my towel and walked down to the pool, sucking in the already hot air, excited to do nothing but soak up the serenity.

Four elegant oryxes bounded across the desert in front of us as we navigated the sandy track at first light the next morning. Their long black horns and black-and-white faces were a stark contrast to their sandy coloured coats that blended into the environment.

From the campsite we climbed a few kilometres on tar to reach the top of the Spreetshoogte Pass, where we paused to look over the series of steep switchbacks that transitioned into a straight dusty road disappearing into the desert.

We would drop 1,000 metres down into the desert that day. The top part was steep and we were nervous but we'd read that it was paved and that the views were amazing. Rumour had it that the pass was built in World War II by a farmer, Nicolaas Spreeth, who was tired of having to do a thirty-kilometre diversion to collect goods. Ironically, he was killed in a motor car accident on this road.

That morning we witnessed the sun rise seven times. As we descended around a steep corner, the sun disappeared behind the rocks only to rise again moments later. It was strange and magnificent. Now fully rested, our senses were sharply attuned to our environment. After several careful turns with our fingers squeezed tight around the brakes, we let go and allowed ourselves to gather speed as we plummeted deeper into the desert.

"Let's check out this place," I said to Joe, pulling into the gate of a padstal (farm stall), which was the only sign of habitation we'd seen all morning.

"I wonder why there's a life-sized sculpture of a Russian rocket in the driveway?" Joe said as we approached.

Once inside the store we could have been in rural Australia. Beautiful cushions, candles and locally made food were for sale. We ordered coffee and cake and sat down on the large colonial-style terrace outside.

"My son went to university and studied space science," explained the white Namibian woman who served us. "So my husband thought he could do one better and built a rocket in the yard. It's just a bit of fun."

"Pretty quirky," I agreed. "We probably would have ridden past if we hadn't seen it and been curious."

"I'm glad you stopped," she said. "We need the business. It's getting harder and harder for white Namibians to live here."

A German colony from 1884 until after World War II when South Africa was given a mandate to administer the country, Namibia has been independent from South Africa since 1990. During apartheid as part of South Africa, its black people were systematically excluded from participating in economic activities. Deep inequalities continue, with Namibia ranking as one of the most unequal countries in the world, according to the OECD.[xxvii] Government land reform policies since 1990 have been attempting to redistribute land, most of which was owned by the white minority, but progress has been slow. Attempts at forced expropriation since 2005 have resulted in ongoing tensions and lack of investment in the farming community.

Two Bugs on Bikes

Wherever we stopped we seemed to be in places run by white Namibians and each of them had a different story about how hard things were getting. Paradoxically, these Namibians continue to control the economy and have a standard of living comparable to well-off European countries or Australia, compared to the rest of the population of Bantu (60 percent) and indigenous Khoi and San people, who make up around 30 percent.

"Where did all these people come from?" I said to Joe as we stopped at the small settlement of Solitaire on the edge of the Namib-Naukluft National Park. We had pulled into a fancy boutique bakery where tourists in smart safari attire were sampling the savoury treats. Next door was a gourmet butcher with a queue of customers waiting outside, ready to purchase overpriced kudu steaks to cook on the bush braai.

"They are on their way to Sossusvlei, like us. They probably took the faster route from Windhoek rather than driving over the Spreetshoogte Pass," he said. "The roads will be a bit busier now."

Having shared a sausage roll and an apple pastry washed down with a banana milkshake, and filled up our water bottles, we were back on the road, battling the heat and the dust as we bumped over the corrugations and slid through the sandy patches.

That night, the campsite we'd headed to was closed, so we stayed in a nearby lodge, languishing by the pool in the afternoon and watching the sun go down over the desert rocks. We watched the wildebeest come by to drink at the waterhole and mongooses pop up and take turns to scuttle over to our terrace to hunt for food.

The next day we reached Sossusvlei, which was like another world. Bikes aren't allowed into the national park, so we joined a tour with the Sossusvlei Lodge. The park officially opens as soon as the first rays of sunlight appear, so we queued with the tourist vehicles waiting for the sun to rise over the Naukluft Mountains. We were joined on our tour by a lovely older French couple – Yves and Dani – and the driver Pietras, an encyclopedia of local information.

Speeding through the dusty sand towards the dunes in our open-sided Jeep reminded me of our four-wheel drive trip around K'gari (Fraser Island) about eight years ago when we'd joined a bunch of backpackers on an awesome island adventure. There the sand was golden. Here the sand turned rusty red as the towering dunes got bigger and the sky deepened into an intense blue, creating a vivid contrast.

"Look, ostriches!" I called out to everyone. The huge birds trotted alongside the Jeep, turning their heads to look at us before increasing their speed.

On the way through the national park, we stopped to climb Big Daddy, one of the highest sand dunes in Namibia. Reaching the peak at 325 metres, we swivelled around to see the trail of footsteps we'd left in the sand as we'd traversed the ridge. We ran down the other side to Deadvlei, a dry salt pan in the valley between the dunes.

Deadvlei means "dead marsh" and it felt appropriate here, where charred tree trunks stood like statues in the salty-white clay that sparkled in the sunshine. The trees died around 700 years ago, when there was no longer enough water to survive. The contrast between the stark black trees planted in the white ground, against a backdrop of red sand and blue sky, is a photographer's paradise. We snapped a few shots in the surreal landscape before walking back to the rest of our party.

Very few plants or animals can survive in the desert. Yet the indigenous San people, the oldest tribal group in Africa, have long had a presence in the desert area, surviving as nomadic hunter-gatherers, utilising the desert's natural resources for thousands of years.

In stark contrast, Joe and I were continually battling the harsh but beautiful environment.

In Betta, we camped on a raised platform under the stars. The sun was barely setting, casting a red glow over the dusty horizon, when our eyes closed in exhaustion and we tumbled into a deep sleep. Halfway through the night I was woken by the wind and had to move downstairs to shelter in the camp kitchen. I should have seen the wind as a warning sign for the day to come.

"The last five kilometres took us forty minutes," said Joe the next day. "We'll never make it at this rate."

We still had over fifty kilometres to go. The combination of the terrible road surface, the heat and the wind, was making it impossible to ride. We'd taken as much air out of our tyres as we could; now we worried that riding on the rims would lead to more punctures.

"Let's stop for a while," Joe said. "We're not getting anywhere at the moment. The wind is forecast to change direction at lunchtime, so it should be better after that."

We set down our bikes at the side of the road and Joe lay down to rest, covering his face with his shirt. I wrapped a sarong around my head to protect it against the wind, which was whipping sand around my face. I took out the stove to make a cup of coffee. Flies bombarded me, buzzing around my face. I brushed them away, trying to relax. I envied Joe for his ability to sleep at the side of the road.

Later, he reached for the water bottle, took a big gulp, then spat out the water with a yelp. "It's boiling!"

"I've hardly got any left since we cooked lunch," I confessed.

There had been no bread at the shop where we'd camped the night before so we'd had to resort to cooking instant noodles with a tin of tuna for lunch. The ride was taking much longer than we'd expected. We were out of snacks and nearly out of water.

"I hope this farmstay place has food," I said.

Back on our bikes, we tried to flag down a truck that was coming in the other direction, but it didn't stop. Eventually we managed to stop a camping Jeep and a lovely Greek couple gave us water.

"It's just fifteen kilometres now," said Joe. "I think we'll make it."

Fifteen kilometres has never seemed so long. The dusty red sand turned golden, then grey. Eventually we saw the sign for Barbie's Farm in one kilometre, and allowed our spirits to lift again.

"I hope there are air-conditioned rooms," said Joe as we pedalled up the bumpy drive.

I parked my bike against the fence outside a small hut that looked like it might be the reception area.

"There's no one here," I said.

"There must be!" said Joe.

Just then a small, dilapidated car appeared and a shirtless grey-haired man wound down the window.

"What do you want?" he asked.

"We're looking for somewhere to stay. We read this was a guesthouse," I said.

"Can't stay here. It's closed!" he said gruffly.

Joe slumped visibly and went to get back on his bike. It was thirty kilometres to the next town and I didn't think we could make it.

I put my hand on the driver's window.

"We just need somewhere to rest and get water," I said. "We can't go any further without water. Otherwise, we have everything we need."

"Where are you from?" he asked.

"Australia," we answered together.

"Australia?" he repeated. "Nothing good ever came out of Australia."

He laughed at his own joke and I sensed he was starting to soften.

"I'm Leslie," he said. "I'm heading out for three hours. My farmhouse is around the corner there. You can rest under my pergola. There's a tap just nearby for water. If you're still here when I get back, I'll see what I can do for you."

We hadn't moved when Leslie got back. We'd filled all our water bottles under the tap and downed two each, trying to rehydrate. I'd taken a strip wash under the tap while we were boiling the water for our last pot noodle. We'd eaten quickly, trying to replenish our energy, to no avail. Joe fell asleep on the cool concrete floor.

Two Bugs on Bikes

I sat and wrote in my journal and finished reading *Mama Namibia*,[xxviii] a book about a young Herero girl who struggles to survive as she wanders in the Omaheke desert, trying to escape the soldiers that are brutally slaughtering the Nama and Herero peoples as part of the first genocide committed by the Germans in 1904. She was saved by a simple act of kindness by a Jewish doctor serving in the German army.

"You still here?" grunted Leslie as he walked into the house carrying bags of shopping. It didn't feel like we were going to be saved by any acts of kindness today.

Joe woke up, and we sat at the table discussing what to do. Leslie was busy inside the house. It wasn't clear if or where we could stay. We were still tired and it was getting too late to cycle another thirty kilometres.

After a while, Leslie came outside and sat at the table with us. Still seeming somewhat reluctant to engage, he asked the usual: Where have you come from? How far do you travel each day? Where are you going next?

Then, "You're not vegans are you?"

"No," we answered, bemused.

"I can't stand bloody vegans." He went on to tell us about four American girls who'd come to stay. "They seemed alright enough," he said, "but then I asked them what they wanted to eat and they said they were vegans. This is a sheep and goat farm. We do meat and dairy. What the hell do you think I'm going to cook for bloody vegans!"

We laughed.

Leslie put his head back and laughed loudly with us. "You two seem alright," he said after a while. "Now, I don't have any beer but would you like vodka and coke?"

I don't know whether it was the thought of the alcohol or the sugar spike, but at that precise moment a vodka and coke sounded like a great idea.

"Sure!" I said.

"Sounds great!" Joe added.

Time passed quickly after that. Joe and Leslie discovered they had quite a bit in common. Joe is a descendent of Irish convicts on his dad's side of the family. Leslie is the fifth generation of farmers descended from Scottish convicts.

"My great-great-great-great-grandfather was on a convict ship destined for Sydney," he said, "but it sank off the Cape of Good Hope. They thought that everyone had drowned, but my grandfather and another chap survived and swam to the shore, where they escaped, never to be found. They managed to get work on a farm in South Africa for a while, but the Afrikaners hated the British and treated them like slaves. Eventually they stole a horse and cart and ran away to Namibia, where they were able to find work. They were given this land, which has since been passed down through the generations."

"So I guess you should have been Australian too?" I said.

"That's right," said Leslie. "And lots of people are trying to move to Australia now. It's not so good for us white people here. The government's trying to give the land back to the black people but it's not happening very quickly and some of the black people are getting angry. When I think about how my grandfather treated his farm workers, I can't say I blame them. Something has got to be done to make things right. I'm just not sure giving them farms is going to work when they don't have the skills or money to farm."

Leslie seemed to have a fairly balanced view on race issues in the country. We asked about his family and why the guesthouse was closed. We learnt that his sister, who usually ran the guesthouse, was overseas, his wife was away in Windhoek, and his housemaid had been in hospital for a week. He couldn't cook for us because there were no clean plates or pans to cook with.

"I'm not a chauvinist," he said. "I can cook, but I don't make beds and I don't wash dishes."

I'd had a few vodkas by now and was feeling hungry.

"How about I come in and wash the dishes while you cook for us?" I said.

"Are you serious? Would you do that?"

"Sure. I don't mind washing up if you don't mind cooking for us."

"Deal!" he said.

Several hours later, after a good feed and a few too many vodkas, we followed Leslie to the guesthouse, struggling to stay upright on our bikes in the dark on the soft sand.

"Here you go!" said Leslie, waving goodbye as he drove back to the house.

The beds were unmade and there was no electricity or running water.

"Let's just pull the mattress onto the porch and sleep under the stars again," I said to Joe.

We woke blurry-eyed the next morning to the sound of goat bells just as the sun was peeking over the hillside.

"What a bizarre evening!" Joe said, rubbing his eyes.

That night, after another long day in the saddle battling headwinds, we stayed at Bethanie Guesthouse, the oldest hotel in Namibia, which had recently been renovated and was beautifully styled with gorgeous crisp and clean air-conditioned rooms – such a treat after three nights under the stars.

From there we headed out towards the Fish River Canyon, camping in the quirky Canyon Roadhouse on the way. The hardest part of the desert was behind us now, but the roads were still tough and it seemed to be getting hotter each day.

The Fish River Canyon is the largest canyon in Africa and the second-longest canyon in the world after the Grand Canyon. It's also the second-most visited tourist attraction in Namibia. The red layered crater was formed 500 million years ago when Africa split from Asia and is more than 500 metres deep in places and around 800 kilometres long.

"We should have camped here!" said Joe when we arrived. "Imagine how spectacular it would have been cooking here and looking out over this view."

We'd been looking out for places to wild camp in the desert but hadn't been brave enough.

"But all the tourists would have arrived just as we were settling in around sunset time," I pointed out.

For the next two nights we slept at Canyon Lodge, the most expensive place on our trip, but well worth it for the amazing food and beautiful oasis swimming pool set in the rocks overlooking the valley.

"This is our treat for making it through the desert," said Joe as we cooled down in the pool.

"I feel like the luckiest person alive," I told him, my skin tingling in response to the cool, clean water washing away the sticky sweat and sand from the desert.

"It's been a tough few days and I don't think I could have done it without you. Thank you for staying positive and encouraging me to keep going," said Joe, nuzzling my neck as we gazed into the dusty red sunset haze over the horizon.

I felt closer to him than I'd ever felt before. "It's always worth it," I said. "It's bizarre how much more amazing everything seems, knowing that we've travelled by bike to get here.

"I'm starting to feel sad that our trip is nearly over," Joe added. "I'm going to miss the routine of getting up early so we can start riding before first light and then going to bed exhausted just after sunset."

The next day's ride started off totally awesome and ended in heat-induced pain. We left Canyon Lodge at 6.40 am after an early breakfast, carrying a packed lunch. The track out of the lodge was easier than we remembered, no doubt because we were well rested on fresh legs.

All types of antelopes – cool kudus, elegant oryxes and sprightly springbok – bounded across our path. Zebras cavorted in the sand by the side of the road. The morning air was cool and the light accentuated the red hues of the canyon to the west as we meandered down the dusty brown road towards the Orange Rover with the high mountains of the Richtersveld in the background.

"Do you realise that those mountains you can see are in South Africa?" said Joe.

I sighed, taking in the moment. "I can't believe we did it," I said. "We cycled 1,500 kilometres through Namibia across the Namib Desert. We didn't think we'd make it. And now the end is in sight. It feels a bit surreal."

~28~

UNUSUAL ESCORTS

"**L**ook at this place – it's spectacular," I said to Joe, showing him an Instagram picture from another Australian cycle tourist. Their tent was pitched on a ledge with amazing views over the mountains. The next shot was of the cyclist bathing in a waterfall in the evening sunlight.

"Wow! That looks like the Cederberg," said Joe. "We are heading that way but I'm not sure we're taking that road."

There are two main roads through the Cederberg mountain range in South Africa. Neither are particularly easy but the higher road through Wupperthal has fewer paved roads and more climbing.

"Why take the easy way when you can take the hard way!" joked Joe as we pushed our bikes through sand.

I chuckled nervously, knowing it was my fault this time. I'd persuaded him that we needed to find the place where the other cyclist had wild camped near the wonderful waterfall. We'd only wild camped nine nights during our whole trip and this was our chance to make it to double figures before we reached the end.

We'd had to push our bikes up a really steep path for several kilometres and were now on sand. Huge red boulders towering over the yellow sand reminded me of the remarkable rocks on Kangaroo Island off South Australia. But we were still some distance from the camp spot we were trying to reach, and running out of daylight.

The ride through South Africa had been cruisy until then. The main road through Namaqualand on the N7 from the border with Namibia into South Africa was relatively quiet, and the climbs were steady. While still stark, the desert landscape started to display new colours as we headed towards Springbok. Patches of yellow and purple gorse clung to the hillsides, and indigenous quiver trees, whose branches were used by the San people to hold their arrows (hence quiver), stood naked on the Kamiesberg mountains.

We'd reached Springbok exhausted after a 124-kilometre day. My bike needed fixing (the chain kept dropping off) so we headed to the bike shop, where the shop assistant Pete discovered it needed a new front chain ring.

After two more long days on the N7 through Kamieskroon (famous for wildflowers in September) and Nuwerus, we'd headed southwest towards the coast, where we'd camped for two nights at Strandfontein. The beach was spectacular and for the first time on this trip we had a proper swim in the ocean, accompanied by a pod of playful dolphins. Elna and Mauricio, an Afrikaans couple who were camping in an elaborate new motorhome behind us, had taken pity on us in our simple tent and adopted us. They gave us a bottle of wine to have with our dinner and invited us and some of the other campers to join them for a traditional South African breakfast the next morning.

Mauricio was a big, warm-hearted Afrikaans farmer with a gutsy laugh. Over a delicious slow breakfast of boerewors (a type of sausage), mieliepap and tomato and bean sauce, he shared a funny story about a French cycle tourist he'd offered to host at his farm a few years ago.

"The guy was stuck on the side of the road, exhausted, having run out of food. So I offered him a place to stay," he explained. "He was keen to stay but refused to get a lift, determined to cycle all the way. I gave him directions. When he arrived a few hours later, he smelled dreadful, like he hadn't showered for weeks. I offered him a shower and said we could put his clothes in the washing machine. But he refused to let us wash his cycling shirt. He said his plan was to cycle for the whole year wearing the same shirt and then at the end of the trip he was going to frame it in a glass frame and mount it on the wall! Can you imagine!"

"It would smell so bad and probably go rotten after a while!" I said.

"I know!" he said. "I think some people who cycle around the world on their own must be a bit crazy. You guys seem to have your heads screwed on. Have you had any problems in South Africa?"

"Nothing so far," said Joe.

"Most of the people we've met are white South Africans who seem concerned about the state of the country and are thinking about leaving," I said. "What about you?"

"We love this country," Mauricio said. "The government needs to do more to address the inequalities that persist since apartheid, but we will never leave."

Even decades after the end of apartheid rule, white South Africans, who only make up about 7 percent of the population, still own most of the country's farmland. As in Namibia, attempts to redistribute have been slow and hampered by gaps in skills and knowledge to support high-tech farming, leading to poor productivity, increased food insecurity and growing unrest.

Failure of the current government to address these and other systemic challenges was evident to us through the energy shortages. Many of the places we stayed, regardless of whether they were cheap backpackers or middle-range lodges, had to apologise that there would likely be a power outage for two to three hours that afternoon. Load shedding, where the government cuts off the power supply for a certain amount of time to avoid running out of electricity completely, has been happening since 2007 and is extremely disruptive and costly for businesses. Unemployment rates in South Africa are already the second-highest in the world, at more than one-third of the overall population, and 60 percent of young people are unemployed.[xxix] The new Government of National Unity formed in June 2024 following elections in May has committed to addressing some of these challenges, but previous weak management of infrastructure, including roads and transport, mean there is a long, tough road ahead.

Finally, we reached the map coordinates where the other cyclist had wild camped in the Cederberg. The ground was rocky with lots of spiky plants. It was going to be hard to find a flat place for the tent.

"This will have to do. It's getting dark," said Joe.

"But where's the waterfall?" I said, feeling a bit despondent.

"I'll go for a wander once we've put the tent up," said Joe. "Maybe it's over the other side of that valley there."

There was no waterfall nearby. We had barely enough water to cook and drink, let alone wash the sweat and sand from our bodies.

"It looked so good in the Instagram photos!" I moaned.

Joe pulled a face as if to say *I told you so*. I laughed.

We sat on a rocky ledge, watching the sun set behind the impressive sandstone rock formations as we waited for the stove to heat up.

"It's hard to get my head around the fact that the trip is nearly over," Joe said as he was stirring the sauce on the camp stove.

"I know," I replied. "People keep asking how I'm feeling about going home. I feel like I'm ready for home because that's always been the plan. We always said we would travel for a year and then go home. But if someone told me tomorrow that we had to keep travelling for another year I'd be happy."

"Same here," said Joe. "Where would you want to go?"

"There's still so much more of Africa I'd love to see, particularly more of the west. But I'd also like to come back and work here and spend time with a local community, rather than just passing through."

"Me too," said Joe.

I looked at him, surprised. "That's great!" I said. "Before this trip I'd never imagined that you might want to come and work in Africa with me."

"I guess it's changed us in many ways," he said.

"That's why when people talk about our trip ending, I say it doesn't feel like the end of anything," I said. "It feels like we set off on a journey that we'll be continuing even after we go home."

He nodded. "We need to find a way of holding onto these dreams and not just getting sucked back into normal life."

As I drank my coffee in the tent's vestibule the next morning, absorbing the wilderness with absolutely no one else around, I silently committed to spending more time in nature, even if it wasn't wild camping.

You'll need to be careful in Cape Town.

Our homestay host's warning circled through my head as Table Mountain came into view. Our last stop was now less than eighty kilometres away.

Situated on the edge of Cape Town's urban sprawl, a few streets back from the beach, the campsite at Melkbosstrand was physically and culturally cold. There were no views and the only facilities were a few plastic tables around a tatty kids' swimming pool and a small shop selling sweets and ice creams. The beach, renowned for being the playground of the rich and famous thanks to its proximity to the city and views of Cape Town, was vast and empty, with large houses along the coast shuttered to maintain the privacy of their residents. Even the water of the Atlantic Ocean seemed uninviting. I was feeling particularly low and anxious.

"I didn't expect to feel like this at the end of the ride," I told Joe. "I think I'm nervous about riding into the city tomorrow. I know we've researched the route but there are still some horror stories, and it'd be so sad for something bad to happen when we're so close to the end of the trip."

We'd heard some terrifying tales about the notorious route into Cape Town and the risk of being robbed, or worse. Our host's warning hadn't helped my nerves.

"It's only the last part through the city that might be tricky," said Joe. "I'm sure it'll be fine."

It was more than fine. The forty-kilometre ride into Cape Town, with glimpses of Robben Island to our right and the iconic Table Mountain getting closer and closer, was unforgettable. It was a Saturday morning. Lots of lycra-clad cyclists were out on the track and everyone shouted *well done* or gave us the thumbs-up.

"It feels like everyone knows what we've done and are congratulating us," I said to Joe.

"I guess most people who cycle Cairo to Cape Town, or even Kigali to Cape Town, finish here," he replied.

Tears pricked my eyes as the enormity of what we'd achieved and the experiences we'd racked up over the last twelve months started to hit me.

"Where have you guys come from?" asked a cyclist who'd been trailing behind us for a while. He was lean and fit with a weathered face. He must have been around eighty, riding a cool Bianchi bike that looked about the same age.

We explained that we'd ridden from Kigali. He asked lots of questions about our trip. It turned out he'd been spending the summers in Cape Town and cycling around there for years. His name was Sergio Bianchi. He'd won his age group in the Cape Town Cycle Tour.

"It was a few years back now," he said. "I'm too old to race now!" He continued to chat to us as we cycled towards the City.

A little further on his voice dropped. "Stay with me for this part," he said. "We're going to go quite quickly. I'm glad I met you here as I don't like cycling this part alone. We really don't want to stop here."

I looked at Joe; he shrugged his shoulders to say *let's go* and we both pedalled faster, following Sergio as we zigzagged across the road onto a littered pathway that ran alongside the disused railway line.

Cape Town's Central Line, stretching from the city centre to Khayelitsha and Mitchells Plain, has been closed since 2019. Initially a temporary measure for repairs, illegal occupation and vandalism scuppered any plans to reopen the railway line. The situation escalated during the COVID lockdowns when people had nowhere to go, resulting in thousands of families occupying the space along the railway line.[xxx]

But the impacts of the railway closures go way beyond the families living on the tracks, who are now being relocated. The cost of commuting has more than quadrupled for more than half a million commuters who used the Central Line to get to work in Cape Town before it was derailed in 2019.[xxxi]

A tall metal fence separated the path from the tracks but there were gaps in sections where people had broken through, and we could see glimpses of corrugated iron shacks. There were few people around and my pulse was racing. I prayed that we wouldn't get a flat tyre and need to stop, my mind full of the stories of people being mugged and even shot here.

In no time at all we were in town, weaving through the traffic. I was struggling to keep up with Sergio as we dodged the pedestrians on the way to the Waterfront.

And suddenly there it was: the famous big frame where we could pose for photos with Table Mountain in the distance. We had arrived in Cape Town. Thanks to Sergio, the route through had been uneventful and now, mingling with the tourists at the Waterfront, our journey felt even more surreal.

We had a coffee with Sergio, then we were joined by Tom and Charlotte, other cyclists we'd met in Namibia and who were now living in Cape Town for a few months. Kicking off our cycling shoes, we shared a celebratory lunch overlooking the boats on the harbour, exchanging stories of our cycling adventures and discussing what to do in Cape Town.

But our trip still wasn't over. Our agreed final destination was the Cape of Good Hope, where we would head after a few days staying in Cape Town with friends.

Plus, of course, we had to climb Table Mountain. While the main route was destroyed due to a recent fire, we circled round the back and took the Platteklip route. It was a steep hike with breathtaking views back over the bay. We then continued to Maclear's Beacon at the pinnacle, from where we could see the city beaches stretching out along the coast towards the Cape. Everyone had told us that this last ride would be stunning. So, naturally, a thick fog cloaked the coastline, obscuring all but the briefest glimpses of the landscape as we headed past Hout Bay and Chapman's Peak towards the Cape of Good Hope.

"This reminds me of Cinque Terra," I said to Joe.

"Jeez, that seems ages ago now," he said, shaking his head. "I was just thinking about when we said goodbye to Trevor and Simon after our week on the yacht in Türkiye. They were so worried about us coming to Africa. But Africa has been amazing. I've felt just as safe here as I did in Europe and the people we've met have been so generous and kind. It just goes to show how our perspectives are influenced by the news and negative stories we hear."

"And there are so many beautiful places," I said. "We've seen so much and yet I feel like there's still so much more to see and experience."

"One thing that's really struck home with me is how privileged we are to be able to do this," Joe said. "At home we just take it for granted that we can jump on a bike or even on a plane and go and explore. But for most people here, and even many people in Europe, it's not even conceivable. Even for people who do have money in Africa, the currency exchange means it's impossible to travel abroad."

"It's definitely inspired me to refocus my work on my original passion of food security," I said. "I'd also be really keen to back to East Africa to live and work someday."

"Me too," said Joe. "It's going to be hard getting back into work in Australia. You know, I was surprised how easily you managed to leave your job behind. I hope we don't both get sucked back into normal life when we get back. We need to keep checking in to make sure we keep our dream alive of returning and going on other adventures."

We were in a long queue of cars and campervans waiting to pay the fees to get into the Cape of Good Hope National Park for our final fifteen kilometres. Once through the gates we jumped on the pedals and flew along the undulating road, looking out over the rocky headlands on the Atlantic coast. The fog had cleared and the azure waters were sparkling in the sunshine as we hit the coast road, turning west for the last kilometre.

"Watch out!" I shrieked as a large female ostrich bounded out onto the road behind Joe. He looked back, grinning, as the ostrich followed him.

"There's more!" I shouted as another four female ostriches emerged from the grassy scrubland and joined the procession behind Joe.

Cars stopped to watch as the cyclist in the bright yellow T-shirt, laden down with touring bags, made his way down the road followed by five large ostriches. I hung back nervously, enjoying the spectacle while filming with my phone, but aware that these were potentially dangerous animals that could turn on us at any minute.

But they just trotted along, heads held high, turning to the right and then the left as if scanning for danger. It was as though they had come to protect us.

"It feels like someone arranged an escort for us!" I called out to Joe, laughing.

Suddenly a male ostrich jumped out and ushered the females to the other side of the road, out of the way.

And then we arrived and queued up for our photo at the famous sign marking the most south-western point in Africa. Everyone else there had just got off a bus or out of a car but we waited our turn. No one there had any idea what we had done. But we knew, and it felt awesome.

We'd cycled 18,000 kilometres over thirty countries, camping 100 nights under the stars. We'd watched a hundred sunsets, returned millions of smiles, and made countless new friends along the way.

We'd had endless debates during the hours of cycling, and some incredible experiences, bringing us even closer as a couple. Two bugs on bikes, humbled by the beauty of the world and the compassion of people, infinitely grateful for one another and our exhilarating year on the road.

Eric makes us breakfast at Eric's cliffside camping near Nyaru overlooking the Rift Valley, Kenya.

Kids crowd around Joe and his bike outside a cafe (which are often called hotels in Kenya) in the village of Torongo, just off the main road between Nyaru and Eldama Ravine, C55, Kenya.

Kids play a game with me whilst Joe tries to recover at the top of one of the hills in the Usambara mountains in Tanzania.

Jacqui soaks up the sunlight descending from the summit of Mt Kilimanjaro with Mt Meru in the background, Kilimanjaro National Park, Tanzania.

Breakfast of champions with our guide Armani from Solo Adventures, Barafu Base camp, 4673 metres, Kilimanjaro National Park, Tanzania.

Our guide, Pablo, explains how trading fish with the mainland on the MV Ilala, provides a livelihood for the people who live on the island, Likoma Island, Lake Malawi, Malawi.

Saying goodbye to Harold, the vice captain of the MV Ilala, after our three-day trip along the lake.

Fishing guide, Benjamin Kumz, one of three guides on the River Horse canoe safari organised by River Breezes Lodge, Chirundu, Zambia. Photo credits Julia Lewis.

The Zambezi cruise was a good way to see the animals from a different perspective, Mana Pools National Park, Zambia/Zimbabwe border

Young men transporting 25kg bags of charcoal to sell in the city. Lusaka, Zambia

Precious cooking Ncima (ground maize meal dish which is the main staple in East and Southern Africa), which we enjoyed with vegetables and chicken! Changa, Zambia.

Meeting Memory and her children with Andrew and Theo from Overflow Mission, Christmas day, Zimba, Zambia.

Two Bugs on Bikes

The Makgadikgadi Salt Pans National Park, Botswana

Riding through the arid Namib desert which stretches for more than 2000 kilometres, Namibia.

Our tenth night wild camping, unfortunately we never found the waterfall we were looking for! Cederberg mountains, South Africa.

Arriving at the Cape of Good Hope having cycled 18000 kilometres across 30 countries, Cape of Good Hope National Park, South Africa.

ACKNOWLEDGEMENTS

Writing this book has felt like a continuation of our adventure and been more rewarding than I could have imagined. I'm extremely grateful for everyone who has been part of the journey.

Joe has supported me completely. Not only did he inspire and plan the whole trip, he has encouraged me to write, put up with my five o'clock starts, answered all my questions over breakfast each day for the last year, and read various drafts and provided suggestions for improvement. Thank you for always being there for me and making sure I'm going in the right direction!

Thanks to all my family and friends in Australia and the UK for the love and inspiration you give me and for allowing me to be me.

Thanks to Mum and Dad for always letting me know I have a place to come back to and call home, however far away I've travelled.

Thanks to The George Institute for Global Health for supporting me to take a year off work and to colleagues in the Australia, India and UK offices who came to listen to my slide show when I returned – your positive feedback provided much-needed encouragement for me to write this book.

Publishing a book is a complex process and is not something I could have done alone. Thanks to Jessica Muddit, book coach and founder of Hembury Books, for persuading me I needed to write a memoir and for coaching me through the journey of writing and publishing. You always helped to put things into perspective and I appreciated the pep talks whenever I've had a confidence crisis.

To my editor, Penny Carrol. Your expert approaches to cutting out surplus detail while retaining my voice, and your attention to sensitivities were spot on and helped me craft the book into something I'm proud of.

Thanks to proofreader Alison Hill and the rest of the Hembury Books team for helping me through the production and publishing process.

Thanks to Ann for being a trusted friend and advisor throughout our journey, for organising the awesome Zambezi canoe safari, and for providing insightful comments on the final draft of this book.

To my former colleague and friend Aylin Dulagil for believing in me, encouraging me to write this book and providing feedback on the final draft. Your book is next!

To Helen Croydon, fellow author, book coach and friend, for critical feedback on the final draft.

To my work colleague and friend Maree for always having my back and inspiring me through your own creativity.

To my team members, supervisors, mentors and colleagues I've worked with over the years. I'm grateful for your support and look forward to working with many of you in my new role.

Thanks to Bianca from Serendis Leadership Consulting for leadership coaching and advice– your support invaluable and it was great to discover a Spanish connection!

Thanks to our Balance Triathlon Club friends for being like an extended family, seeing us off and welcoming us home in style, including escorting us back from the airport on bikes and organising the slideshow and book reading.

Thanks to our neighbours at Mackenzie Street, Leichhardt, for friendship and neighbourly love over the years. A particular thanks to Alice and Amelie for the welcome home banner.

Thanks to my godchildren Mac and Heidi Walker in Sydney, Australia and Georgia and Charlie in the Cotswolds, UK for following us on the map, and to Mila Linder for coming by bike to meet us at the airport. Thanks to Luca and Lilah and all the other gorgeous children in our lives. We are privileged to share such love with the next generation of adventurers.

Thanks to Connie and Jim for the Christmas gift that we used to take a helicopter ride over the Okavango Delta and to the extended Gooley family for accepting me into the family.

Thanks to the MacMasters Beach "Craic" swimmers, Mac's Maniacs and the Macmasters Beach Surf Life Saving Club for welcoming us into the community and giving us a reason to get out of bed every morning, whatever the weather. Saltwater therapy really is the best way to start the day!

To Omafiets bike shop for helping to set up our bikes before our trip, and answering enquiries while we were away.

To all of our friends and who gave us support and encouragement along the way. We enjoyed sharing our stories and your feedback and encouragement often helped to carry us through the tough times.

Thanks to Betty, Jean and Graham, Mum's sisters and younger brother, for reading my journal extracts, encouraging me to keep writing and sharing your own travel stories.

Thanks to Jocie Evison for giving me your favourite socks for the trip. That's true friendship!

Thanks to Di Brown for looking after our home at Macs and gifting us the money that planted the seed for us to support a few families in Zimba for Christmas. From little things big things grow...

Thanks to Trevor Potts for buying us new gear and sending it over to Kigali by FedEx after we'd lost our bag on the plane.

A big thanks to all the people who came to meet us on the way! This includes my sister Sam and her partner Simon, niece Ella and boyfriend Oliver, who travelled from the UK to join us for a few days in Split; Trevor and Simon who travelled from Australia to meet us for a week's sailing in Turkey and Greece; and Joe's son Jesse and his girlfriend, Isabella, who came to meet us in Istanbul.

Thanks to all the other travellers who we met or who shared information online or on the Cairo to Cape Town Whatsapp group. It was great to be able to reach out for advice and we loved reading about other people's (mis)adventures!

Big thanks go to Paul McEvoy, the Irish traveller we met at the Elite Backpackers in Masaka and who inspired us to visit the Masaka Kids, to visit Brother Colm and the home of the Kenyan runners in Iten and climb Mt Kilimanjaro with Solo Adventures. Sometimes you meet people who change the course of your journey and you were certainly one of those guys!

Thanks to Clive for inspiring us to be more intrepid wild campers and for being a good source of amusement when the going got tough. We can't wait to read your book one day.

Thanks to all the people who helped, hosted, and shared your stories with us along the way. It is not possible to list everyone but a few special mentions go to:

- Abdul from La Grotte D'Auberge for cooking us amazing food while we rested and sheltered from the rain after descending from the Tizi n'Ouano pass.
- Steve (Stik) and Christine (friends of more than thirty years!) and their twins Sid and Sam, and Steve's father David, for hosting us for a lovely lunch with fabulous views over the Alhambra in Granada.
- The Africa Rising Cycling Centre and Olivier, for hosting and guiding us in Musanze, Rwanda.
- Brother Colm, the godfather of Kenyan runners in Iten, for spending a whole morning sharing your story and insights into the Kenyan runners' success.
- Eric and Mary from Eric's clifftop camping in the Rift Valley in Kenya, and John and Lily from Yefuka farm in Tanzania, for inviting us into your homes and sharing dinner with us.
- Wilson, our Maasai guide in Amboseli, Kenya, for being such an informative guide including sharing so much about your life and family and the transitioning Maasai culture.
- Shabani Isanga, Amani Sedenga and all the porters and chefs from Solo Adventures who helped us to climb Mt Kilimanjaro in Tanzania. I am still singing Jambo Bwana!

- Captain Harold Chigona of the MV Ilala ship in Malawi for taking an interest in my writing whilst I was on the ship, insisting I send regular updates, and suggesting I write a book called *Two Bugs*!
- CB (Cathberg Nyamunda), our guide from River Horse Safaris who kept us safe on the Zambezi river. Thank you for sharing your knowledge and insights about life in Africa and on the river.

Thanks to all the other community health projects we visited. This includes the Masaka Kids and Bwindi Community Hospital (Uganda), Sister Josepha at Nazareth Guest House and The Floja Foundation (Malawi), Tikondane Community Centre and Overflow Mission (Zambia).

Thanks to our Warm Showers hosts in South Africa, Nicolene and Harem in Springbok and Margarita in Yzerfontein. We learnt a lot staying with you and hope you can continue your own adventures.

To Sergio Bianci, for guiding us through the backstreets to avoid the potential danger spots on the way into Cape Town. You are amazing and we are so grateful for meeting you when we did.

To Ann's sister Jean, husband Jeremy, and their children Sam and Kate, for hosting us in Cape Town.

To Jess, for putting us up in Kalk Bay and sharing your beautiful morning swim routine.

Thanks to the people who stopped just to check we were okay or to give us food or water along the way. As much as the food or water, often these spontaneous acts of kindness were exactly what we needed to keep going.

Lastly, to all of you who have bought and read this book. Thank you! I hope you enjoyed the journey.

EPILOGUE

Coming home was always going to be challenging. We'd grown comfortable spending all our time together, and every day was different. We felt changed by the journey and were anxious about falling back into the same routines, doing similar things.

I had to make the difficult decision to fly straight back to Australia without first returning to the UK to see my family on the farm. While I'd lived in Australia for eighteen years now and built my life there, I still felt a strong pull towards my family in Yorkshire and it was hard not to reconnect with them in person at the end of such an epic adventure. But we'd maxed out our time travelling and needed to get back to start work on the first of March.

Arriving at the airport in Sydney, we were met by many of our Balance Triathlon Club friends, who had come to the airport on bikes and helped us unpack and reassemble our bikes so they could escort us home. Arriving in Leichhardt, we were welcomed by yet more friends and neighbours. Joe's family had also come to meet us. Amelie and Alice, our neighbours' beautiful kids, had made a welcome home banner that was strung across our doorway. More friends joined us in the Royal Hotel in Leichhardt for a surprise welcome home party that evening. It was wonderful reconnecting, telling our stories and catching up on everything that had happened while we were away.

Settling back into work was a different story. Joe came back to a promotion (go figure!). I'd come back from my travels feeling fitter than I'd ever been, not just physically, but also emotionally and spiritually. I was inspired to work really hard to grow my program of work on food and water security and was expecting this to be easy given that I had my own funding to support this.

But things didn't go to plan. Something wasn't right and I wasn't getting the support I needed. Within a few months I was super stressed. After a year of riding around on a bike feeling free, I was reminded of what it was like to live with anxiety, always looking over my shoulder. After a few months, I felt completely demotivated, was struggling to sleep properly and started gaining weight.

At fifty-three years old, everything was probably made worse by perimenopause. I thought I'd sailed through this difficult life transition by riding a bike every day for a year, but back in the throes of normal life, it hit me with a vengeance. I wasn't coping and needed to make some changes.

I decided to leave my job of eighteen years and look for a new position elsewhere.

It's a well-known cliche that travel broadens the mind. In the same way, time away from everyday life helps you see things from a different perspective. Like many people who do similar work to me, my identity was linked to my work. Taking a year off helped me to reconnect with myself outside of my profession and gave me strength to make changes I didn't previously see as possible.

We sold our house in Leichhardt and made the Central Coast our home. That way we could spend more time in nature, swimming in the sea most mornings, running in the bush, and spending time establishing our veggie garden. A year away together on our bikes also helped us see the value of making time to read, reflect and write. But avoiding getting pulled back into the busyness of everyday life and staying focused on our shared dreams feels like a constant battle.

Joe, while doing great at work and still fairly fit by most standards, is continuing to struggle with long-COVID symptoms, including periodic bouts of fatigue and shortness of breath. He is currently undergoing every type of test (cardiology, endocrinology, respiratory and rheumatology) to try and understand the causes, but so far everything is coming back clear. It is frustrating not really understanding what the problem is or how to address it.

Writing this book was the best antidote for the challenges I was facing at work, and helped us both keep the memories alive. I'd wake up early most mornings and fire up my computer and would have a hundred questions for Joe by breakfast. I had my notes on the journey, but Joe always remembered the details of the routes and the people we met. Every day we relived our adventures.

And then there was Olivier, the young kid we'd met interning at the Africa Rising Cycling Center (ARCC) in Musanze, Rwanda, who we'd decided to fund so he could finish his final year at school. Olivier wrote to us every week, sending pictures of him at school, sharing news about how he was going and always wanting to know how we were doing back home in Australia. When he finished school, we decided to continue giving him a small amount of money each month so he wasn't forced to work for a dollar a day to buy food for him and his family. It meant he could instead spend time getting useful work experience, continuing to intern at the ARCC or helping friends with tourism-related activities. He decided to use some of the money for his family to rent land to grow food. They are just about to harvest their first crop of sorghum, which will bring them an income that will help support Olivier's brothers and sister to finish school. We have since agreed to support Olivier through college to study tourism.

We have also kept in touch with Ashley and Andrew, who we stayed with for Christmas in Zimba, Zambia. We've learned that Memory, who we gave a small amount of money to for Christmas so she could buy new clothes and food for her children, instead bought 6,000 bricks so she could build her own house. This Christmas we helped raise some additional funds from friends and family so she could put a roof on her house. We've been astonished to see how far such a small amount of money can go.

I didn't write this book because I thought it would be a bestseller. I just wanted to document our trip so I could record the memories and maybe inspire a few people. Now I realise it was the start of a new journey. We are not sure how yet, but we plan to use any funds from sales of this book to set up a charity to continue to support education and health programs in Africa.

JACQUI WEBSTER

So the adventure continues. At the start of 2025, I handed in my notice at work and signed a contract for a new academic role in Sydney for four years. After that Joe and I want to do another long cycling journey, and who knows where that will take us.

REFERENCES

[i] R Steves, n.d., "Cinque Terre", *Rick Steves' Europe* https://www.ricksteves.com/europe/italy/cinque-terre (accessed 03.01.2025)

[ii] A McCall Smith, *My Italian Bulldozer*, London: Abacus, 2017

[iii] J Horncastle, "Croatia's bitter harvest: Total National Defence's role in the Croatian War of Independence", *Small Wars & Insurgencies*, 26(5), 744–763. https://doi.org/10.1080/09592318.2015.1072320 (accessed 13 March 2025)

[iv] C McClain Brown, *Chasing a Croatian Girl: A Survivor's Tale*, South Carolina: CreateSpace, 2015

[v] R Carver, *The Accursed Mountains: Journeys in Albania*, New York: Harper Perennial, 1999

[vi] R Lowe, *The Slow Road to Tehran: A Revelatory Bike Ride through Europe and the Middle East*, London: September Publishing, 2022

[vii] G Maddox, "A lockdown project gets serious, novice kayakers take on the Bass Strait", *Sydney Morning Herald,* March 13 2021: https://www.smh.com.au/lifestyle/health-and-wellness/a-lockdown-project-gets-serious-novice-kayakers-take-on-bass-strait-20210219-p5746b.html (accessed 17 September 2024)

[viii] M Huband, "12 April 1994: A report from Rwanda", *The Guardian*, https://www.theguardian.com/theguardian/from-the-archive-blog/2011/jun/06/guardian190-rwanda-genocide-1994 (accessed 3 October 2024)

[ix] UNICEF, "Water, Sanitation and Hygiene: Clean water, basic toilets and good hygiene practices are essential for the survival and development of children" https://www.unicef.org/rwanda/water-sanitation-and-hygiene (accessed 8 November 2025)

[x] D Mousa, "This African Lake may literally explode and million are at risk", *National Geographic*, January 2024: https://www.nationalgeographic.com/environment/article/africa-lake-kivu-explosion-energy (accessed 12 January 2025)

[xi] L Watts, "The Congo Nile Trail", *Bikepacker.com*: https://bikepacking.com/routes/congo-nile-trail/ (accessed 23 November 2024)

[xii] K Coats, "The inside story of Rwanda's lost cycling generation", *Escape*, 2023, https://escapecollective.com/the-inside-story-of-rwandas-lost-cycling-generation/ (accessed 6 October 2024)

[xiii] S Kokunda et al. "Batwa Indigenous Peoples forced eviction for 'Conservation': A qualitative examination on community impacts", *PLOS Global Public Health* 2023 3(8): 16 August 23 https://doi.org/10.1371/journal.pgph.0002129 (accessed 13 March 2025)

[xiv] I Yussuf, "Kizimkazi Festival: Let's exploit opportunities – Samia", *Daily News*, 25 August 2024, https://dailynews.co.tz/kizimkazi-festivallets-exploit-opportunities-samia/ (accessed 7 September 2024)

[xv] N Avieli and T Sermoneta, "Maasai on the phone: materiality, tourism and the extraordinary in Zanzibar", *Humanities and Social Sciences Communications*, 2020, DOI: 10.1057/s41599-020-00607-7 (accessed 13 March 2025)

[xvi] World Bank Group, "Towards a more inclusive Zanzibar economy, Zanzibar Poverty Assessment 2022" Washington, DC. http://hdl.handle.net/10986/38262 (accessed 3 March 2025).

[xvii] Global Hunger Index, "Malawi, a Closer Look at Hunger and Undernutrition", June 2019 https://www.globalhungerindex.org/case-studies/2018-malawi.html (accessed 1 December 2024)

[xviii] J Nyambose, "Preserving the Future for Lake Malawi", *Africa Technology Forum* 1997, https://web.mit.edu/africantech/www/articles/Lake_Malawi.html (accessed 1 March 2025)

[xix] UNICEF Malawi *Budget scoping on programmes and interventions to end child marriage in Malawi*, 2019 https://www.unicef.org/esa/media/7446/file/UNICEF-Malawi-End-Child-Marriage-Budget-Scoping-2020.pdf (accessed 23rd December 2024)

[xx] Ripple Africa, "Healthcare in Malawi",: https://rippleafrica.org/healthcare-in-malawi-africa/ (accessed 1 March 2025)

[xxi] N J Parkinson, "Malawi steps up action against illegal charcoal trade (analysis)", *Mongabay Media*, 12 May 2022: https://news.mongabay.com/2022/05/malawi-steps-up-action-against-illegal-charcoal-trade-analysis/ (accessed 27 June 2025)

[xxii] H E Smith et al., "Criminals by necessity: the risky life of charcoal transporters in Malawi", *Forests, Trees and Livelihoods*, 24 (4) 2015, doi.org/10.1080/14728028.2015.1062808 (accessed 13 March 2025)

[xxiii] U Azele, "Vinchenzo M'bale, Yo Maps and Peter Gabriel: 'Don't Give Up, You are Not Alone'!", *News Diggers!*, 14 September 2023: https://diggers.news/guest-diggers/2023/09/14/vinchenzo-mbale-yo-maps-and-peter-gabriel-dont-give-up-you-are-not-alone/ (accessed 3 April 2024)

[xxiv] H D Mazigo et al, Gaps in healthcare workers' knowledge about female genital schistosomiasis in Tanzania", *PLOS Global Public Health* 23 Mar 23 2022; 2(3): doi:10.1371/journal.pgph.0000059: https://journals.plos.org/globalpublichealth/article?id=10.1371/journal.pgph.0000059 (accessed 13 March 2025)

[xxv] Wateraid, Things are changing in Zambia, *Wateraid* :https://www.wateraid.org/us/where-we-work/zambia (accessed 6 March 2025)

[xxvi] World Population Review, "Botswana" 2024 (live) https://worldpopulationreview.com/countries/botswana-population (accessed 17 November 2024)

[xxvii] K Schade, J La and A Pick, "Financing Social Protection in Namibia", *OECD Development Policy Papers*, 19, 2019: https://www.oecd.org/content/dam/oecd/en/publications/reports/2019/04/financing-social-protection-in-namibia_a98552b8/6957c65a-en.pdf (accessed 7 May 2024)

[xxviii] M Serebrov, *Mama Namibia*, Louisiana: Kamel Press, 2013

[xxix] The World Bank in South Africa, *World Bank Group*, February 2025: https://www.worldbank.org/en/country/southafrica/overview (accessed 24 February 2025)

[xxx] News 24, *Blood on the Tracks: The battle for Cape Town's Central Line*, News24, https://specialprojects.news24.com/blood-on-the-tracks/index.html (accessed 6 March 2025)

[xxxi] S Phaliso, "Thousands of people still living on Cape Town's Central Line", *GroundUp*, 14 March 2024 https://groundup.org.za/article/thousands-of-shack-dwellers-are-still-living-on-prasa-rail-lines-in-langa-philippi-and-khayelitsha/ (accessed 6 March 2025)

Two Bugs on Bikes

www.ingramcontent.com/pod-product-compliance
Lightning Source LLC
Chambersburg PA
CBHW020518080526
44583CB00013B/642